Whores of Babylon

ALSO BY FRANCES E. DOLAN

*Dangerous Familiars: Representations of Domestic
Crime in England, 1550–1700*

The Taming of the Shrew: Texts and Contexts (editor)

WHORES OF BABYLON

Catholicism, Gender, and Seventeenth-Century Print Culture

FRANCES E. DOLAN

Cornell University Press

ITHACA AND LONDON

First published 1999 by Cornell University Press.

Printed in the United States of America.

Library of Congress Cataloging-in-Publication Data

Dolan, Frances E. (Frances Elizabeth), b. 1960
    Whores of Babylon : Catholicism, gender, and seventeenth-century
print culture / Frances E. Dolan.
        p.   cm.
    Includes bibliographical references and index.
    ISBN 0-8014-3629-X
    1. Catholics—England—History—17th century.   2. Catholic women—
England—History—17th century.   3. Catholic Church—Controversial
literature—History and criticism.   4. English literature—Early modern,
1500–1700—History and criticism.   5. Catholics—England—Public opinion—
History—17th century.   6. Public opinion—England—History—17th century.
7. England—Church history—17th century.
I. Title.
BX1492.D65   1999
305.6'2042'0932—dc21   99-15782

Cornell University Press strives to use environmentally responsible suppliers and materials to the fullest extent possible in the publishing of its books. Such materials include vegetable-based, low-VOC inks and acid-free papers that are recycled, totally chlorine-free, or partly composed of nonwood fibers. Books that bear the logo of the FSC (Forest Stewardship Council) use paper taken from forests that have been inspected and certified as meeting the highest standards for environmental and social responsibility. For further information, visit our website at www.cornellpress.cornell.edu.

Cloth printing   10 9 8 7 6 5 4 3 2 1

FSC FSC Trademark © 1996 Forest Stewardship Council A.C.
SW-COC-098

WHORES OF BABYLON

*Catholicism, Gender, and
Seventeenth-Century
Print Culture*

FRANCES E. DOLAN

Cornell University Press

ITHACA AND LONDON

First published 1999 by Cornell University Press.

Printed in the United States of America.

Library of Congress Cataloging-in-Publication Data

Dolan, Frances E. (Frances Elizabeth), b. 1960
    Whores of Babylon : Catholicism, gender, and seventeenth-century print culture / Frances E. Dolan.
      p. cm.
    Includes bibliographical references and index.
    ISBN 0-8014-3629-X
    1. Catholics—England—History—17th century. 2. Catholic women—England—History—17th century. 3. Catholic Church—Controversial literature—History and criticism. 4. English literature—Early modern, 1500–1700—History and criticism. 5. Catholics—England—Public opinion—History—17th century. 6. Public opinion—England—History—17th century. 7. England—Church history—17th century.
    I. Title.
    BX1492.D65 1999
    305.6'2042'0932—dc21   99-15782

Cloth printing   10 9 8 7 6 5 4 3 2 1

FSC FSC Trademark © 1996 Forest Stewardship Council A.C.
SW-COC-098

For Scott,
and for my parents,
Tom and Mary Dolan

For Scott,
and for my parents,
Tom and Mary Dolan

Contents

Illustrations

Acknowledgments

I am grateful for many kinds of support and help in researching and writing this book. Miami University fostered my earliest research by providing an assistant, the crack researcher Teresa Lyle, and a Summer Research Appointment; Miami later enabled me to complete the manuscript on an Assigned Research Appointment. William Wortman makes Miami's King Library a very congenial place in which to work on the early modern period. A National Endowment for the Humanities Fellowship at the Folger Library not only gave me time to write but also offered access to a wonderful collection, the invaluable assistance of librarians such as Rosalind Larry, LuEllen DeHaven, Betsy Walsh, and Georgianna Ziegler (who located the cover illustration), and a delightful community of fellows.

Audiences at the University of Cincinnati, the Center of Literary and Cultural Studies at Harvard, the University of Maryland–College Park, the University of California–Los Angeles, the Folger Shakespeare Library, Florida State University, the Newberry Library, and the University of Pittsburgh, and meetings of the Society for the Study of Early Modern Women, the Modern Language Association, the Shakespeare Association of America, and the Group for Early Modern Cultural Studies offered helpful comments and thought-provoking questions. I am grateful to those audiences and to the people who facilitated my visits, especially Karen Cunningham, Lowell Gallagher, Marina Leslie, Arthur Marotti, Jodi Mikalachki, Marianne Novy, Maura O'Connor, Mary Beth Rose, Adele Seeff, and Georgianna Ziegler. In these and other places, Susan Amussen, Margaret W.

Ferguson, Mary Fuller, Cynthia Herrup, Megan Matchinske, Robyn Muncy, Laura Rosenthal, and David Underdown engaged me in especially memorable discussions. Part of chapter 4 was published in *Catholicism and Anti-Catholicism in Early Modern English Texts*, ed. Arthur F. Marotti (Houndmills, Basingstoke, Hampshire: MacMillan/St. Martin's, 1999). I am grateful to the press for their permission to reprint it here.

Many people read and commented on chapters of the manuscript. They include colleagues at Miami, such as Mary Jean Corbett, Timothy Melley, Kate McCullough, and Susan Morgan (who offered especially clarifying advice), and generous colleagues farther afield, such as Mario DiGangi, Melissa Mowry, Valerie Traub, and Wendy Wall. Mary Beth Rose read parts of the manuscript, shared her own work in draft, and engaged in many conversations that made the process a richer one. I am also grateful to Theodora Jankowski, Carole Levin, Elizabeth Mazzola, and Rachel Weil for sharing their work in progress. At Cornell University Press, Bernhard Kendler encouraged the project at an early stage and helped shape its form and style. Barbara Salazar edited the manuscript with care, tact, and wit. A few intrepid souls read the whole of the manuscript: Arthur Marotti and Dympna C. Callaghan both offered generous but rigorous readings. They have made the book a better one; the errors and obstinacies remaining are my own. Scott Shershow not only read through multiple versions of the whole manuscript, commenting in detail each time, but also helped me to think and talk through the project from start to finish. In scholarship, as in all else, he is an incomparable partner.

F. E. D.

Whores of Babylon

Introduction

In this project I pursue a long-standing interest in how early modern culture imagined danger and difference. In an earlier book I considered cheaply produced, widely circulated texts (such as pamphlets, ballads, plays, and statutes) about domestic murder. Why, I asked, was English culture so interested in threats that emerged from inside the household? Why did both legal statutes and popular representations grant special significance to the violence perpetrated by domestic subordinates, such as wives and servants?[1] In *Whores of Babylon* I shift my focus from the domestic to the national, although I emphasize throughout how each is defined in relation to the other. I argue that at the national as well as at the domestic level, English culture located threat in the familiar as much as in the strange, and in those who were (apparently) least powerful. Here I focus on the Catholic subject in the English Protestant nation. I use the term "Catholic" because it was the least pejorative name employed in the seventeenth century to identify members of this amorphous group, and it remains the most recognizable to readers today.

This project requires me to survey a larger canvas. Many more texts, in a broader array of forms, were printed about Catholics than about domestic murder. The contrast between Catholics and Protestants was central to the definition of identity and difference in the seventeenth century. Critics and historians have long recognized that without the printing press, that period would have unfolded very differently.[2] If print was crucial to

1. Frances E. Dolan, *Dangerous Familiars: Representations of Domestic Crime in England, 1550–1700* (Ithaca: Cornell University Press, 1994).

2. See Sharon Achinstein, *Milton and the Revolutionary Reader* (Princeton: Princeton University Press, 1994); Elizabeth Eisenstein, *The Printing Press as an Agent of Change* (Cam-

the processes of cultural conflict and change, then Catholicism was central both to those processes and to print culture. Debates about the status of Catholics impinged on, were incited by, or constituted almost every political crisis in the course of the seventeenth century. The specter of Catholicism was the animating and organizing obsession of early modern English print culture.

Yet this project has taught me that the national is not necessarily a bigger topic than the domestic, or even a wholly separate one. Working on Catholicism has returned me to constructions of the domestic and the familiar, which prove to be inseparable from constructions of the difference and threat of Catholicism. For Catholics were not less threatening because they were so similar and well known, but rather more so. This insight has, in turn, enabled me to question the assumption that those English people who persisted in or converted to Catholicism were retreating to the safety of the familiar. Since the familiar was consistently construed as dangerous, to whatever extent Catholicism was associated with it, it was associated with risk as much as with security.

Whores of Babylon is a reconsideration as well as an extension of my earlier work. Although I continue to be interested in disparities among different registers of evidence, I am less confident that there is any kind of evidence that stands before or beyond interpretation. For instance, whereas I once resorted to court records, albeit slyly, for more reliable or more direct access to "what really happened," I now view court records as themselves representations, shaped by occasion and convention, rather than as standards against which to check the accuracy of, say, plays. Published accounts of trials can stand as one example of how indistinguishable are "documents" and "representations." Multiple narratives about the most notorious crimes and trials survive, each inflected by its author, its authorization, its intended audience, its timing. Yet we do not have "transcripts"; that is, official, exhaustive manuscript accounts that purport to record verbatim what happened in the courtroom. Furthermore, the fullest accounts of witnesses' testimony are often those published in pamphlet form. If transcripts existed, they would not necessarily offer the historian any greater certainty. Yet their absence reminds us that we have no recourse outside of representation. I am arguing not that representations offer direct access to what really happened, but rather that even legal records, widely employed as the most reliable of documents, are "representations" that we must read

bridge: Cambridge University Press, 1979); and Tim Harris, *London Crowds in the Reign of Charles II: Propaganda and Politics from the Restoration until the Exclusion Crisis* (Cambridge: Cambridge University Press, 1987).

with caution. In viewing legal evidence with suspicion, I am in accord with many historians who work with these records.

Why would an inquiry into representations of Catholicism lead me to reconsider my standards of evidence and notions of history? Because early modern debates about Catholics and Catholicism were simultaneously debates about England's history and about what might constitute knowledge. If seventeenth-century English men and women had been certain of the outcome of religious and political struggles, if they had even been certain that Catholicism should or would recede into the margins and into the past, they would not have needed to write so voluminously and vituperatively against it. Since their uncertainty drove their prolixity, I make that uncertainty my subject, rather than attempting to correct or compensate for it.

On the basis of surviving evidence, historians cannot determine exactly what it meant to be a "Catholic" in early modern England, how many Catholics there were, or the extent to which Catholic subjects actually engaged in the conspiracies of which they were constantly suspected. What is clear, however, is that whoever they were and whatever they did, Catholics were central figures in narratives and fantasies—the obstacles to and underminers of England's peace and progress. Early modern discourses, ranging from ballads, broadsides, plays, and newspapers to parliamentary speeches, statutes, and sermons, often cast Catholics as officious spoilers who attempted to interfere in and reverse the course of English history. Created in the mind and through the word, "Catholics" were stock characters inserted into conventional, highly popular narratives; by holding the positions of villains, however unwillingly, they performed their most important work as historical agents.

In the history of seventeenth-century Catholics, then, there is no smoking gun; that is, no definitive cache of physical evidence that could prove, once and for all, who they were and what they were really up to. Even searching for such proof suggests that the physical would always be more incontrovertible, less open to interpretation, than the discursive. But consider for a moment the Gunpowder Plot, the most fully documented conspiracy attributed to Catholics. This purported plot by Guy Fawkes and others to blow up the king and his lords when Parliament assembled on November 5, 1605, was baptized when Fawkes was discovered guarding thirty-six barrels of gunpowder in a vault under a building next door to the House of Parliament. Certainly this was damning evidence (if we assume that it was indeed found, not planted or fabricated). But while it confirmed the fears and suspicions of Catholic conspiracy, it proved little else. Where had the gunpowder come from? What was it to be used for? With whom was Fawkes working? Investigators needed Fawkes's confession to confer meaning on the gunpowder and to implicate other conspirators. State papers suggest that the king authorized the use of torture to compel Fawkes to yield up this needed confession; the remarkable and notorious degeneration of Fawkes's signatures on his statements as the torture progressed further attests to the coercions that motivated and shaped his testimony. How much, then, can even these barrels of gunpowder prove? How separable are they from the discourses that placed them within a narrative of Catholic conspiracy? Such "evidence" is as remote and unverifiable for us now, and as contested, as the official account of the plot and its discovery. We cannot get to the bottom of the Gunpowder Plot. For me, the dearth of historical certainty and the superabundance of representation are twinned methodological advantages. In regard to Catholics in seventeenth-century England, the representations of events such as the Gunpowder Plot are not less reliable forms of evidence—colorful elaborations on or illustrations of less slippery "facts"—but, for the most part, the only available evidence.

Furthermore, perceptions and representations participate in cultural process whether or not they are "accurate." After all, fears and hatreds are always "real," their targets always significant, whether or not the threat can be corroborated. Consequently, I attempt here not to recover or reconstruct a lost or suppressed past, or to advocate the inclusion or increased prominence of Catholics in existing histories, but rather to use Catholics to interrogate the grounds on which we have written our histories of this period. Many studies of Catholics and Catholicism in the early modern period have reproduced the assumptions and conventions of contemporary anti-Catholic writing, repeating stories of Catholic menace. Thus, in many recent historical narratives, as in early modern ones, Catholics and Catholicism stand as the "before" photo (arbitrary, tyrannical, superstitious, bigoted) to be contrasted to new, improved versions of England (parliamentarian, rational, enlightened). By identifying with and perpetuating early modern prejudices, scholars lose sight of the extent to which the formation of an English national identity is a history of fear and hatred, a history in which attitudes toward Catholics and Catholicism played a crucial role. I am neither offering a history of Catholics and Catholicism in this book nor disparaging others who may wish to do so. Instead, I consider the role Catholics played in the English Protestant imagination and in English print; I focus particularly on how often fantasies and representations linked Catholics and Catholicism to disorderly women.

I have organized this book around the discursive constructions of Catholics and Catholicism and the uses to which these constructions were put during three crises in Protestant / Catholic relations: the Gunpowder Plot (1605); Queen Henrietta Maria's open advocacy of Catholicism (in the

1630s and 1640s); and, finally, the Popish Plot and the Meal Tub Plot (1678–80). In each of these crises, fear was the event, not a fog preventing us from apprehending that event accurately. I do not offer exhaustive narratives of these crises, nor do I survey all of the representations of Catholics and Catholicism available at these moments. Instead, I use each as a jumping-off point, an opportunity for speculation, just as contemporary writers did. How did each allegation against Catholics provoke representation, and what forms did those representations take?

Rather than offer an oppositional or corrective narrative, I seek to demonstrate that the oppositions and the narratives that still structure our understanding of the English past are inadequate. Such categories as winners and losers, center and margins, progress and regress, white and black, Christian and non-Christian—the categories through which many early modern polemicists understood their experience and to which modern critics and historians return—cannot adequately describe the position of Catholics. Since Catholics were woven into families and communities and were prominent at court, the threat they offered was precisely that they could not be readily separated out. Both laws and polemic struggled to identify and vilify Catholics. But neither succeeded in drawing an indisputable or uncrossable line between Catholics and everyone else. Catholics were both highly influential (especially at court, where they were literally in bed with Stuart monarchs) and oppressed (the victims of legal penalties and local prejudices, and the scapegoats accused of everything from plotting to blow up monarchs to setting London on fire). The minority in England, they had previously been the majority, as they continued to be in those countries England feared most: France, Italy, and Spain. Suspected of great privilege, they lived under the threat of harsh penalties. Their status changed not only from reign to reign but from year to year. Attitudes toward Catholicism in the abstract differed significantly from attitudes toward known, local Catholics; attitudes toward Catholics in Yorkshire, where many were members of families of discretion and property, with long-standing ties to their communities, differed from those toward Catholics in London, where it was possible to attend mass openly in royal and embassy chapels and where many Catholics were aristocratic, attached to the court, or foreign. Undermining Englishness and Protestantism by not being different enough, English Catholics unsettled the nation's relation to its own past and, with their allegiances divided between England's sovereign and Rome's pope, blurred the distinction between the English and foreigners, loyal subjects and traitors, us and them. It was in the tension between the foreign and the familiar, the different and the same, that the particular threat of Catholicism lay. The term "Whore of Babylon" expresses this tension. Appropriated from the Book of Revelation to describe corruption within the church long before the Reformation and widely used after the Reformation to denounce the Roman church, the pope, and particular Catholics, especially women, this epithet conjoins the familiar language of gender abuse and a reference to an exotic place. The "Whore of Babylon" is thus one of the usual suspects and an outlandish stranger, a person and an abstraction, from here and from there.

In imagining Catholics and Catholicism as icons of a feared otherness, effigies to be burned, so to speak, early modern discourses mobilized all of the available strategies for conceptualizing difference. Some of these strategies were venerable, such as that which David Underdown has called "the gendered habit of mind."[3] In constructions of Catholicism, gender is the most fully developed and consistently, if unevenly, deployed system for re-marking difference. It works in anti-Catholic discourses, as it does in many others, to represent "the destructive potential of strangeness, disorder, and variety" through "the familiar, and familiarly threatening, unruliness of gender," to use Kim Hall's terms.[4] If there was widespread anxiety about the gender order from about 1560 to 1660, then Catholicism was one important discursive site of this gender "crisis" or "panic."[5] Anti-Catholic discourses sometimes marked Catholicism as different and inferior by associating it with blackness, backwardness, monstrosity, and filth; more pervasively, they used religion to create distinctions within the increasingly self-conscious and vexed category of whiteness. Hostility toward the elite and the foreign conjoined in the frequent denunciations of an international court Catholicism. This quick overview, on which I elaborate in Chapter 1, suggests how Catholicism works not as a coherent identity but as a site at which available systems of distinction intersect; as a focus, it thus enables an inquiry into how these systems create and maintain difference, what "difference" meant in this period, and the cultural resources required to make "difference" out of shared blood, origins, and history. As Roger Castlemaine reminded readers in 1666, Catholics are "both fellow sub-

---

3. David E. Underdown, *A Freeborn People: Politics and the Nation in Seventeenth-Century England* (Oxford: Clarendon, 1996), p. 62 and passim.

4. Kim F. Hall, *Things of Darkness: Economies of Race and Gender in Early Modern England* (Ithaca: Cornell University Press, 1995), p. 28.

5. For the argument that there was a "gender crisis" in this period, see Susan D. Amussen, "Gender, Family, and the Social Order, 1560–1725," and David E. Underdown, "The Taming of the Scold: The Enforcement of Patriarchal Authority in Early Modern England," in *Order and Disorder in Early Modern England*, ed. Anthony Fletcher and John Stevenson (Cambridge: Cambridge University Press, 1985), pp. 116–36, 196–217; and Anthony Fletcher, *Gender, Sex, and Subordination in England, 1500–1800* (New Haven: Yale University Press, 1995).

jects, and your own flesh and bloud also. . . . If we err, pitty our condition, and remember what your great Ancestors were."[6]

As many scholars have argued, English national identity emerged in the early modern period as white, Protestant, and masculine; Catholics figured prominently among the "definitional others" against whom the English nation so defined itself.[7] Linda Colley, discussing a later period (1707–1837), has argued that "Britishness was superimposed over an array of internal differences in response to contact with the Other, and above all in response to conflict with the Other," and that, in the formation of British identity, "a strong sense of dissimilarity from those without proved to be the essential cement."[8] Several subsequent studies with an earlier focus, however, emphasize that contact and conflict with "the Other" could occur inside England itself, and that the opposition between external and internal differences was highly unstable. More specifically, several scholars have focused on particular groups defined as "other" in Renaissance England, including Africans and Jews. Rather than argue for a considerable African or Jewish presence in Renaissance England, these investigators demonstrate how those who are very much in the minority, and who are socially marginal and powerless, can be symbolically central.[9] Groups such as Africans and Jews were perceived to pose a threat disproportionate to their actual numbers or resources. To a certain extent, this was also true of Catholics, whose discursive presence seems, at first, out of proportion to their numbers. Yet Catholics had dominated the country just a few generations earlier; they continued to dominate on the Continent. They not

6. *To All the Royalists That Suffered for His Majesty . . . the Humble Apology of the English Catholicks* (London, 1666), sigs. A4v, A2.

7. This phrase is from the "Introduction" to *Nationalisms and Sexualities*, ed. Andrew Parker, Mary Russo, Doris Sommer, and Patricia Yaeger (New York: Routledge, 1992), p. 5. On the relationship between Protestantism and nationalism, see Linda Colley, *Britons: Forging the Nation, 1707–1837* (New Haven: Yale University Press, 1992), chap. 1; Patrick Collinson, *The Birthpangs of Protestant England: Religious and Cultural Change in the Sixteenth and Seventeenth Centuries* (New York: St. Martin's Press, 1988); Stephen Greenblatt, *Renaissance Self-Fashioning from More to Shakespeare* (Chicago: University of Chicago Press, 1980); Liah Greenfeld, *Nationalism: Five Roads to Modernity* (Cambridge: Harvard University Press, 1992), pp. 51–66; and Richard Helgerson, *Forms of Nationhood: The Elizabethan Writing of England* (Chicago: University of Chicago Press, 1992).

8. Colley, *Britons*, pp. 6, 17. In contrast, Greenfeld argues in *Nationalism* that English nationalism emerged organically and consensually from within.

9. Hall, *Things of Darkness;* and James Shapiro, *Shakespeare and the Jews* (New York: Columbia University Press, 1996). On the symbolically central and socially marginal, see Barbara Babcock, "Introduction," in *The Reversible World: Symbolic Inversion in Art and Society*, ed. Babcock (Ithaca: Cornell University Press, 1978), esp. p. 32; and Peter Stallybrass and Allon White, *The Politics and Poetics of Transgression* (Ithaca: Cornell University Press, 1986), p. 20 and passim.

only appeared in the nightmares and on the pages of those who feared them; they also held positions in court, walked the streets of London, lived next door, slept in the same bed; their names were listed in the front of the family Bible.

Catholics were not, then, as socially marginal or as powerless as other demonized groups; consequently, examining how they were represented reveals that even this widely used, helpful formulation—that those who were demonized in the early modern period were socially marginal yet symbolically central—cannot account for Catholics. The position of Catholics was unique. There were far more of them in England than of Jews, Africans, Moors, or Turks, yet their compatriots found them much harder to recognize. Perhaps because of their greater numbers but less visible presence in England, their resemblance to their antagonists, and their problematic status as "natives," Catholics provoked more prolific and intemperate visual and verbal representation and more elaborate and sustained legal regulation than any other group.

While Catholics did not share the social and symbolic position of many "definitional others," they were persistently linked to women: similar yet different, familiar yet threatening, a subordinated group who yet dominated the culture's imagination, oppressively restricted at the level of prescription yet maneuvering to achieve some influence and autonomy in practice, talked about yet talking back. Many seventeenth-century texts made this connection between Catholicism and disorderly women; many scholars have observed it, usually in passing. In *Whores of Babylon* I make this association my focus, examining it from three angles. First, anti-Catholic polemic often represents its object as feminine, despite the fact that men dominated the institutional church. In associating Catholicism with traditionally feminine attributes as well as with female agents, anti-Catholic polemic responds, on the one hand, to the perceived importance of women in Catholic theology, iconography, and post-Reformation English practice, and ignores, on the other hand, Catholicism's patriarchalism. The widespread assumption that masculinity and femininity should be related hierarchically enables anti-Catholic polemicists to describe the inversions they fear from Catholicism in the familiar terms of women who are not only "on top" but also outsized.[10] Especially in the case of icons of the Virgin Mary, the female figure is literally larger than the male, dwarfing him. The problem with Catholicism, from this point of view, is that it inappropriately empowers women, spiritually, symbolically, and socially. This vo-

10. Natalie Zemon Davis, "Women on Top," in her *Society and Culture in Early Modern France: Eight Essays* (Stanford: Stanford University Press, 1975), pp. 124–51.

cabulary of gender inversion figures the triumph of Catholicism as a disaster simultaneously apocalyptic and domestic. For if Catholicism is the "Whore of Babylon," larger than life, monstrous, foreign, grotesquely feminine yet not human, she is also a wife and mother in England, sheltering inside English homes, lying even in the king's own bed.

Second, I consider how this representation of the Catholic threat justified sporadic attempts to control Catholics through penal legislation, which proposed to invade Catholic families, but only to restore gender hierarchy there. This legislation itself contributed to the very gender inversions Protestants most feared in Catholicism, attributing influence and authority to Catholic wives and mothers by making them a focus of legislation and debate, and curtailing the privileges of Catholic men.

Finally, I am interested in representations of specific Catholic women, particularly Charles I's Catholic wife, Henrietta Maria, and Elizabeth Cellier, who was tried for both treason and libel in 1680. These were two of the most controversial and most widely discussed and depicted Catholic women in seventeenth-century England. Exceptional in so many ways, they cannot stand for all Catholic women of the period. While the many texts about them do not show what it would have been like to be a Catholic woman in that time and place, they do reveal how contemporaries perceived, responded to, and described notorious women associated with Catholicism. Since I am focusing here not on the history of Catholic women but on the association of Catholicism with femininity and disorderly women in print culture, I offer two case studies of women who dominated imaginations, conversations, and representations.

From this third angle, I continue to attend to how anti-Catholic polemic holds a distorting mirror up to the prominent role of women in Catholic belief and practice; I also examine Catholic apologies for and defenses of particular women and of female authority more generally. If anti-Catholicism mobilized misogyny to discredit such women as Henrietta Maria and Elizabeth Cellier, as well as the cause they promoted, did Catholicism offer them or their defenders any positive ways to construe female authority? My conclusion is that sometimes pro-Catholic discourses did defend and revere female authority. In a culture that most often construes female power negatively, Catholic apology is one discourse that justifies women's influence as wives and mothers, their authority as queens of heaven or of earth.

Though to some extent Catholicism was a household religion, in that it had to be practiced at home and in secret, it could never be "private." Penal laws attempted to intervene in Catholic families and households, especially in respect to the rearing of children and the harboring of priests; they also pushed men out of public office and into the home, and pushed priests out of monasteries and into domestic dependency, thus inadvertently making the home the cell of Catholic resistance. Catholicism also pushed Englishwomen out into the world—into court, into print, across the seas—offering them access to activism in an international arena, an occasion for resistance both domestic and political, the opportunity for influence and significance, and the prospect of communities of women. Because of the ultimate defeat of the Catholic cause in the political and dynastic struggles of English history and the high risks public exposure entailed, these appearances in court or in print should not be lauded uncritically as opportunities for self-expression or self-determination. Through them, however, these women went on the record; their words and their acts were taken into evidence. That is why we can see them now.

Just as the domestic sphere was neither private nor safe for Catholic women, the public sphere did not welcome them. Since Catholic women emerge into (usually hostile) public notice when they parlay domestic intimacy and authority into political influence, consigning them solely to one history or "sphere" or the other misses the point. So, too, does announcing that the domestic and the political were indistinguishably intertwined. Both approaches obscure the particular scandal attributed to these women. Their straddling of spheres was so persistently demonized because, by the mid– and late seventeenth century, the domestic and the political were beginning to be constructed as separate; yet the border between the two was also perceived as unstable and at risk. Seventeenth-century discourses often organize anxieties about Catholic women's straddling of supposedly distinct categories—such as private and public, domestic and political, familiar and foreign—around particular places on the fault lines: Henrietta Maria's marital bed; Somerset House, which is the residence first of Henrietta Maria, then of Catherine of Braganza, the site of an elaborate chapel, and the center of Catholic worship in London; Elizabeth Cellier's house in Arundel Street, from which evidence against her is collected and from which she sells her controversial text; the particular house of office in which Mary Hobry, the "French midwife," disposed of the remains of the husband she had just murdered. These spaces provide a way of thinking about the place of the feminine in polemic for and against Catholicism, or in the Protestant imaginary, as well as those locations of Catholic female power that have since been paved over and forgotten.

The association between Catholicism and femininity was (and is) tenacious. So were some of the historical women who became figures for the threat of Catholicism in the English Protestant imagination and seventeenth-century print culture. Long-lived women, such as the queens Henrietta Maria and Catherine of Braganza, exceeded their historical moments. Surviving their husbands and living on past the watershed events that were supposed to close eras (Charles I's execution, the Glorious Revolution), such tenacious "relicts" disrupt the neat borders we erect to divide one historical period from another. Although from one perspective they can seem like the mothers in Shakespearean romance, popping up in Act V, alive after all, they do not disappear in the interval, allowing the next generation to get on with things without their interference. Even Henrietta Maria, who did disappear from the London scene during the interregnum, was entirely too busy to be mistaken for a statue in the meantime. Standing for the sometimes disturbing resiliency of the past, its refusal to stay buried, these women, like Catholics more generally, suggest that our attempts to make a coherent "history" out of the chaos of the past is a violent, fantastic, and inadequate process.

Though standard literary and historical periodizations often tie the Restoration to the eighteenth century, divorcing it from what came before, I have drawn the chronological boundaries of my project to sweep from the early to the late seventeenth century, but also to stop just short of the "Glorious" Revolution in 1688.[11] This approach helps me to remember the Gunpowder Plot in 1605 as I consider the Popish Plot in 1678. It also licenses me to forget, for the purposes of argument, that there was either a Glorious Revolution or an Enlightenment. Ignoring the outcome to focus on the process, I wonder: What if one did not know that a Protestant succession and a parliamentarian government would be secured? How would both Catholics and their cause, on the one hand, and narratives of England's past, on the other, look then? In Chapter 1 I draw on texts spanning the century to explore the abundant, diverse, yet curiously consistent representations of Catholics. This surfeit of representations attempted to compensate for a dearth of unambiguous information. After entertaining some pressing but unanswerable questions—exactly who counted as a Catholic? and how many of them were there?—I consider how the press and penal laws exploited uncertainty as an opportunity to imagine or invent the threat Catholics posed.

Having surveyed the conventions that shaped anti-Catholic discourses throughout the century, I narrow my focus to how gender operated in con-

11. Caroline M. Hibbard, *Charles I and the Popish Plot* (Chapel Hill: University of North Carolina Press, 1983); Jonathan Scott, *Algernon Sidney and the Restoration Crisis, 1677–1683* (Cambridge: Cambridge University Press, 1991); and Steven Zwicker, *Lines of Authority: Politics and English Literary Culture, 1649–1689* (Ithaca: Cornell University Press, 1993) similarly insist that the late seventeenth century is best understood as the culmination of a long seventeenth century, rather than the start of an even longer eighteenth century.

structions of Catholicism during three distinct moments. Although there were notorious Catholic plots before 1605 (many seventeenth-century histories of popish atrocities begin with the St. Bartholomew's Day massacre, the various attempts on Queen Elizabeth's life, and the Armada), in Chapter 2 I turn to the Gunpowder Plot as my first crisis because it occurred in England and its alleged perpetrators were all English. As a result, it became a focus for the threat offered by familiar Catholics. Despite the fact that the Gunpowder Plot was purportedly a conspiracy of men against men, much anti-Catholic discourse after the "discovery" of the plot inserted a bossy woman or women into the group of scheming men, often figuring the threat of Catholic conspiracy as the threat of the unruly heterosocial couple.

The demonization of the Catholic couple, whether the husband and wife or the woman and her priest, is surprising. One might expect Catholic women to be associated with virginity and a renunciation or disparagement of marriage; one might expect the Protestant emphasis on the prestige of marriage to make the rhetorical strategy of demonizing the couple deeply problematic and unappealing. Yet, while even the earliest reformers complained that the valuing of virginity and celibacy twisted lives, they did not talk and write about that, or about "unnatural" same-sex alliances, as much as they did about women in disturbing intimacy with men and with alarming power over them. Jacobean penal laws, too, expressed particular concern about married women.

In Chapter 3 I continue to look at the scandalous heterosociality that polemic associated with Catholicism. Here I focus on a particular person, Charles I's wife, Henrietta Maria, charting the relationships among debates over Marian devotion, Henrietta Maria's "intercessions" with Charles, and penal legislation to regulate Catholic parents', especially mothers', control over their children. While anti-Catholic and anti-Caroline rhetoric proclaims the scandal of heterosociality, lamenting the Virgin Mary's dominance in Catholic devotions and Henrietta Maria's influence in the Caroline court, Catholic apology defends both queens. To do so, it appropriates conventional constructions of gender and sexuality to defend the normality of heterosexual intimacy and influence, the naturalness of maternal power, the possibility of heterosocial friendships.

In Chapter 4 I focus on a particular Catholic activist and polemicist. Elizabeth Cellier, a midwife implicated in the Meal Tub Plot, achieved extraordinary visibility, far more than that accorded to even the most revered or disorderly Protestant women (other than Elizabeth I). She stood on the pillory (as punishment for libel); she was depicted in numerous woodcuts; she was included, in effigy, in a pope-burning procession; she was the topic of almost thirty broadsides and pamphlets. For the most part, Cellier's gender and religion combined to make her a particularly scandalous, ridiculous, and vulnerable figure. Yet Cellier was not only a spectacle and the subject of gossip. She also wrote her own account of her treason trial, had it printed, and sold it from her home; it was for this text that she was subsequently tried for libel.

Cellier's case reveals that Catholics were not only the central bogeywomen of Protestant England's print culture but producers and consumers of print as well. We know about groups that were symbolically central but socially marginalized, even criminalized, almost exclusively through representations that contributed to their being both—that is, hostile or fearful representations that conferred difference and justified oppression or exclusion. But Catholics, while most often the objects of representation, also sometimes represented themselves in court and in print; they used litigation and publication, as well as less visible and fully documented strategies, to contest and counter the constructions made of them. Pro-Catholic representations are, of course, no less interested, no more accurate than anti-Catholic ones. Yet by contradicting dominant discourses, these Catholic texts offer startling reminders that there were alternatives to the dominant ways of constructing Catholicism; it was imaginable to characterize Catholics differently, to position them in new roles, to tell other stories.

By 1680, however, it was almost impossible to defend a Catholic woman publicly and credibly. It was not only the political climate that had changed. The genres on which Catholics had previously relied had been so widely appropriated, parodied, and discredited that it had become difficult to reclaim them. Furthermore, if anti-Catholic polemic since at least the 1630s had associated Catholic women with the scandalous intermingling of public and private, as I argue, then by 1680 a surer conviction that the public and private should or could be distinct underlies a more vehement outrage at a woman such as Cellier for conflating them.

While Henrietta Maria and Elizabeth Cellier certainly suffered, they survived opposition and pain to turn up again and again. No single text or moment can represent their long, complicated lives. Neither virgins nor martyrs, and identified as much by their relationship to a cause as by their relationship to husbands or families, such women found none of the predictable conclusions for their stories. In fact, the end of Cellier's life is not known; I happily end on that indeterminacy, rather than on the executions that invariably closed the lives of the criminalized women I've worked on previously. Yet part of the indeterminacy of my conclusion is that I reopen the relationship between criminal women and Catholic women, arguing that the two categories overlap because both groups of women allow the private to erupt into public scrutiny and discussion, and reveal the shameful intimacy that is a part of the most public and political concerns. Thus I conclude with Mary Hobry, the "hellish midwife," finding in her murder of her husband political meanings that emerge into visibility and significance only when her story is viewed as part of a history of the representations of Catholicism, as well as a history of the representations of criminal women. In the end, I ask, how distinct are the criminal and the Catholic, especially at the level of representation? How does the feminine work to link the two? If the history of representing Catholicism is a history of inventing and enforcing distinctions, how does our own scholarship perpetuate that process? To what end?

Since I have organized *Whores of Babylon* around moments of crisis, I do not offer a continuous narrative here, and certainly not a history of Catholicism and anti-Catholicism in early modern England. Many years intervened between one crisis and the next; there are many gaps in my story. The moments on which I focus were exceptional by definition; these were the moments in which anti-Catholicism was most virulent and volatile, in which more texts were printed and circulated than usual, in which the law and its enforcement corresponded most closely. The discursive violence of shifting from one crisis to another, without a chance to catch one's breath, highlights the discontinuities in the meanings and manifestations of Catholicism and anti-Catholicism from one cultural crisis to the next, the changes that occurred across time. I also employ the gaps in my story to acknowledge that my account of these discursive and ideological contests in the seventeenth century is partial, partisan, and contingent on factors as far outside my control as the survival of some texts and the disappearance of others. In this respect, my handicap is not much more burdensome than that under which the original participants in these debates labored.

My emphasis on gaps and discontinuities, not just from moment to moment but in our very knowledge of the past, does not mean that I think the chronological sequence of these crises is random or meaningless. Each successive crisis builds on the last. Stories of Catholic conspiracy persistently double back to recount past plots, always imagined as predicting and explaining the present moment. This circularity and the strikingly consistent conventions that molded representations of Catholicism throughout the century counter the apparent linearity of my structure. Charges of Catholic conspiracy became ever more compelling as they became more familiar through repetition. Although Catholics were often accused of "backwardnesse in Religion" and of impeding England's spiritual and political progress, it was Protestants who constantly looked backward, to reclaim the elusive purity of the once-shared origin of their faith and to understand present intrigues through past experience.[12] Past offenses were obsessively remembered and retold so that shared blood and history might be repressed and forgotten. Yet the constant repetition of the increasingly conventional stories of Catholic conspiracy never seemed to confine Catholics to the past. The reformed and repressed kept returning.

12. This phrase is quoted from John Foxe, *Actes and Monuments* (London, 1641), continuation, p. 88, but it was pervasive. On this habit of thought, see David Cressy, *Bonfires and Bells: National Memory and the Protestant Calendar in Elizabethan and Stuart England* (Berkeley: University of California Press, 1989); and Jonathan Scott, "England's Troubles: Exhuming the Popish Plot," in *The Politics of Religion in Restoration England*, ed. Tim Harris, Paul Seward, and Mark Goldie (Cambridge: Basil Blackwell, 1990), pp. 107–32. On the important role of forgetting in the creation of a nation, see Ernest Renan, "What Is a Nation?" in *Nation and Narration*, ed. Homi K. Bhabha (London and New York: Routledge, 1990), pp. 8–22, esp. 11.

CHAPTER ONE

"Home-Bred Enemies":
Imagining Catholics

The Catholics who skulk across the pages of pamphlets, broadsides, statutes, and sermons have the vivid contours and extraordinary powers of cartoon villains. Always covert, they are masters of disguise, equivocation, poison, and arson. They superstitiously overvalue objects such as relics and rosaries, investing them with agency and animation, yet hold cheap the lives and goods of Protestants. Their extrascriptural, occult rituals are hideous parodies of Christianity, perhaps even Satanic. Although they give lip service to celibacy and virginity, they copulate promiscuously. They honor fellow Catholics over their own family members and countrymen. Even the most violent act, if committed for their pope and his cause, instills no guilt. They are cunning, indefatigable, and industrious opponents. As William Bedloe declares, "there can be none more *cursedly ingenious* in inventing and promoting the most exquisite, various, and to us still *new* methods of doing mischief."[1] Why? Why would they work so assiduously against their countrymen?

In anti-Catholic discourses, the answer is, above all, misplaced optimism. *Reflections upon the Murder of S. Edmund-Bury Godfrey* (1682), which rehashes the "evidence" of a popish plot, describes papists as "a People generally of debauch'd and murderous Principles, that bear no Consciences towards Hereticks, persecuted by Penal Laws, allur'd by the recovery of their Abby-

---

1. Capt. William Bedloe, *A Narrative and Impartial Discovery of the Horrid Popish Plot* (London, 1679), sig. B; see also Ev.

Lands, encourag'd and supported by great Interest in the Kingdom."[2] Without sympathy, this writer acknowledges that the status quo does not serve Catholics, who have much to gain and nothing to lose by reversing the Reformation. Catholics want to reclaim the abbey lands, the resources lost to fines, the kingdom, and they are willing to work tirelessly and skillfully to do so. Miles Prance cautions that

> no Defeat can *daunt* them, nor scarce any Disappointment *discourage* them; no sooner is one Plot discovered, but they presently lay another. For 'tis a Rule that their Priests injoyn their people to believe, I may I am confident say of most, as firmly as their Creed, That their Religion shall infallibly one day or other be restored and established again in *England;* and being thus verily perswaded, they bear up under all Miscarriages, and still vigorously pursue the *main design,* though in *New Methods,* and with different Instruments.[3]

The problem, then, is that Catholics do not take their grievances lying down, but instead are "busy." In response, Protestants, committed as they are to faith rather than works, can only wait for Providence to intervene on their behalf. "Again and again," as Carol Wiener writes, the English "rewrote their history as the tale of the last-minute salvation of a bumbling and helpless people by a bountiful God."[4] Print materials such as those I have been quoting here vilified Catholics and justified their persecution, yet they were hardly flattering to Protestants, since they promoted the sense that Catholics monopolized cleverness, competence, and industry.

Although the character of the print papist was graphically described, who belonged in the maligned group was not. Obsessive detail and endless repetition could not compensate for the mystery lurking beneath the surface of anti-Catholic discourse. Who counted as a Catholic (or a "Romanist" or a "papist")? How might one recognize him or her? How many Catholics plagued England? The lack of any clear definition of "Catholic" and of incontrovertible evidence regarding Catholic numbers nagged at the impassioned certainty of anti-Catholic writers. Yet the unknown was also an opportunity. Since neither visible signs nor foolproof tests separated Catholics from Protestants, Catholics were who Protestants imagined

---

2. *Reflections upon the Murder of S. Edmund-Bury Godfrey* (London, 1682), sig. E2.
3. Miles Prance, *A True Narrative and Discovery of Several Very Remarkable Passages Relating to the Horrid Popish Plot* (London, 1679), sig. A2v.
4. Carol Z. Wiener, "The Beleaguered Isle: A Study of Elizabethan and Early Jacobean Anti-Catholicism," *Past & Present* 51 (1971): 55.

them to be. Representations locate the threat of Catholicism in the perception that Catholics are rarely one thing or another, but usually both, thus blurring needful distinctions between categories. The categories that they combine most disturbingly, and those that are most often used to describe them, are the familiar and the strange.

WHO WAS A CATHOLIC?

Exactly who was a Catholic? The identity is born through the putting asunder of what once had been one flesh. I am less interested in how Henry VIII's desire to divorce Catherine of Aragon worked as a catalyst for the Reformation in England than in how Henry's announcement, in 1536, that he was now head of the Church of England itself effected a kind of divorce, not just between England and Rome but between some English subjects and others. From that time on, except for the brief reign of Henry's Catholic daughter, Mary Tudor, England was a Protestant country. English subjects owed religious and political allegiance to their sovereign rather than dividing their allegiance, as they once had done, between sovereign and pope. Before 1536, most English subjects were either Catholics or heretics; after 1536, most were Protestants or Catholics (and thus proto-traitors).

The story I have so condensed here is, of course, far more complicated. Where did the Reformation in England come from? How did it happen? Some scholars claim the Reformation was imposed from above on a reluctant populace.[5] Others have stressed the broad appeal of Protestantism and the role of accessible forms of oral and print vernacular discourse, such as sermons and ballads, in widely disseminating and popularizing the new religion.[6] Whether the Reformation moved from the top down or the

---

5. Eamon Duffy, *Stripping of the Altars: Traditional Religion in England, c. 1400–1580* (New Haven: Yale University Press, 1992); Christopher Haigh, *English Reformations: Religion, Politics, and Society under the Tudors* (Oxford: Clarendon, 1993); and Ronald Hutton, "The English Reformation and the Evidence of Folklore," *Past & Present* 148 (August 1995): 89–116, and *The Rise and Fall of Merry England: The Ritual Year, 1400–1700* (Oxford: Oxford University Press, 1994), chap. 3.

6. Patrick Collinson, *The Birthpangs of Protestant England: Religious and Cultural Change in the Sixteenth and Seventeenth Centuries* (New York: St. Martin's Press, 1988); and Peter Lake, "Deeds against Nature: Cheap Print, Protestantism, and Murder in Early Seventeenth-Century England," in *Culture and Politics in Early Stuart England*, ed. Kevin Sharpe and Lake (Stanford: Stanford University Press, 1993), pp. 257–83. On the "popular" and "elite," see Scott Cutler Shershow, "New Life: Cultural Studies and the Problem of the 'Popular,'" *Textual Practice* 12.1 (1998): 23–47.

bottom up, or, like so many other revolutions, occurred through a considerably messier process, it can hardly have transformed or reformed beliefs and practices overnight. Who, then, was a Catholic? Was it anyone who retained some sympathy with the old religion, or with particular beliefs or practices? If so, then that category would include many people, especially in the years just after the Reformation.

Laws intervened to draw boundaries between old and new, them and us, by marking those who resisted the change—who excused or withheld themselves from Church of England services—as "recusants." This strategy was not particularly successful. Not all who retained loyalty to the pope or reverence for Catholic theology, or who continued to observe some Catholic practices, became recusants. Nor did everyone who later converted to Catholicism become a recusant. Recusants were not only those who refused to attend their parish church but those whose absence was observed and prosecuted and who, in the face of accusation or conviction, refused to conform. "Church papists," those who conformed outwardly and occasionally while maintaining private observance of their Catholic faith, were subject to comment but not to the laws; nor were those whose neighbors chose not to pursue them. Since recusancy was more about public observance than private belief, many residual beliefs, inclinations, and observances persisted invisibly beneath the law's scrutiny. Finally, while repeat offenses accrued ever stiffer penalties, conformity could reverse this process in a moment. Thus "recusants" were a smaller, constantly shifting subset of Catholics; many who viewed themselves as Catholic may not have been recusants. Furthermore, just as not all Catholics were recusants, not all recusants were Catholics; there were other religious dissidents who refused to attend Church of England services.[7]

Brisk traffic back and forth blurred whatever line divided Catholics from Protestants. Conversions to Catholicism became especially fashionable in the 1620s, in anticipation of Charles's marriage to the Spanish infanta, and then, in the 1630s, in response to his French queen, Henrietta Maria, and the prestigious presence of Catholics at the Caroline court and in London; they also increased in some circles in anticipation of and during

---

7. On the slipperiness of religious categories in this period, see Thomas H. Clancy, S.J., "Papist-Protestant-Puritan: English Religious Taxonomy, 1565–1665," *Recusant History* 13.4 (1976): 227–53; P. R. Newman, "Roman Catholics in Pre–Civil War England: The Problem of Definition," *Recusant History* 15.2 (1979): 148–51; and David L. Smith, "Catholic, Anglican, or Puritan? Edward Sackville, Fourth Earl of Dorset, and the Ambiguities of Religion in Early Stuart England," *Transactions of the Royal Historical Society*, 6th ser., 2 (1992): 105–24.

James II's brief reign as an openly Catholic king.[8] Conversions also went the other way. Apostates from Catholicism peddled "inside information" that purportedly confirmed Protestants' darkest suspicions; their scurrilous reports were popular, even profitable, and could earn them considerable influence. Titus Oates, whose accusations constituted the "Popish Plot," is probably the most infamous and powerful of these tattling apostates.

Definitional dilemmas made it difficult to determine how many Catholics there were in England. The apostate Thomas Abernethie warned that in England there were "five or six thousand" Jesuits and priests, and that the "populous multitude of Papists" extended "to many thousands."[9] Witnesses testifying to the cause of the London fire in 1666 claimed that there were 7,000 Catholics in London and 100,000 in England; they also reported Catholics' boast that they were "able to raise Forty thousand men" within twenty-four hours.[10] Protestant writers advised that Catholic estimates were exaggerated, and that such exaggerations served to inflate Catholics' sense of their own power. Writing around the time of the Gunpowder Plot (in 1605), Gabriel Powel cautioned that "Papistes . . . bragge much of their number and multitudes within this Kingdome, whereby they have encreased their malicious zeal, insomuch as they seeme to be even almost ready to breake forth into actuall Rebellion."[11] Seventy years later, at the time of the Popish Plot, Joseph Glanvill similarly urged his readers not to overestimate the numbers of Catholics: "People are mightily given, and generally so, to *multiply* the number of *Papists,* and they do it in common talk, at least ten-fold." By doing so, even Protestants were inadvertently encouraging Catholics' self-importance and dangerous officiousness: "Did they know how *inconsiderable* their real numbers are, they must certainly sit down, and be quiet."[12]

Twentieth-century estimates, which suggest that the number of practicing Catholics may have been as low as 1.5 percent of the population, are, of necessity, inconclusive and speculative.[13] More interesting than the hypothetical numbers are the theories about why contemporaries seem to

8. Michael C. Questier, *Conversion, Politics, and Religion in England, 1580–1625* (Cambridge: Cambridge University Press, 1996).

9. Thomas Abernethie, *Abjuration of Poperie* (Edinburgh, 1638), sig. F3v.

10. *Londons Flames Discovered by Informations Taken before the Committee* (London, 1667), pp. 12–13.

11. Gabriel Powel, *A Refutation of an Epistle Apologeticall Written by a Puritan-Papist* (London, 1605), sig. *3v.

12. Joseph Glanvill, *The Zealous and Impartial Protestant, Shewing Some Great, but Less Heeded Dangers of Popery* (London, 1681), sigs. G4v, G3v.

13. Robin Clifton, "Fear of Popery," in *The Origins of the English Civil War,* ed. Conrad Russell (London: Macmillan, 1973), p. 153.

have thought they were so much higher. First, although Catholics, however defined or counted, seem to have been a small percentage of the total population, they were a far larger percentage of the landed gentry and peerage, in part because financial penalties for recusancy drove the less privileged into conformity. Lawrence Stone has speculated that "in 1641 something like a fifth of the 121 peers were Roman Catholics";[14] focusing on the latter half of the century, John Miller describes the "social top-heaviness" of English Catholicism, conjecturing that perhaps 10 percent of peers and gentry were Catholics.[15] Another explanation for the exaggerated perception of the Catholic threat is that missionary efforts in Stuart England were succeeding. In the first half of the seventeenth century, according to John Bossy, both the Catholic population and the presence of clergy increased: "The real membership of the Catholic community, considered as the more or less regular clientele of the missionary priests, was something like 35,000 in 1603 and something like 60,000 in 1640; the number of its priests increased a good deal faster, from about 250 to about 750." As a consequence, "those who thought that popery was increasing were right, though their notions about the absolute number of its adherents were wildly exaggerated and their ideas about why it was increasing were usually wrong."[16] Finally, Catholics were powerful and visible at court; they were also on the rise in Europe. Therefore, even toward the end of a century during which, according to J. P. Kenyon, Catholics were "steadily declining in numbers and morale," they were still perceived as growing and prospering.[17]

Despite the elusiveness of its object, anti-Catholicism became a dominant strain in post-Reformation discourse almost immediately. Did anti-Catholicism emerge spontaneously as an organic expression of popular sentiment? Or was it whipped up to mobilize an ambivalent populace? As in the case of the Reformation itself, the most likely answer seems to be something in between the popular groundswell and the elite conspiracy. However it happened, anti-Catholicism rapidly became so much a part of English culture that, during James II's brief reign, a Catholic writer speculated that it was hereditary. How could the English fall for the calumnies

14. Lawrence Stone, *The Crisis of the Aristocracy, 1558–1641* (Oxford: Clarendon, 1965), p. 742.

15. John Miller, *Popery and Politics in England, 1660–1668* (Cambridge: Cambridge University Press, 1973), p. 12; see also J. P. Kenyon, *The Popish Plot* (London: Heinemann, 1972), p. 25.

16. John Bossy, "The English Catholic Community, 1603–1625," in *The Reign of James VI and I*, ed. Alan G. R. Smith (New York: Macmillan, 1973), pp. 101–2.

17. Kenyon, *Popish Plot*, p. 21; see also Miller, *Popery and Politics*, chap. 4.

against Charles I, or for the "Popish Plot," except that "the Frenzy of our Fathers is *Hereditary* . . . the extravagant Apprehensions of the Danger of Popery being that natural imperfection that the generallity of *English* Men are as much born to, as men are to a Club-Foot, or a Hunch-back, or any other Deformity; and really, which they are almost as hardly to be cured of."[18]

Even if anti-Catholicism quickly became a given of English political culture, it was no less assiduously inculcated. Nor did it maintain a consistent meaning or use. In pursuit of a moving target, anti-Catholic discourse, too, shifted shape. Indeed, several historians suggest that by the late seventeenth century anti-Catholicism had become a labile polemical resource. Writers of various ideological and political positions and with diverse agendas might use "popery" as what Peter Lake calls "a free-floating term of opprobrium" to discredit an opposing position and to solicit the support of readers.[19] One consequence of this lability was that anti-Catholicism became a less effective means of unifying an increasingly diverse English populace against a shared enemy. As Tim Harris explains, "this shared hatred did not serve as a unifying force, smoothing over the tensions within English protestantism, since both anglicans and nonconformists used the rhetoric of anti-catholicism to justify their opposition to each other."[20] But the omnipresence and elasticity of anti-Catholicism by the late seventeenth century do not mean that Catholicism had become evacuated of meaning or apolitical. Indeed, it was saturated with meaning, overdetermined.

Thus, while some religious differences were associated with outsiders and aliens (Moors, Turks, Jews), the most hotly contested differences in the early modern period were those within Christianity. Protestants and Catholics disagreed among themselves, of course, and those disagreements shaped the course of seventeenth-century Anglo-American history. Still, as Linda Colley asserts, "the most striking feature in the religious landscape" was the opposition of Protestant and Catholic.[21] Indeed, Protes-

18. *The Memoires of Titus Oates* (London, 1685), sig. B3v.
19. Peter Lake, "Anti-Popery: The Structure of a Prejudice," in *Early Stuart England: Studies in Religion and Politics, 1603–1642*, ed. Richard Cust and Ann Hughes (London: Longmans, 1989), pp. 96, 79–80; see also Rachel Weil, "Sometimes a Scepter Is Only a Scepter: Pornography and Politics in Restoration England," in *The Invention of Pornography: Obscenity and the Origins of Modernity*, ed. Lynn Hunt (New York: Zone Books, 1993), pp. 125–153, esp. 145.
20. Tim Harris, *London Crowds in the Reign of Charles II: Propaganda and Politics from the Restoration until the Exclusion Crisis* (Cambridge: Cambridge University Press, 1987), p. 156; Wiener, "Beleaguered Isle," p. 60.
21. Linda Colley, *Britons: Forging the Nation, 1707–1837* (New Haven: Yale University Press, 1992), p. 19; see also Colley, "Britishness and Otherness: An Argument," *Journal of British Studies* 31 (October 1992): 309–29, esp. 316–23; and Lake, "Anti-Popery," pp. 73–74.

tantism could be defined only in relation to Catholicism. *The Protestant Tutor* (1679), for instance, instructs children that the appropriate response to the question "What religion do you profess?" is "The Christian Religion, commonly called the Protestant, in opposition to Popery."[22] While this opposition was fundamental to the processes of making meaning and creating conceptual order, it was so subtle and shifting that it had to be reasserted or recreated constantly. Indeed, the difference between the two categories existed largely in such reassertion.

CATHOLICISM AND PRINT CULTURE

In seventeenth-century England, the printing press and penal laws were particularly important vehicles for asserting the difference of Catholicism. Seventeenth-century Catholic conspiracies and their representations cannot be clearly distinguished; most of the "plots" attributed to Catholics in the seventeenth century existed largely at the level of suspicion, conjecture, and narrative. The remarkable resemblances among these alleged plots suggest the extent to which Catholic conspiracy developed as a genre with well-codified, consistently deployed conventions. Though representations of the Catholic menace seem to have expressed and exacerbated fears of what *might* happen rather than dispassionately describing what *had* happened, they were not divorced from the material world. The charges that constituted the "Popish Plot," for instance, while apparently groundless, caused enormous political turmoil and resulted in at least twenty-two executions. Thus, in crises such as the Gunpowder Plot and the Popish Plot, representations are what "really happened."

Public spectacles obviously played a crucial role in both Catholicism and anti-Catholicism, even in post-Reformation England. Catholics celebrated the mass in London chapels. What Leah Marcus has called "Protestant ceremony against ceremony" was even more prominent: public burnings of Catholic ritual objects and effigies of the pope; processions of floats, late in the century, loaded with effigies of the whole Catholic clerical administration, also destined for the flames; public punishments and executions of supposed conspirators and other criminalized Catholics.[23] In many ways,

22. Benjamin Harris, *The Protestant Tutor* (London, 1679), sig. E7v.
23. Leah Marcus, *Puzzling Shakespeare: Local Reading and Its Discontents* (Berkeley: University of California Press, 1988), p. 90. See also David Cressy, *Bonfires and Bells: National Memory and the Protestant Calendar in Elizabethan and Stuart England* (Berkeley: University of California Press, 1989); and Hutton, *Rise and Fall of Merry England*. On an effigy burning, see *The Burning of the Whore of Babylon* (London, 1673).

anti-Catholic rituals parodied and replaced Catholic ones; this is particularly clear in the way the Protestant burning of objects and images replaced the Catholic burning of heretics as a ritual of punishment, purification, and expulsion.

The theater similarly seems to have emerged from, criticized, and replaced the Catholic mass. Its resemblance to what it replaced was one reason that Catholicism's harshest critics reproved it. Just as the mass was attacked as theatrical, the stage was reviled as popish; both were criticized for their reliance on the visual, material, and superficial.[24] Yet the association of the theater with Catholicism and antitheatricality with Protestantism, especially "Puritanism," is too simple, since in the late sixteenth and early seventeenth centuries the stage helped to create a Protestant aesthetic and a Protestant visual imaginary. This Protestant aesthetic, which developed also in the anti-Catholic public spectacles I have just mentioned and in Protestant woodcuts and engravings, reclaimed the visual and the material for Protestantism, rather than ceding them entirely to Catholicism.[25] As one Catholic writer complained, Protestants attacked the Catholic use of images in worship, "yet can their *Fox* set them out the pictures of his Martyrs, and his people may gaze upon them."[26]

Several important studies have insisted that public spectacle was more important than print as a medium of social contestation and construction. Focusing on the late sixteenth and early seventeenth centuries, Jean Howard, for instance, argues that "while the ensuing bourgeois era would rely more and more heavily upon an expanding print culture to create self-regulating subjects, the Renaissance employed spectacles."[27] In her work on that "ensuing bourgeois era," Paula Backscheider retains the emphasis on public spectacle, claiming that "literary critics and historians have probably overestimated the part that printed texts and literacy played—

---

24. Jean E. Howard, *The Stage and Social Struggle in Early Modern England* (London: Routledge, 1994), chap. 2; Katharine Eisaman Maus, *Inwardness and Theater in the English Renaissance* (Chicago: University of Chicago Press, 1995), chap. 1; and Louis A. Montrose, *The Purpose of Playing: Shakespeare and the Cultural Politics of the Elizabethan Theatre* (Chicago: University of Chicago Press, 1996), pt. 1.

25. Collinson, *Birthpangs of Protestant England*, chap. 4; Huston Diehl, *Staging Reform, Reforming the Stage: Protestantism and Popular Theater in Early Modern England* (Ithaca: Cornell University Press, 1997), esp. chaps. 1 and 2; Alexandra Walsham, "'The Fatall Vesper': Providentialism and Anti-Popery in Late Jacobean London," *Past & Present* 144 (August 1994): 36–87, esp. 63–64; and Tessa Watt, *Cheap Print and Popular Piety, 1550–1640* (Cambridge: Cambridge University Press, 1991), chaps. 4 and 5.

26. Robert Chambers, "Translator's Preface" to Philippe Numan, *Miracles Lately Wrought by the Intercession of the Glorious Virgin Marie, at Mont-aigu*, trans. Chambers (Antwerp, 1606), sig. D6v.

27. Howard, *Stage and Social Struggle*, p. 4.

and play—in the formation of public opinion and of a politically involved public"; "In this time before mass literacy and a well-developed press and propaganda network, the best means of mass communication available was public spectacle."[28] Yet in both periods, print culture and public spectacle coexisted. Much of what we know about spectacles is mediated through print; we know spectacle as it was translated into words, as it was described, verbally and visually, by those who designed, participated in, or observed it.

Rather than view public spectacle as *the* "public sphere" in early modern England, the most efficient means of mass communication, of subject or nation formation, I join those who see the press as crucial to the processes of political and social change that characterize the century. Two influential accounts of the growth of nationalism, for instance, argue that it could not have developed without the printing press. Benedict Anderson claims that "print-capitalism . . . made it possible for rapidly growing numbers of people to think about themselves, and to relate themselves to others, in profoundly new ways." Anderson even proposes newspaper reading as a version of the daily mass; although it is a "ceremony . . . incessantly repeated" in "silent privacy," each "communicant" is yet aware that it is "being replicated simultaneously by thousands (or millions) of others of whose existence he is confident, yet of whose identity he has not the slightest notion." Linda Colley, too, discusses the role played by "cheap printed matter" in disseminating stories of England's past and constructions of its enemies.[29] Although both Anderson and Colley chart the emergence of nationalism in the eighteenth and nineteenth centuries, their emphasis on the importance of print pertains even as early as the seventeenth century. In the contacts between Protestants and Catholics in England, the challenge was not how to speak across difference, or to create an imagined community out of distinct linguistic and imaginative resources, but rather how to invent and articulate difference within an already shared history, imaginary, and vocabulary.

If Catholics were identified with a language other than English, it was usually Latin. Latin was, however, troublesome as a marker of inferiority and backwardness, since it also continued to be the language of English universities and professions, a lingua franca uniting people by class and education across national boundaries. On the one hand, Latin prayers

28. Paula R. Backscheider, *Spectacular Politics: Theatrical Power and Mass Culture in Early Modern England* (Baltimore: Johns Hopkins University Press, 1993), pp. xv, 1–2.

29. Benedict Anderson, *Imagined Communities: Reflections on the Origin and Spread of Nationalism*, rev. ed. (London: Verso, 1991), pp. 36, 35; Colley, *Britons*, p. 20 and chap. 1 passim. Both are indebted to Elizabeth Eisenstein, *The Printing Press as an Agent of Change*, 2 vols. (New York: Cambridge University Press, 1979).

were often ridiculed as "lip-labour" that speakers mumbled and garbled without understanding; Latin was the language of witchcraft, incantation, Catholic prayer, and other superstitious and residual practices.[30] In this view, Latin is a dead language, spoken over bones and nail parings. It is, according to Thomas Hobbes, "but the *Ghost* of the Old *Romane Language*" and thus appropriate to a pope who is "the *Ghost* of the deceased *Romane Empire*, sitting crowned upon the grave thereof."[31] Yet Latin lived on vigorously as the language of learning and law, even as the Bible was translated into English and the vernacular came to dominate the expanding print market.

The increasing significance of English as the language of public discourse and print as its medium did not mean that literacy was no longer a barrier. Of course it was. Yet the inability to read did not necessarily exclude an early modern person from all participation in print culture. Since a visual vocabulary for anti-Catholicism developed in tandem with a verbal one, the woodcuts in many polemical publications drew in those who were more comfortable with images than with words, acclimating them to print, and, because so many images were recycled, drawing visual connections among texts and between stories. Those members of a household or neighborhood or village who could read might read aloud to those who could not; some who learned news and rumors through print might then disseminate them orally.[32]

Such processes, which combined the verbal and the visual, written and oral transmission, provided access not only to the illiterate but to those who could not afford to buy news sheets or news books, pamphlets or broadsides. The briefest of these texts, however, were not much more expensive than the cheapest admissions to theaters. Joy Wiltenburg estimates that ballads and broadsides—both printed on one side of single sheets of cheap paper—cost a penny apiece, the same as the cheapest theater admission in the late sixteenth century; short pamphlets cost about 3 or 4 pence, but could get more expensive as they got longer. As the century

---

30. Andrew Willet, *A Catholicon, That is, a Generall Preservative or Remedie against the Pseudo-catholike Religion* (Cambridge, 1602), sigs. L5r–v.

31. Thomas Hobbes, *Leviathan* (1651), ed. C. B. Macpherson (Harmondsworth: Penguin, 1983), 4.47.712.

32. Roger Chartier, "Leisure and Sociability: Reading Aloud in Early Modern Europe," trans. Carol Mossman, in *Urban Life in the Renaissance*, ed. Susan Zimmerman and Ronald F. E. Weissman (Newark: University of Delaware Press, 1989), pp. 103–20; Keith Thomas, "The Meaning of Literacy in Early Modern England," in *The Written Word: Literacy in Transition*, ed. Gerd Baumann (Oxford: Clarendon, 1986), pp. 97–131. On how print and word of mouth overlap in the transmission of news, see Richard Cust, "News and Politics in Early Seventeenth-Century England," *Past & Present* 112 (1986): 60–90.

progressed, print became less expensive than the theater, since theater admissions climbed while the price of print held fairly steady, and would have been more affordable in any case, since wages were rising.[33] Furthermore, coffeehouses emerged as places in which one might read the news, in print and in manuscript, without having to purchase it.

My focus on print works against the long-standing association of Catholicism with spectacle. Certain contrasts between Protestant and Catholic belief and practice underlie this association, giving it some validity. One of the most basic initiatives of the early reformers was a turn away from the accretion of extrascriptural tradition and back toward Scripture; to facilitate wider access to the Bible, they promoted its translation into vernaculars and the broader dissemination of reading skill, so that, as William Tyndale promised, "a boy that driveth the plough" might know more of the Scripture than a priest.[34] In contrast, Catholic churches employed stained glass, paintings, and sculpture to engage even illiterate believers, and placed more emphasis on oral instruction than on independent Bible study. The title page of John Foxe's *Actes and Monuments* makes this conventional contrast visible in its opposition between Protestants holding books and Catholics fingering rosaries.[35] To accommodate illiteracy, however, is not to promote it. Yet this was what many anti-Catholic polemicists claimed the Catholic church did.

The assumption that women were more likely than men to stick with Catholicism, or to convert to it, often corresponded to the assumption that women were illiterate and unlearned, and thus were loyal to a religion that coddled their incapacities, or, in the case of converts, were vulnerable to one that preyed on their ignorance. Furthermore, it was widely believed that Catholicism lured women with its ritual paraphernalia, offering them trinkets and toys rather than a Bible they could not read. Samuel Torshel, for instance, expresses concern about "popish Ladies" who "have had the same curiosities about their *Disciplining whips,* as about their *fannes,* their *praying beads* as rich as their *neck-laces* and *bracelets,* and their *Crucifixes* made into *Iewels.* Judge whether this be not rather a *courting* of pleasure, then the

33. Joy Wiltenburg, *Disorderly Women and Female Power in the Street Literature of Early Modern England and Germany* (Charlottesville: University Press of Virginia, 1992), p. 30. On theater admissions, see J. Leeds Barroll, "The Audience," in *The Revels History of Drama in English,* vol. 3, *1576–1613,* ed. Clifford Leech and T. W. Craik (London: Methuen, 1975), pp. 48–49; and John Loftis, "The Audience," in *The Revels History of Drama in English,* vol. 5, *1660–1750,* ed. T. W. Craik (London: Methuen, 1976), pp. 23–24.

34. John Foxe, "The Life and Story of the True Servant and Martyr of God, William Tyndale," in *Actes and Monuments* (London, 1641), vol. 2, p. 362.

35. Eisenstein, *Printing Press as an Agent of Change,* p. 415; see also pp. 344, 355. For the most part, Eisenstein accepts and perpetuates the association of print with Protestantism.

worshipping of God."[36] Prohibitions against Catholic ritual objects promoted a fashion for small wearable objects that could be kept on the person, and concealed if need be. Yet these objects, in turn, provoked vitu-
peration. Other writers agreed with Torshel in censuring the fashion for
crucifixes worn as necklaces. Henry Ainsworth shuddered that "this in-
satiable whore [of Babylon] doteth on and adoreth the Divils own engin,
the Crosse or Gibbet whereby he killed Christ the Saviour of the world."[37]
Sir William Moore condemned both the opulence of some crosses and the
fact that they were being manufactured for the broadest possible audience.

> Enricht with gold or Iewels, *These* are borne
> The breasts of *Dames* of *Honor* to adorne,
> Which not beseeming *Vulgars* (as too deare),
> The *Poorer* sort doe *Poorer Christlings* weare
> Of polisht *Ivorie*, of gilded *Glasse*,
> Of glistring *Horne*, of *Copper, Tinne*, or *Brasse*,
> Which by the *Priest* if hallow'd, so much more
> Held worthie are of *Worship*, than before.[38]

Such fulminations operate on the assumption that women are vain and
fashion-conscious, drawn to ornaments and objects rather than the Word.
They also register an anxiety that, this being the case, Roman Catholicism
has the advantage when it comes to recruiting women.

Some early modern writers connected Catholic women not just to illiteracy and materialism but also to superstition, oral transmission, and the
occult. This set of associations, in which old wives' tales and old papists'
tales are the same, works to discredit Catholicism and relegate it to the
past. Reginald Scot offers a particularly vivid version of the progress narrative in which Catholic women represent "before": "In our childhood our
mother's maids have so terrified us with an ugly Devil having horns on his
head . . . that we are afraid of our own shadows, insomuch as some never
fear the Devil but in a dark night. . . . Well, thanks be to God, this wretched
and cowardly infidelity, since the preaching of the gospel, is in part forgotten, and doubtless, the rest of those illusions will in short time, by God's
grace, be detected and vanish away."[39] John Aubrey refers to "the old, ignorant times, before women were readers," when "the history was handed

---

36. Samuel Torshel, *The Womans Glorie* (London, 1645), p. 205.
37. Henry Ainsworth, *An Arrow against Idolatrie. Taken Out of the Quiver of the Lord of Hosts*
(London, 1624), sig. G6.
38. Sir William Moore, *The True Crucifixe for True Catholickes* (Edinburgh, 1629), sig. I.
39. Reginald Scot, *The Discovery of Witchcraft* (London, 1584), in *Witchcraft in England,
1558–1618*, ed. Barbara Rosen (Amherst: University of Massachusetts Press, 1991), p. 179.

down from mother to daughter."[40] In these optimistic narratives of Protestant progress, print dispels superstition, defeats Catholicism, and robs old women of their power to terrify. Surprisingly, the assumption that when women become readers they necessarily also either become Protestants or cease to be storytellers (or both) still informs histories in which Catholicism remains rooted in a fairytale world before print—a world dominated by women.

But Catholics never really inhabited this fantasyland. Like everyone else in the period, Catholics existed in the midst of a sloppy transition from image to word, a transition that, of course, can never be complete. Since to abstain from print would have been to retreat from the field of contestation for England's future, Catholics had to take the plunge. As one Protestant polemicist summarized the situation in 1616, "The *Presse* is the worlds *Stage.*"[41] Perhaps more than the pulpit, certainly more than the stage, the press was the vehicle of religious controversy and instruction in early modern England; the majority of works printed in England were religious.

While Protestants dominated publication, they did not monopolize it. Catholics may have been resistant readers of anti-Catholic discourses, engaging in the revisionary, appropriative consumption that, according to Roger Chartier, is also a kind of production.[42] Catholics' resistant readings are available for discussion only to the extent to which their polemic and marginalia register them; Catholics' resistant writings are surprisingly profuse. Just as Protestantism used image and spectacle, the resources most associated with Catholicism, Catholicism, in turn, used the press, the resource most associated with the Reformation, to create and record what Nancy Fraser has called a "subaltern counterpublic."[43] The Pollard and Redgrave and Wing short title catalogs grossly underestimate the number of Catho-

---

40. John Aubrey, *The Natural History and Antiquities of the County of Surrey* (written 1673–92) (London, 1792; facs. ed. Dorking, 1975), 3: 93, 99, as quoted in D. R. Woolf, "The 'Common Voice': History, Folklore, and Oral Tradition in Early Modern England," *Past & Present* 120 (August 1988): 50; cf. Hobbes, *Leviathan*, 4.44, 46.

41. Richard Sheldon, *A Survey of the Miracles of the Church of Rome* (London, 1616), sig. gg4.

42. Roger Chartier, "Culture as Appropriation: Popular Cultural Uses in Early Modern France," in *Understanding Popular Culture: Europe from the Middle Ages to the Nineteenth Century*, ed. Steven L. Kaplan (Berlin / New York: Mouton, 1984), pp. 229–53, and "Communities of Readers," in *The Order of Books: Readers, Authors, and Libraries in Europe between the Fourteenth and Eighteenth Centuries*, trans. Lydia G. Cochrane (Stanford: Stanford University Press, 1994), p. 23. On appropriation, see also Houston A. Baker Jr., "Critical Memory and the Black Public Sphere," *Public Culture* 7 (1994): 3–33; and Scott Cutler Shershow, *Puppets and "Popular" Culture* (Ithaca: Cornell University Press, 1995), chap. 3.

43. Nancy Fraser, "Rethinking the Public Sphere: A Contribution to the Critique of Actually Existing Democracy," in *Habermas and the Public Sphere*, ed. Craig Calhoun (Cambridge: MIT Press, 1996), p. 123.

lic texts written in English and intended for English audiences, but printed secretly or printed abroad, most often at Douai or the English Jesuit College at St. Omer in the Spanish Netherlands, but also in Amsterdam and Louvain, and smuggled into England. Often the imprints on such books are missing or falsified. For a more thorough listing, one must turn to references such as A. F. Allison and D. M. Rogers's *Contemporary Printed Literature of the English Counter-Reformation between 1558 and 1640* and Thomas H. Clancy's *English Catholic Books, 1641–1700.* The on-line English Short Title Catalogue is attempting to bridge this divide by including all works printed in English anywhere in the world. This is an important step forward, since works printed in English for Catholic readers constitute "a corpus of writings far larger than those of the Baptists and Quakers and second only to the established church," according to Caroline Hibbard.[44]

It is difficult to imagine what would constitute a secret public spectacle; hence, public spectacle could not enable Catholics to participate in a "subaltern counterpublic," as print did. Catholics simply could not risk their own parallels to pope burning, except perhaps briefly during James II's reign. While they could attend mass at royal and embassy chapels in London, they were always at risk of assault upon leaving these chapels; furthermore, this option was not available to those living outside of London. In contrast, through the oxymoron of the "secret press" Catholics could participate in shaping the terms of public debate. As the press gradually took its place beside the stage and the street as arenas of struggle, it also became harder and harder to regulate. As one supposed exposé of Catholcism reports, "they have *Printing-presses* and *Book-sellers* almost in every corner."[45] Protestants read, responded to, and berated what Benjamin Harris described in the late seventeenth century as the "vast number of Popish Primers, Catechisms, Manuals, and a multitude of such Romish Trash and Trumpery . . . dispersed like a General Infection among the youth of this Nation."[46]

Just as women often have more symbolic visibility than real power, so the prominence of positive and negative images of Catholicism as feminine— the Virgin Mary and the Whore of Babylon—did not necessarily authorize actual women to participate in print culture as producers and consumers.

---

44. A. F. Allison and D. M. Rogers, *The Contemporary Printed Literature of the English Counter-Reformation between 1558 and 1640: An Annotated Catalogue,* 2 vols. (Brookfield, Vt.: Gower, 1990–94); Thomas H. Clancy, *English Catholic Books, 1641–1700: A Bibliography* (Chicago: Loyola University Press, 1974); and Caroline M. Hibbard, "Early Stuart Catholicism: Revisions and Re-Revisions," *Journal of Modern History* 52.1 (1980): 13.

45. John Gee, *The Foot Out of the Snare: With a Detection of Sundry Late Practices and Impostures of the Priests and Jesuits in England* (London, 1624), sig. D3.

46. Harris, *Protestant Tutor,* sig. A3v.

Indeed, quite the opposite. Yet many Catholic women participated significantly in writing, translating, printing, and reading religious and controversial texts. Many converts, such as Elizabeth Cary, read their way into Catholicism. Margaret Clitherow took her imprisonments for recusancy as an opportunity to learn "to read English and written hand."[47] Some who knew Latin translated texts into English to make them more readily available; the movement into vernaculars enabled more Catholics, as well as more Protestants, to participate in print culture as readers and writers. Some Catholic women acted as patrons for texts; others secretly harbored presses in their houses, smuggled Catholic books over from the Continent, and engaged in printing and selling Catholic books in England.[48] Furthermore, Catholic women and those Catholic men excluded from official participation in many of the arenas of public life might have found print their easiest means of access to debates to which they were central, but from which they were often excluded.

PENAL LAWS

Catholics in early modern England also developed and exercised legal knowledge, turning to the courts, as they did to the press, to represent themselves. "The law" that expressly targeted recusants was actually a group of constantly expanded but sporadically enforced statutes that came to be known as "penal laws." These laws targeted only those Catholics who were convicted recusants. Although others, such as Protestant dissenters who refused to conform to the Church of England, also came within the purview of these laws, the legislation was enacted and enforced in response to crises around Catholicism and was often expressly directed at *"popish* recusants."[49]

These laws were not the reality behind or against representations that circulated in print, but rather legal fictions on a continuum with other negative representations of Catholics. Constructing the Catholic menace

47. Fr. John Mush, "Life of Margaret Clitherow," in *The Troubles of Our Catholic Forefathers Related by Themselves*, ed. John Morris, 3 vols. (London: Burns & Oates, 1877), 3: 375.

48. Leona Rostenberg assembles considerable evidence that women played an active role in the printing and distribution of Catholic books in England. See *The Minority Press and the English Crown: A Study in Repression, 1558–1625* (The Hague: Nieukoop, 1971), pp. 22, 24, 26, 101–7, 116, 204. On Protestant women's activities as printers, see Paula McDowell, *The Women of Grub Street: Press, Politics, and Gender in the London Literary Marketplace, 1678–1730* (Oxford: Clarendon, 1998).

49. *Statutes of the Realm. Printed by Command of His Majesty King George the Third* (1819), vol. 4, pt. 2, Index.

in strikingly similar terms, penal laws presented themselves as a response to the problem identified (or created) in polemic; they then fed back into those constructions, adding urgency to them and, when enforced, adding teeth. When the stories England told itself about who its enemies were, where they were located, and how they were most likely to do harm were enacted into law, they became no less fictional but more efficacious. Any of the representations of Catholics could have real consequences, as hate speech always can. Penal laws gave the hate speech against Catholics official sanction; they elevated it from rumor and cheap print to statute. Their impact on Catholics' lives and English culture in the early modern period, like their value as evidence now, lies precisely in their status as authorized articulations of perceived threat and official fantasies of control and punishment; they set the limits of imaginative possibility, and by this indirect means shaped daily experience by perpetuating a climate of fear and endorsing prejudice. Thus they might have material consequences without being consistently enforced.

Many historians have emphasized both that the penal laws were enforced irregularly and that they hung over Catholics as a form of harassment.[50] The laws were sporadically enforced because, in part, England's system of law enforcement was still too scattered and undeveloped, its sovereigns were too often ambivalent about Catholics and Catholicism, and its foreign policy was too dependent on Catholic countries to put fully into practice the persecution it fantasized in legal statutes. In a single work, James I, for instance, both justifies the severe penal laws he enacted after the Gunpowder Plot and points out their status as threats: "So farre hath both my heart and government bene from any bitternes, as almost never one of those sharpe additions to the former Lawes have ever yet bene put in execution."[51] Even Protestants who vilified Catholicism in the abstract might be unwilling to persecute their Catholic neighbors as fully as the law allowed, even encouraged, and might protect local Catholics.[52] Some writers feared that this disparity between the laws and their enforcement would promote a disrespect for the law among Catholics and other dissenters.[53]

One way of demonstrating the limited scope and force of penal law enforcement is to chart those Catholics who were executed for treason, for

50. Miller, *Popery and Politics*, chap. 3; J. A. Williams, "English Catholicism under Charles II: The Legal Position," *Recusant History* 7.1 (January 1963): 123–43.

51. James I, "A Premonition to All Christian Monarches," in *The Political Works of James I*, ed. Charles Howard McIlwain (Cambridge: Harvard University Press, 1918), p. 113.

52. Hibbard, "Early Stuart Catholicism," pp. 3–4; Kenyon, *Popish Plot*, p. 6; and Miller, *Popery and Politics*, pp. 1, 16, 58.

53. Glanvill, *Zealous and Impartial Protestant*, sig. B2.

being a priest, or for harboring one in the course of four reigns, from Elizabeth to Charles II. In his "statistical review" of English martyrs, Geoffrey Nuttall calculates that there were 189 martyrs under Elizabeth; 25 under James I, most in relation to the Gunpowder Plot; 24 under Charles I; and 24 under Charles II. Of these martyrs or traitors, depending on your perspective, most were clergy members; very few were peers; and even fewer were women—only four in total, all executed under Elizabeth in connection with hiding or helping priests.[54] The marked decline in executions under the Stuart kings, despite the increasingly ferocious and far-reaching penal laws enacted during their reigns, suggests, again, that these laws registered the nightmare of Catholic disorderliness and the fantasy of retribution far more than they described or dictated the actual punishments being meted out.

If Catholics were relatively unlikely to die for their faith, they were considerably more likely to pay for it. Penal laws were so named because they established specific penalties for behaviors such as absence from Church of England services. By doing so, they suggested that such conduct was morally neutral, that it was a nuisance to be discouraged rather than a crime to be prohibited outright. If one were willing and able to pay the fine, £20 per month, one could continue in the conduct; it was almost as if wealthy recusants could rent from the state the right not to go to church. As Thomas Abernethie complains, penal laws grant wealthy Catholics a "pecuniall libertie of conscience."[55] Penal laws sent the message that Catholic observance was not quite wrong, and placed the state in the position of profiting from, even licensing Catholic recusancy.[56] Yet these laws also made Catholic observance costly and inconvenient, and offered both the state and the community material rewards for scrutinizing Catholic conduct. In sum, although the various laws passed to penalize recusants were not consistently effective, and therefore are not accurate gauges of legal practice or of recusants' experience, they were capable of placing considerable pressure on Catholics to conform. Considered in the context of

54. Geoffrey F. Nuttall, "The English Martyrs, 1535–1680: A Statistical Review," *Journal of Ecclesiastical History* 22.3 (July 1971): 191–97; see also Martin Havran, *The Catholics of Caroline England* (Stanford: Stanford University Press, 1962), pp. 111–12; and Marie B. Rowlands, "Recusant Women, 1560–1640," in *Women in English Society, 1500–1800*, ed. Mary Prior (London: Methuen, 1985), pp. 149–80, esp. 158–59.

55. Abernethie, *Abjuration of Poperie*, sig. F4.

56. Elliot Rose, *Cases of Conscience: Alternatives Open to Recusants and Puritans under Elizabeth I and James I* (Cambridge: Cambridge University Press, 1975), chap. 5, esp. p. 68. In chap. 6 of *Conversion, Politics, and Religion*, Questier makes a strong case that enforcement of the laws, especially as regards financial penalties, was more consistent and efficient than has been claimed.

other printed vilifications of Catholicism, as products of and contributors to the English Protestant imaginary, these statutes provide further evidence of how English Protestant culture understood the threat of Catholicism and how strenuously it attempted to limit that threat.

REPRESENTATIONS OF CATHOLICS AND CATHOLICISM

At this point I would like to survey some of the ways in which seventeenth-century English culture construed the difference, and therefore the menace, of Catholicism. One pervasive assumption was that Catholics were not fully or dependably English, and therefore could not be trusted to be loyal subjects. In contrast to Jews, who, according to James Shapiro, as "an anomalous international nation" could not "owe allegiance to a foreign prince," Catholics were assumed to divide their allegiance between the pope and the English sovereign, at best, or to devote themselves entirely to the pope, at worst.[57] Because of their divided allegiance and their inscrutability, English Catholics' loyalty was constantly questioned; although they were undeniably subjects, they were assumed to be bad ones, since, as Alexander Chapman announced in 1610, "it is impossible to be of *their religion, and heere to be a true subject in Civill Obedience.*"[58]

Their familiarity and proximity made them especially threatening. In 1600, John Baxter warned his readers that "home-bred enemies" and "household foes" were "most hurtfull to the health of the Church."[59] *Admirable and Notable Things of Note* (1642) cautions that "of our enemies, the civill enemy is the most dangerous, and as his practice hath the least suspition, so have they the most danger, by this means working his designes from all means of p[r]evention."[60] Catholics depend on their very proximity to infiltrate and distract their opponents. Joseph Glanvill alerts his readers: "We look so intently at the danger that makes the loud Noise, that we little heed the Enemy behind the Bush, that is ready to shoot us off."[61] The only protection is a vigilant scrutiny of those close at hand. A 1679 commentary on an Elizabethan act of Parliament "to preserve the Queens

57. James Shapiro, *Shakespeare and the Jews* (New York: Columbia University Press, 1996), p. 191.

58. Alexander Chapman, *Jesuitisme Described under the Name of Babylons Policy* (London, 1610), sig. D3v. For Michael Dalton, "recusant" and "traitor" seem to be virtually synonymous (*The Countrey Justice* [London, 1618], p. 200).

59. John Baxter, *A Toile for Two-Legged Foxes* (London, 1600), sigs. Kv, L4v, B8v.

60. *Admirable and Notable Things of Note: viz. . . . a Horrible Treason Discovered from Holland, Which Was Plotted by a Company of Jesuites and Papists* (London, 1642), sig. A4.

61. Glanvill, *Zealous and Impartial Protestant*, sig. B.

person, and Protestant Religion and Government, from the Attempts of the Papists" seizes the opportunity to recommend that readers watch out for "the restless attempts of . . . an Inveterate, Implacable Enemy within us" as well as "the present Threats, and great Preparations of a Successfull Potent Enemy without us."[62] The purported scheme of the Gunpowder Plotters—to dig tunnels under the House of Parliament and blow it up from below, literally becoming "the secret Underminers of our Quiet," as *A Moderate Expedient for Preventing of Popery* (1680) described them—gave vividness and legitimacy to such anxious imaginings, and haunted anti-Catholic discourses throughout the century.[63]

From a Protestant perspective, what was particularly objectionable about Catholics was that they directed their animosity against their own kind. (The same might be said, of course, for the very Protestant vituperations from which I will now quote, but their authors did not see it that way). Comparing the days of Purim to the Gunpowder Plot to the detriment of the latter, for instance, George Hakewill explained that the "powder treason" was worse because "there [Purim], *Pagans* and *Infidels, Persians* and *Amalakites* conspired against the *Israelites:* heere native *English* and professed Christians, (though in truth most unworthy of the name of either) conspired against their own Countreymen."[64] Similarly, fifty years later Andrew Marvell explained that papists were worse than pagans, Jews, or Muslims, because "these were all, as I may say, of another Allegiance and if Enemys, yet not Traytors."[65] Catholicism, in contrast, claimed to be a branch of Christianity yet flouted its principles; worse, the pope wanted to police the Christianity of others, labeling them heretics. In 1680, Henry Care complained in even more vivid terms about the way Catholics turned their animus against other Christians rather than against "infidels," assumed here to be an appropriate target of antagonism. "There are swarms of Catholick *Bog-Trotters,* desperate *Monsieurs,* roaring *Bullies,* and Atheistical *Swaggerers* in all Corners of the Town, that no doubt had rather be *Riffling* their Neighbours, and *Cutting of Throats by Surprize* here at home, than venturing their *rotten* Carkasses in the field against the dreadful *Black Folks* of the Land of *Fez.*"[66] On the one hand, Care associated murderous

62. *The Act of Parliament of the 27th of Queen Elizabeth* (London, 1679), p. 6.

63. *A Moderate Expedient for Preventing of Popery, and the More Effectual Suppression of Jesuits and Priests, Without Giving Them the Vain-glory of Pretending to Martyrdom* (London, 1680), p. 7.

64. George Hakewill, *A Comparison Betweene the Dayes of Purim and That of the Powder Treason, for the Better Continuance of the Memory of It* (Oxford, 1626), sig. A4v.

65. Andrew Marvell, *An Account of the Growth of Popery, and Arbitrary Government in England* (Amsterdam, 1677), sig. B.

66. Henry Care, "The Popes Harbinger," appended to *The Weekly Pacquet of Advice from Rome* 3, no. 9 (Sept. 3, 1680): 71.

Catholics with foreigners, the Irish ("bog-trotters") and French ("monsieurs"). The difference and inferiority of the Irish, often associated with their Catholicism, was already sometimes understood as racial; that is, as a matter of blood. This racialization would gain momentum in the following centuries.[67] On the other hand, the whole thrust of Care's passage is to censure Catholics for assaulting their neighbors "here at home," rather than killing "dreadful black folks" elsewhere, which, he assumed, was an acceptable, indeed laudable, activity. All of these texts presume that it is appropriate to turn against those who are unlike you but "unnatural" to turn against your own kind. Yet they also articulate their fear that Catholics are unnatural in just this way; they are natives, Christians, neighbors here at home as well as traitors and murderers.

The widespread interest in domestic insubordination and familial murder provided polemicists with a rich stock of images and terms for describing what I have called elsewhere the "dangerous familiar."[68] Drawing on this stock, Protestant polemicists persistently constructed Catholics as domestic insubordinates: servants who served two masters, or treacherous wives, empowered by their intimacy with their intended victims. One vision of the apocalyptic consequences of the Gunpowder Plot, had it succeeded, prognosticates that "servants had ruled over us: and none could have delivered us, out of their hands: our inheritance had bene turned to the straungers, and our houses, to the Aliants."[69] Even the pope, who usually stood for the strangers and aliens who would enter in once the unruly servants opened the doors, is cast as himself an insubordinate. In 1602, Andrew Willet related that "Professing himself a servant, [the pope] doth his own will and not his masters"; *The Araignement and Execution of the Late Traytors* (1606) concurred that "*servus servorum* saies hee that would be *Dominus dominorum* servant of servants, that would be maister of maisters."[70] Such descriptions of the pope cast him as the insubordinate de-

67. On constructions of Irish difference, see Michael Hechter, *Internal Colonialism: The Celtic Fringe in British National Development, 1536–1966* (London: Routledge, 1975); Ann Rosalind Jones and Peter Stallybrass, "Dismantling Irena: The Sexualizing of Ireland in Early Modern England," in *Nationalisms and Sexualities*, ed. Andrew Parker et al. (New York: Routledge, 1992), pp. 157–71; Michael Neill, "Broken English and Broken Irish: Nation, Language, and the Optic of Power in Shakespeare's Histories," *Shakespeare Quarterly* 45.1 (1994): 1–32; and William Palmer, "Gender, Violence, and Rebellion in Tudor and Early Stuart Ireland," *Sixteenth Century Journal* 23.4 (1992): 699–712.

68. Frances E. Dolan, *Dangerous Familiars: Representations of Domestic Crime in England, 1550–1700* (Ithaca: Cornell University Press, 1994).

69. William Leigh, *Great Britaines Great Deliverance from the Great Danger of Popish Powder* (London, 1606), sig. B4, referring to Lam. 5:8.

70. Willet, *Catholicon*, sig. C5; *The Araignement and Execution of the Late Traytors* (London, 1606), sig. C4v.

pendent who haunts so many English stories of domestic violence and disorder. Representations of the Catholic threat were thus simultaneously stories of national and of domestic betrayal, emphasizing undermining from within as much as invasion from without. Hakewill, for instance, fantasized that if the Gunpowder Plot had succeeded, "wee should neither have lyen quietly in our beds, nor have sate quietly at our tables, nor have walked quietly in our streets, nor have travelled quietly in our waies, much lesse have mett quietly in our temples but every place would have beene full of feare and danger and horror and bloud."[71] The familiar is not always more frightening or contemptible than the strange, nor did early modern English culture inevitably locate threat in the known rather than the unknown. But in the particular situation of Catholics and Catholicism in early modern England, familiarity, similarity, and proximity were not a comfort.

Catholicism was also associated with the unfamiliar and foreign, as Care's reference to "bog-trotters" and "monsieurs" suggests. This association offered the reassurance that Catholicism was not a residual English belief and practice, at war with a newer arrival, but rather something that people believed elsewhere and tried feloniously to import into England.[72] From this perspective, the threat lay not in local, known Catholics but in what Caroline Hibbard terms "the specter of international Catholicism, both monolithic and conspiratorial."[73] This specter haunting the English Protestant imagination corresponded to the real power of Catholic countries, especially if they mobilized English Catholics as a potential fifth column, creating an alliance between *"Rome's* Rogues abroad, and Plotters here at home," to quote a 1679 broadside.[74] The part of English Catholics that enabled them to conspire with foreigners could be understood as itself foreign; John Baxter, for instance, referred to the "Italianated" hearts of English Catholics.[75] In some texts, all that was wrong with Catholicism could be summed up as "Roman"; in others, "the Spanish Inquisition" stood for all of the violence, injustice, and corruption associated with (and displaced onto) Catholicism.

71. Hakewill, *Comparison Betweene the Dayes of Purim and That of the Powder Treason,* sig. D2r–v; see also John Heath, *The Divell of the Vault; or, The Unmasking of Murther in a Briefe Declaration of the Cacolicke-Complotted Treason, Lately Discoverd* (London, 1606), sig. D.

72. Collinson, *Birthpangs of Protestant England,* pp. 16, 11; Lake, "Anti-Popery," pp. 79, 94.

73. Hibbard, "Early Stuart Catholicism," pp. 28, 29, 31; see also Hibbard, *Charles I and the Popish Plot,* p. 3.

74. "A Tale of the Tubbs; or, Rome's Master Peice Defeated" (London, 1679). On how fears of internal conspiracy increased in the seventeenth century, see Clifton, "Fear of Popery," p. 150; Harris, *London Crowds,* p. 112; Kenyon, *Popish Plot,* p. 3; and Miller, *Popery and Politics,* p. 7.

75. Baxter, *Toile for Two-Legged Foxes,* sig. K6v.

The focus for xenophobia shifted from year to year, depending on both conflicts and potential alliances. The fear and hatred of Spain, for instance, was aroused as much by Mary Tudor's marriage to Philip II and the proposed "Spanish match" between the infanta and Prince Charles as by the Armada.[76] The court under the Stuart kings became a focus for anxieties about this international Catholicism because, according to Miller, "the Catholicism of the court tended to be alien and cosmopolitan; the court was full of foreigners and Irish."[77] Here, too, the privileged position of Catholics in relation to other nonconformists provoked more hostile antagonism because it made them seem more powerful. Viewed as participants in international (indeed, antinational) communities and conspiracies, Catholics could never be viewed as loyal and trustworthy members of the English nation. Thus their recourse to a constellation of leaders outside of England, which distinguished them from other religious nonconformists, also made them more suspect.

At the level of conduct, this desire to associate Catholicism with strangers made "unknown Catholics" more vulnerable to attack, more likely to be singled out in moments of crisis. According to Robin Clifton, for instance, "many alarms centred on Catholics who were strangers locally, often because they were refugees or vagrants. When a disturbance centred upon Catholics known to the locality they were almost invariably recusants living just beyond the town affected. . . . Where the Catholics suspected of conspiracy fell into neither category, the reason for alarm was usually some striking and alarming departure from their customary behaviour."[78] Perceiving Catholics as foreign and unfamiliar rendered volatile an intransigent yet dormant anti-Catholicism through the animating power of xenophobia.

If anti-Catholicism in the abstract persisted alongside relatively peaceful coexistence with known Catholics, and if known Catholics were less threatening (and therefore less vulnerable) than strange ones, then anti-Catholicism was not a prejudice nurtured in ignorance that could be ameliorated by new knowledge. Split off from lived experience, anti-Catholicism could coexist with tolerance and remain unaltered. As a con-

76. On the persistence of hostility toward Spain, see William S. Maltby, *The Black Legend in England: The Development of Anti-Spanish Sentiment, 1558–1660* (Durham, N.C.: Duke University Press, 1971).

77. Miller, *Popery and Politics,* p. 26.

78. Clifton, "Fear of Popery," p. 165; see also Robin Clifton, "The Popular Fear of Catholics during the English Revolution," *Past & Present* 52 (1971): 23–55, esp. 38, 49; Harris, *London Crowds,* p. 198; and Lake, "Anti-Popery," p. 94.

sequence, Catholics themselves might fear strangers. Roger Castlemaine, for instance, alleges that, since Catholics know they are good companions, hosts, and neighbors, "our acquaintance therefore we fear at no time, but it is the stranger we dread: (that taking all on Hear-say,) zealously wounds, and then examines the business when 'tis too late, or is perchance confirm'd by another, that knows no more of us then he himself."[79] In Castlemaine's view, a stranger might not be able to balance prejudice against local knowledge, and might respond to the abstraction of antipopery rather than to the daily encounters that were supposed to temper that prejudice.

Another way in which Protestants associated Catholicism with the stranger was by associating it, in subtle and inconsistent ways, with monstrosity, contamination, and blackness. When this association was made, it was often via imagery of "unnatural" congress, not between individuals but between abstractions, resulting in monstrous conceptions. Catholic plots were widely described as monstrous births; Catholics from Guy Fawkes to Elizabeth Cellier were described as "midwives" who presided over the travails through which Catholics' plots were born.[80] In anti-Catholic polemic, as elsewhere, images of pregnancy and childbirth are more versatile than one might expect, and therefore more confusing. Sometimes the mother is the Whore of Babylon, her pregnancy revealing her sinfulness and deflating her pretensions to virtue. In such cases, the whore mother transmits her own corruption to her offspring. Elsewhere, polemic casts England itself as the mother, harboring Catholicism as a monstrous child that grows inside its parent but is not like it. At Henry Garnet's trial for his involvement in the Gunpowder Plot, the Earl of Northampton wondered: "What spirit moved you and yours (*M. Garnet*) to dissolve the quiet of a State, that never conceived you in her wombe, with a purpose that (like the broode of Vipers) you should make your issue into life by eating out the bowels of the Damme that gave you both creation and nourishment?"[81] When England stands as mother, the means of conception (rape) or the attitude of the progeny (matricidal) make the birth monstrous; the rapist father puts his stamp on the fetus, erasing the impress of the virtuous English mother. Whether Catholicism is the mother or the father, then, it

79. *To All the Royalists That Suffered for His Majesty . . . the Humble Apology of the English Catholicks* (London, 1666), sig. A4.

80. *Novembris Monstrum; or, Rome Brought to Bed in England, with the Whores Miscarying* (London, 1641), sig. C5; *A Letter from the Lady Cresswell to Madam C. the Midwife* (London, 1680), p. 4.

81. *A True and Perfect Relation of the Whole Proceedings against the Late Most Barbarous Traitors, Garnet a Jesuite, and His Confederats* (London, 1606), sig. Ccc4.

determines the shape of the offspring that are born of its coupling with England. Such monstrous births warn of the dire consequences of a very common occurrence: the congress between English Protestants and Catholics.

All Catholic plots, whether real or imagined, were "abortive" in that none of them came to fruition; sometimes the horror and harmlessness of these abortive stillbirths were located in blackness. In descriptions written eighty years apart, for instance, Catholic conspirators produce only an "Affrick Birth," or "a few *Abortive Blackamores.*"[82] Discouraging England's toleration of its Catholic population, such imagery warned that incorporating Catholics' difference into a definition of England could alter, indeed sully or blacken, England's complexion.

An alleged episode in which some of the Gunpowder Plotters were drying their powder by the fire when it exploded, besmirching their faces, offers another image of the way Englishmen, through Catholic conspiracy, might lose their whiteness. Since Protestants repeatedly expressed anxiety that Catholics were so adept at disguise that they were unidentifiable, such a marking of their difference and danger might be seen as useful. But this besmirching of English whiteness would not stop with the conspirators themselves. In *Great Britaines Great Deliverance*, for instance, William Leigh informs "Romish Aramites" that "the prints of your former cruelties have pierced our hearts, but this last impression [from the Gunpowder Plot] hath even wounded our soules, wherin we see nothing but traces of blood, and (as it were) the blacke face, and countenance of confused desolation." Leigh confers on the "Romish Aramites" the power to print their cruelty in black letters inside of white Englishmen, on their hearts and souls; his grammar also confuses whose faces are black. Does Leigh's "we"—that is, the Protestant English—see its own face as black or has it been invaded by the enemy's image, the smudged faces of the Gunpowder Plot conspirators? Whose is the "countenance of confused desolation"? Leigh later warns that the threatened triumph of Catholicism will first result in economic disaster and consequently will blacken all English people: "Our skinne had bene blacke as an Oven, because of the terrible famine." For Leigh, this blackening symbolizes the degradation that would be wrought by a return to Rome. Leigh's depiction of Catholics as black-faced, his suggestion that this blackness could spread to other people through toleration, and his description of the deprivation and loss that would be its inevitable consequence build toward the lesson he draws from the Gunpowder Plot: "Be-

---

82. *Novembris Monstrum*, sig. D3; Miles Prance, *Mr. Prance's Answer to Mrs. Cellier's Libel* (London, 1680), sig. E2v.

ware of mixture, and shun the sinnes of *Samaria*, who were a mixed people, and of a confused Religion, tollerating both the persons and causes of Idolatry."[83]

Although the feared "mixture" might take many forms and blur various boundaries, it was most often depicted in visual terms not just as the co-existence of different groups but also as the resulting erosion of needful distinctions. Toleration does not improve the inferior category (whether women or black people or Catholics) as much as it disparages the privileged group (men, white people, Protestants). In early modern England, "mixture" threatened "the absorption of 'white' European by the foreign other," as Kim Hall has said.[84] As Patricia Parker demonstrates, "the language . . . of contaminating, sullying, or mixing is part of a series of distinctions already in place before *miscegenation* (literally 'mixing') became the historically later term for the adulterating or sullying of 'white.'"[85] Thus, in the "mixture" Leigh warns against, not only do boundaries dissolve but the "inferior" category obscures the "superior" one. This fear of subsumption often suggests that the inferior yet magnetic category that pulls the unsuspecting into it is somehow prior; this is especially the case in anti-Catholic discourses, since English Protestants could readily understand themselves as having been Catholic. In the "mixture" of Catholic and Protestant, the Catholic threatens not only to subsume or absorb the Protestant but to mirror something already within him and return him to a former self, repudiated but not erased. English Protestants could and did convert (or revert) to Catholicism; they not only lived among Catholics but married or became them. The language of mixture, used rarely in descriptions of Catholicism, provided one way of insisting on an absolute difference between Catholics and Protestants, and a way of demonizing the congress and traffic between the two. Yet at the very time that this imagery insisted on distinction, it registered the fact that this boundary could be crossed and the difference become blurred.

83. Leigh, *Great Britaines Great Deliverance,* sigs. Bv–B2, B4, E.

84. Kim F. Hall, *Things of Darkness: Economies of Race and Gender in Early Modern England* (Ithaca: Cornell University Press, 1995), p. 95.

85. Patricia Parker, *Shakespeare from the Margins: Language, Culture, Context* (Chicago: University of Chicago Press, 1996), p. 5; see also p. 276n12. On the early modern conceptualization of miscegenation, see also Lynda E. Boose, "'The Getting of a Lawful Race': Racial Discourse in Early Modern England and the Unrepresentable Black Woman," in *Women, "Race," and Writing in the Early Modern Period,* ed. Margo Hendricks and Patricia Parker (London and New York: Routledge, 1994), pp. 35–54, esp. 41–46; and Margaret W. Ferguson, "News from the New World: Miscegenous Romance in Aphra Behn's *Oroonoko* and *Widow Ranter,*" in *The Production of English Renaissance Culture,* ed. David Lee Miller, Sharon O'Dair, and Harold Weber (Ithaca: Cornell University Press, 1994), pp. 151–89.

Associating Catholics with the foreign, the strange, and the black helped to make them less disturbing, and to mark them out as more acceptable targets of aggression. If their home was someplace other than England, then perhaps they could be sent back there; certainly they could be clearly identified and expelled from England without loss. Yet, just as, under controlled conditions, blackness could be fashionable, so the strangeness conferred on Catholicism could give it panache. In Thomas Scott's popular satire _The Second Part of Vox Populi_ (1624), the wily Gondomar explains to the Spanish parliament that "the English naturally are desirous of novelties, and innovations. . . . Hence are strangers the most admired and entertayned amongst them, and if of quality preferred many times to place and preferment before the English, though perhaps there are many who deserve better." Even in this satirical view, the taste for the strange is an urban and elite phenomenon. English ladies would compete to serve as "Groomesse" to the infanta should she become the English queen, yet the "common people" have an antipathy to Spaniards.[86]

Other kinds of evidence also suggest that while local prejudices scapegoated the stranger, the "strangeness" of court Catholicism was precisely what made it fashionable. Crowds flocked to the royal and embassy chapels with their highly theatrical, gorgeous stagings of the mass. Queen Henrietta Maria's sumptuous new chapel at her Somerset House residence was staffed by Capuchins, whose "strangeness" made them spectacles in themselves. Fr. Cyprien of Gamache, the queen's Capuchin confessor, described the response: "They said that they [the Capuchins] were persons so strange, wearing dresses so extraordinary, leading so austere a life, that every one conceived a desire to see them. Accordingly, persons of quality, ministers, people of all conditions, who had never been out of the kingdom, came to see them, as one goes to see Indians, Malays, Savages, and men from the extremities of the earth." Since Londoners came "in crowds" to see the Capuchins, the Capuchins "resolved by common consent to add something striking to their austerities," and thereby to amplify the difference that made them a draw. "To edify" the English and "to render them the more disposed to a holy conversion," or perhaps just to keep the spectators coming, the Capuchins stripped their beds down to bare boards to impress sightseers with their asceticism.[87]

---

86. Thomas Scott, _The Second Part of Vox Populi; or, Gondomar Appearing in the Likenes of Matchiavell in a Spanish Parliament_ (London, 1624), sigs. B2, B3. On Scott, see Maltby, _Black Legend_, pp. 102–9.

87. Fr. Cyprien of Gamache, "Memoirs of the Mission in England of the Capuchin Fathers," in _The Court and Times of Charles the First_, ed. Thomas Birch, 2 vols. (London: Henry Colburn, 1848), 2: 309.

Of course, anti-Catholicism, always in the mainstream, could also be trendy. In January 1679, for instance, fashionable ladies carried daggers bearing the name of the supposed victim of the Popish Plot conspirators, Sir Edmundbury Godfrey, as protection against murderous papists.[88] But anti-Catholicism was so hardy a strain of English national identity and English public discourse that Catholicism itself, for the most part, had the monopoly on exoticism and fashion. It also had an advantage denied to other forms of religious dissent, since it could mobilize the resources of queens, courtiers, ambassadors, and aristocrats in London, as well as of foreign kings, to render itself glamorous. Furthermore, by the reigns of the Stuarts, enough time had elapsed since the Reformation that Catholicism might have "nostalgic appeal for the older generation and novelty value for the younger," as Helen Hackett has claimed was the case by late in Elizabeth's reign.[89] Thus, whatever "strangeness" could be attributed to Catholicism worked as much to enhance its fascination as to justify its persecution[90]—perhaps because any distance imposed between Catholics and their countrymen, any defamiliarization, might make them less disturbing and amorphous. If they were like "Indians, Malays, Savages, and men from the extremities of the earth," then, however frightening, at least they would be identifiably different.

Linda Colley tries to resolve the paradox of Catholic English subjects, who interrupt her claim that British national identity was defined against outside others, by engaging in the same strategy that Protestant polemicists sometimes used; she estranges Catholics: "Catholics were beyond the boundaries, always on the outside even if they were British-born: they did not and could not belong."[91] Yet Catholics were such troubling figures precisely because they represented the foreign or strange from inside geographical and conceptual boundaries of Englishness.

In the chapters to come, I investigate how gender serves the project of rendering the familiar threatening and of positioning Catholics as simultaneously familiar and foreign. The epithet "whore of Babylon," widely used to denounce the pope as the Antichrist and the Roman church more generally, yokes together the familiar seduction and corruption of the unruly feminine and the more outlandish threat of the foreign, even fantastical. For where, exactly, is Babylon? In seventeenth-century representa-

---

88. Miller, *Popery and Politics*, p. 161.

89. Helen Hackett, *Virgin Mother, Maiden Queen: Elizabeth I and the Cult of the Virgin Mary* (Houndmills, Basingstoke, Hampshire: Macmillan, 1995), p. 161.

90. G. K. Hunter, "Elizabethans and Foreigners," in *Shakespeare Survey*, vol. 17, ed. Allardyce Nicoll (Cambridge: Cambridge University Press, 1964), p. 45.

91. Colley, "Britishness and Otherness," p. 320.

tions of Catholics and Catholicism, London threatens to become Babylon, or to admit invasion; the apocalypse is imminent. English Catholics are whores of Babylon, feminized, intimate, proximate, yet unknowable: in dramatizations of the Gunpowder Plot, which transport the conspiracy of Englishmen on their native soil to exotic locations, yet also include women among the conspirators to ally the story more closely to typical accounts of domestic conspiracy and insubordination; in attacks on Henrietta Maria, who is French but also the wife of one English king and the mother of two others, and who is accused of gaining political influence by means of "curtain lectures" to her husband; and, finally, in representations of Elizabeth Cellier, whose husband, and therefore surname, are French, but whose notoriety stems much more from her elite London circle and her way with the English tongue and the English law.

CHAPTER TWO

Searching the Bed:
Jacobean Anti-Catholicism and
the Scandal of Heterosociality

The Gunpowder Plot, to whatever extent it existed in the minds of those executed for it and in the discourses describing and lamenting it, was, for the most part, a conspiracy of men against men. Of the conspirators, including three who died before reaching trial, thirteen who were tried and executed, and two who were fined and imprisoned, none was a woman. Of the intended victims, the only woman was James I's wife, Anne. Yet the anti-Catholic discourses that proliferated after the plot was discovered often represented the problem of Catholicism as that of female empowerment and gender inversion. While women were not often blamed outright for the Gunpowder Plot, female figures, abstract and particular, crop up frequently in Jacobean discussions of the threat Catholics and Catholicism offer to England. Why would that be? The answer, I suggest, lies in a polemical tradition that both predates and long survives the alleged Gunpowder Plot.

Representations of the plot take their shape as much from the cultural imaginary and polemical conventions of post-Reformation England as from the contours of an extraordinary event, in part because the Gunpowder Plot never quite existed, except at the level of imagination and representation. It was conceived by or imputed to Catholics, but not enacted by them. According to most versions of the story, the conspirators had secreted barrels of gunpowder in the undercrofts of the House of Parliament, planning to blow it up while Parliament was in session, thus killing James I, his wife and male heirs, and virtually all of the most powerful men in the kingdom (the nobility and clergy, the judges, and the members of

45

Parliament assembled for its opening) and any foreign ambassadors present. As John Heath imagines the outcome in 1606: "Heere armes, there legges, dissevered quite,/lie mangled every where."[1] The explosion would also have destroyed the building James I identifies as that in which "the cruell Lawes (as they [Catholics] say) were made against their Religion" as well as many important documents; had they been lost, according to George Hakewill, "not onely we but the memory of us and ours should have beene thus extinguished in an instant, worse than if we had been invaded or vanquished by the *Turke* or *Scithian.*"[2]

Uncovered before it could do any damage, the Gunpowder Plot produced rather than destroyed laws, books, and proclamations. Although commentators on the plot frequently insisted that its scope was so vast that it was impossible to comprehend or describe it, it was evidently not "unspeakable," for it was much discussed and widely represented, both visually and verbally, throughout the seventeenth century. Illuminations of the subterranean schemes of the powder plotters took many forms: published accounts of trials and James's speeches, sermons and prayers of thanksgiving, ballads, pamphlets, plays, and woodcuts. Retelling this story became the fastest way, throughout the seventeenth century, to explain why Catholics should not be tolerated and exactly what kind of threat they offered. Guy Fawkes Day remains a holiday on which effigies of the chief conspirator are paraded and burned, suggesting the power of this purported plot to provoke rather than to baffle representation.[3]

Many viewed the Gunpowder Plot as a scheme "without any forraine help to replant againe the Catholique Religion." The many representations of and responses to the plot worked to convince many English people still adjusting to the accession of a Scottish king that their greatest enemy was other English people, and that even without foreign assistance English Catholics could be very dangerous, worse than "the *Turke* or *Scithian.*"[4]

---

1. John Heath, *The Divell of the Vault* (London, 1606), sig. C2v.

2. *His Majesties Speach in This Last Session of Parliament, as Neere His Very Words as Could Be Gathered at the Instant* (London, 1605), sigs. B2v, E3v; George Hakewill, *A Comparison Betweene the Dayes of Purim and That of the Powder Treason, for the Better Continuance of the Memory of It* (Oxford, 1626), sig. D3.

3. Although effigies of the pope, the clergy, and the devil began to be burned as part of November 5 festivities during Charles I's reign, effigies of Guy Fawkes himself do not seem to have been burned until the nineteenth century. See David Cressy, *Bonfires and Bells: National Memory and the Protestant Calendar in Elizabethan and Stuart England* (Berkeley: University of California Press, 1989), p. 147.

4. Thomas Wright's "confession" as presented in John Foxe, *Actes and Monuments*, 3 vols. (London, 1641), continuation, p. 90. For early accounts of the plot, see *His Majesties Speach in This Last Session of Parliament*, also known as the *King's Book*, since it was the official government narrative of the plot and its discovery; *A True and Perfect Relation of the Whole Proceedings against the Late Most Barbarous Traitors, Garnet a Jesuite, and His Confederats* (London,

While James and his counselors probably did not make up the Gunpowder Plot out of whole cloth to serve his public relations needs, the timely "discovery" of the plot was certainly opportune.[5]

Many of the otherwise heterogeneous anti-Catholic texts written in response to the plot employ gender as one way of describing a terrifyingly new threat in familiar yet still disturbing terms. On the one hand, the author of *The Women's Sharp Revenge* bolstered a defense of women in 1640 by reminding readers that "we have heard of a Gunpowder Treason plotted by men, but never heard since the beginning of the world such a devilish and damned stratagem devised by women"; later s/he even more vehemently insisted, "I am sure that women were not the complotters or contrivers of the Powder Treason."[6] On the other hand, the plot was persistently associated with women and their sneaky, cunning schemes. Although no women were indicted, convicted, or executed in relation to the plot, many were imprisoned and questioned. Those who came under scrutiny were the wives, servants, relations, and allies of the accused conspirators.[7] Furthermore, the popular imagination came to focus on women with an intensity out of proportion to their presence among those examined about the plot or implicated in it. In John Webster's tragicomedy *The Devil's Law-Case* (1617–21), for instance, Romelio claims that his mother's suit, by which she is attempting to disinherit him,

> Springs from a devilish malice, and her pretence
> Of a grieved conscience, and religion,
> Like to the horrid powder-treason in England,
> Has a most bloody unnatural revenge
> Hid under it. Oh the violencies of women![8]

1606); and *The Araignement and Execution of the Late Traytors* (London, 1606). Much of this material was reprinted around the time of the Popish Plot as *The Gunpowder-Treason: With a Discourse of the Manner of Its Discovery . . . Now Reprinted* (London, 1679).

5. Some historians, such as Francis Edwards, S.J., argue that the conspirators were framed or the cases against them bolstered, and that evidence was forged, manipulated, or produced through torture ("Still Investigating Gunpowder Plot," *Recusant History* 21.3 [1993]: 305–46); others, such as Mark Nicholls, insist that the surviving evidence, while not always conclusive, is reliable (*Investigating Gunpowder Plot* [Manchester: Manchester University Press, 1991]). A. H. Dodd, "The Spanish Treason, the Gunpowder Plot, and the Catholic Refugees," *English Historical Review* 53 (1938): 627–50, esp. 646, and Jenny Wormald, "Gunpowder, Treason, and Scots," *Journal of British Studies* 24 (April 1985): 141–68, both argue that the plot was a "heaven-sent" opportunity.

6. *The Women's Sharpe Revenge* (1640), in *The Women's Sharp Revenge: Five Women's Pamphlets from the Renaissance*, ed. Simon Shepherd (London: Fourth Estate, 1985), pp. 173, 178.

7. The most detailed discussion of the women tangentially related to the plot and the plotters can be found in Antonia Fraser, *Faith and Treason: The Story of the Gunpowder Plot* (New York: Doubleday, 1996).

8. John Webster, *The Devil's Law-Case*, ed. Elizabeth M. Brennan (London: Ernest Benn, 1975), 4.2.285–89.

At first glance, Romelio's rapid slide from his mother's malice to "the horrid powder-treason in England," his conflation of political conspiracy and private revenge, and his leap from a confraternity of men to "the violencies of women" seem quirky. But the slide in this passage is, in fact, quite typical of representations of Catholicism after the Gunpowder Plot. The focus often shifted from the conspirators to the priests—especially Jesuits, who were assumed to be behind most Catholic schemes—to the wives and other women assumed to be in cahoots with the priests. Thus the missing link in Romelio's chain of association is the priest.

I will now explore premonitions and reverberations of the plot in anti-Catholic polemic, in penal laws, and on the stage, rather than the plot itself. In this analysis, the Gunpowder Plot remains elusive; it recedes as we approach, rather than yielding up its secrets. What I seek to discover in the representations of and responses to the plot is not whether there was a conspiracy or who was involved or what they hoped to gain, but rather how the allegation of such a conspiracy served the English Protestant imagination. My particular interest is the ways in which gender inflects these Jacobean constructions of the Catholic threat. The fact that the conspiracy itself, to the extent that we can grasp it, was the work of lay male agents makes it all the better an occasion for considering the tenacity and obstinacy with which anti-Catholic discourses reassert the links between Catholics and disorderly women, between women and priests.

While the centrality of gender disorder in representations of Catholicism seems at first surprising, it is in other ways predictable. To construe the threat of Catholicism as the threat of disorderly women may require a misapprehension of the Gunpowder Plot itself, yet it draws on the most conventional ways of using gender to describe both order and disorder. As in a wide variety of early modern discourses, anti-Catholic representations depict disorder in terms of gender inversion; in Catholicism, its attackers find women on top and men on the bottom. Yet in anti-Catholic discourses, these stock characterizations of gender inversion—so pervasively and obsessively repeated in early modern culture, so much discussed now—are less predictable than they at first seem. While representations of Catholic women link them to other criminalized women in early modern culture—the witch, the scold, the petty traitor—many of these representations also suggest that the problem of the recusant wife is closely related to the legal problem posed by wives in general. Thus Catholic women are not demonic opposites of Protestant women but disturbing reminders of the dilemma created when spiritual equality and wifely subordination, a conscience and coverture, are brought together.

While representations of Catholic men denigrate them as effeminate and domesticated, these representations also suggest that manhood in the early modern period was contingent and precarious. Thus these representations put pressure on the very notion of masculinity, and on the assumption that authority, masculinity, and autonomy inevitably go together. Just as the caricatures of Catholic men and women turn out to be more complicated than the bossy woman and the henpecked man, the relationship between Catholic women and men is not always depicted as one in which gender hierarchy is neatly inverted. In some texts, we glimpse the prospect of men and women in alliance. For all the debate about and reevaluation of marriage in this period, the possibility that a man and a woman, whether husband and wife or priest and penitent, might collaborate as equals was considerably less familiar than the assumption that one or the other must be "on top." In anti-Catholic discourses, we find unease not just about gender inversion but about gender equality and gender integration. This disquiet suggests that, while heterosociality was in many ways the norm in early modern culture, it was also considered scandalous and disturbing. Although "heterosexuality" is a nineteenth-century coinage and "heterosociality" an even more recent one, I use both anachronistic terms as a matter of convenience. Early modern culture did not have a name for attraction, attachment, and congress between the sexes, but it did have a range of terms that focused largely on licit and illicit sexual liaisons: marriage, adultery, fornication. This suggests both that relationships between men and women were so much the norm and so omnipresent that they did not need to be named, and could not be described with a single term, and that certain possibilities between the sexes—such as friendship—were not really on the map. Even if Protestantism and print conjoined to promote a wider dissemination of the ideal of companionate marriage, legal and polemical critiques of Catholic domesticity suggest that the dominant discourses in early modern England sometimes had a hard time imagining and valuing mutuality and cooperation between the sexes. Thus debates around Catholicism brought to the fore contradictions in the prevailing ideologies of gender, sexuality, and the family.

CATHOLIC WOMEN ON TOP?

Given that not only the conspirators but the administrative hierarchy of the Roman church was (and is) entirely male, why would Catholicism be viewed as empowering women any more than Protestantism did? In retrospect, some historians assert that Protestantism offered women new opportunities, new skills, and new respect by raising the prestige of marriage, countering clerical misogyny, arguing for women's spiritual equality, encouraging women's education and Bible study, and offering women fuller participation in public worship. Indeed, the Reformation is often heralded as the harbinger of modernity and progress. When one focuses on Catholicism in the Reformation, however, as in the Glorious Revolution and the Enlightenment, one loses confidence in this progress. Once one does so, the Reformation looks like a mixed bag for women, offering both gains and losses.[9] While they may have experienced some of the benefits I just listed, women lost the convent as an alternative to marriage, and lost as well female objects of worship and a visual culture rich in positive images of femininity.

In the special circumstances of post-Reformation England, married Catholic women may have gained authority and independence. If, as Christopher Hill and Lawrence Stone have claimed, Protestantism empowered the father as priest presiding over the "spiritualized household," Catholicism in a country without monasteries or churches empowered women as custodians of household religion, as Marie B. Rowlands was the first to argue.[10] Catholic women did not look to their husbands as their spiritual teachers and leaders, but turned instead to priests. Yet in England clergymen were scarce. Once the mass was suppressed (everywhere but in royal or embassy chapels in London, that is) and priests were hunted as felons, household observance was the only observance available to most people; in many households, women motivated and facilitated clandestine worship, even when, in the case of sacraments that required a priest, they could not preside themselves. If a priest lived in the house, he was dependent on the mistress's as well as the master's patronage and protection. Consequently, whether the Roman Catholic church liked it or not, many English Catholic women were not clearly under either a husband's or a

---

9. Patricia Crawford, *Women and Religion in England, 1500–1720* (London and New York: Routledge, 1993), chaps. 1 and 2; Natalie Zemon Davis, *Society and Culture in Early Modern France: Eight Essays* (Stanford: Stanford University Press, 1975), chap. 3; Sr. Joseph Damien Hanlon, "These Be but Women," in *From the Renaissance to the Counter-Reformation: Essays in Honor of Garrett Mattingly*, ed. Charles H. Carter (New York: Random House, 1965), pp. 371–400; Theodora Jankowski, "Pure Resistance: Queer(y)ing Virginity in the Early Modern Drama," manuscript; Elizabeth Rapley, *The Dévotes: Women and Church in Seventeenth-Century France* (Montreal: McGill-Queen's University Press, 1993); Retha M. Warnicke, *Women of the English Renaissance and Reformation* (Westport, Conn.: Greenwood, 1983), chap. 9; and Diane Willen, "Women and Religion in Early Modern England," in *Women in Reformation and Counter-Reformation Europe: Public and Private Worlds*, ed. Sherrin Marshall (Bloomington: Indiana University Press, 1989), pp. 140–65.

10. Christopher Hill, *Society and Puritanism in Pre-Revolutionary England*, 2d ed. (New York: Schocken, 1967), chap. 13; Lawrence Stone, "The Rise of the Nuclear Family in Early Modern England: The Patriarchal Stage," in *The Family in History*, ed. Charles E. Rosenberg (Philadelphia: University of Pennsylvania Press, 1975), pp. 13–57; Marie B. Rowlands, "Recusant Women, 1560–1640," in *Women in English Society, 1500–1800*, ed. Mary Prior (London: Methuen, 1985), pp. 149–80.

priest's spiritual governance, or they received spiritual advice from a man whom they also sheltered from the law.[11] In their own households, they could dedicate themselves to piety with less interference, supervision, and restriction than nuns.

Yet these recusant households, far from private or safe, were scrutinized and vulnerable. Servants and neighbors stood to gain a percentage of recusansy fines if they informed. Although, according to Rowlands, the House of Commons was much more comfortable prosecuting Jesuits and seminary priests than it was sanctioning "an intrusion by the state into the family," it is also true that, as Diane Willen has put it, the religious practices of recusants "were perceived as legitimate matters of public concern for the body politic."[12] Penal laws made it their project to divide and conquer recusant families, and sometimes they succeeded. William Allen laments of Catholic families under Elizabeth: "How many godly and honest married couples most dear one to another, by the imprisonment, banishment, flight, of either party are pitifully sundered; how many families thereby dissolved?"[13] With the household serving as base of political operations, place of worship, seminary, and site of various criminal activities, from misdemeanors through felonies, women's authority therein might have far-reaching consequences. Furthermore, when families were sundered, even married women might head their households.

To a certain extent, anti-Catholic polemic responded to Catholic women's household empowerment, holding a distorting mirror up to this phenomenon. But the association of Catholicism with powerful women emerged more from caricatures and fantasies of Catholic theology and iconography than from descriptions of the actual distributions of power in Catholic households or in church administration. For many in post-Reformation England, the church was embodied in the once-loved statues and paintings of the Virgin Mary and other female intercessors, which were now repudiated and even violently mutilated or destroyed. According to

11. The church did not necessarily sanction women's increased authority and independence. The Council of Trent, for instance, strenuously sought to cloister women in holy orders and to curtail the domestic authority of married women. Because of the unique circumstances in England, however, the council's reach did not quite extend there. See Rapley, *Dévotes*, chaps. 1 and 2; Margot Todd, *Christian Humanism and the Puritan Social Order* (Cambridge: Cambridge University Press, 1987), p. 236.

12. Rowlands, "Recusant Women," p. 154; Diane Willen, "Women in the Public Sphere in Early Modern England: The Case of the Urban Working Poor," in *Gendered Domains: Rethinking Public and Private in Women's History*, ed. Dorothy O. Helly and Susan M. Reverby (Ithaca: Cornell University Press, 1992), p. 185.

13. William Allen, *A True, Sincere, and Modest Defense of English Catholics*, reprinted with William Cecil, *The Execution of Justice in England*, ed. Robert M. Kingdon, Folger Documents of Tudor and Stuart Civilization (Ithaca: Cornell University Press, 1965), p. 227.

Huston Diehl, this iconophobic violence accompanied and tried anxiously to suppress an iconophilic longing for these familiar, trusted, still perhaps loved female images.[14] Reforming zeal thus needed to harness misogyny to counter ambivalence and expose the folly of worshiping women. Litanies of objection to Catholic practice often start out with its elevation of women into objects of adoration: *The Araignement and Execution of the Late Traytors* (1606) complains of Catholics' "kissing of babies, their kneeling to wodden Ladies, their calling to Saintes that cannot heare them." According to Richard Sheldon, Catholics "praise and adore wodden and Silvered Ladies, at *Loretto, Sichem, Hall,* &c."[15] While some saints survived the Reformation relatively unscathed—England's patron saint, George, for example—others, especially "ladies," became the focus for iconoclasm and anti-Catholic hostility. The most contested of them all, because most visible and powerful, was the Virgin Mary, as I will discuss in the next chapter. Thus discourses that depicted Catholicism as empowering women responded largely to a theology and an iconography in which women were understood as inappropriately visible, powerful, and esteemed.

Reformers' attacks on the Roman Catholic church also associated it with the Whore of Babylon, borrowing imagery from the Book of Revelation to vivify intensely corporeal denunciations of the church's corrupt and feminized body.[16] The language and associations found in their attacks had been widely used even before the Reformation to denounce corruption within the church, but they accrued fresh force and specificity when the Reformation split Christianity. By persistently associating the Roman church with fallen women, reformers could acknowledge its seductive appeal while simultaneously repudiating it. This strategy of representing difference and disorder through the person of the unruly woman is hardly unique to reformers or, later, anti-Catholic polemicists. A wide range of early modern texts ridicule and disparage change and difference as the carnivalesque inversion of an expected gender hierarchy; that is, as a dominant woman "on top" who subordinates a submissive man "on the bottom." In the various contestations that characterize the early modern period, such as those between Catholics and Protestants, or Anglicans and

14. Huston Diehl, *Staging Reform, Reforming the Stage: Protestantism and Popular Theater in Early Modern England* (Ithaca: Cornell University Press, 1997), esp. chap. 6.

15. *Araignement and Execution of the Late Traytors,* sig. Dv; Richard Sheldon, *A Survey of the Miracles of the Church of Rome, Proving Them to Be Antichristian* (London, 1616), sig. X2v; see also Thomas Abernethie, *Abjuration of Poperie* (Edinburgh, 1638), sigs. C2r–v.

16. On this international tradition, see Julia Gasper, *The Dragon and the Dove: The Plays of Thomas Dekker* (Oxford: Clarendon, 1990), chap. 3; Christopher Hill, *Antichrist in Seventeenth-Century England* (London: Oxford University Press, 1971), chap. 1.

Presbyterians, Royalists and Parliamentarians, Jacobites and Whigs, each side could employ the language of gender inversion to different ends; each could claim that what was wrong with the other was that it inverted the hierarchy in sexual and familial relations. As Peter Stallybrass has shown, this inversion then became the excuse for violent action to restore what had been overturned, even if such action required transgression against hierarchy in another register (such as class or status).[17] Religious reformers justified their rebellion against their parent church, for example, by claiming that it fostered gender inversion; as I will explore in the next chapter, Republicans justified their rebellion against their king by claiming that his Catholic wife dominated him. While the assumption that gender is hierarchical provides the grounds for identifying and attacking difference, it also connects the two opposing groups as mirror images of one another: either men are on top or women are. In such discourses, gender equality is not a conceptual or rhetorical option.

Thus Protestant polemicists described what was wrong with the Roman church by suggesting that its hierarchy was actually dominated by women. In doing so, they observed and exaggerated the significance of women in Catholic worship while ignoring the power of men in the institutional church. Some went so far as to represent the invariably male pope as a woman: the Empress of Babylonia in *The Whore of Babylon,* Duessa in *The Faerie Queene,* Pornopolis in John Foxe's *Christus Triumphans,* and Pope Joan in the many retellings of that apocryphal story. The "truth" about Joan, like the truth of the church's corruption, is revealed at last with humiliating publicness; her birth pangs disrupt a street procession, thus proving that the infallible pope is really, as John Mayo concludes in 1591, "a woman with child, delivered in procession, dead openly in the streetes, and buried without any honour or solemnitie."[18] In his hugely popular *Synopsis Papismi, That is, a Generall View of Papistrie,* which went through at least nine printings between 1592 and 1634, Andrew Willet insists that Pope Joan is not an exception in the history of papal succession but rather a reminder of how many women have determined that succession "by harlots meanes" and how often the "Whore of Babylon's seate" has been "governed by strumpets." In view of this supposed history, which Willet cata-

17. Peter Stallybrass, "The World Turned Upside Down: Inversion, Gender, and the State," in *The Matter of Difference: Materialist Feminist Criticism of Shakespeare,* ed. Valerie Wayne (Ithaca: Cornell University Press, 1991), pp. 201–20. Jill Campbell shows how this focus on inversion continued in anti-Jacobite polemic of the 1740s (*Natural Masques: Gender and Identity in Fielding's Plays and Novels* [Stanford: Stanford University Press, 1995], p. 134).

18. John Mayo, *The Pope's Parliament, Containing a Pleasant and Delightful Historie* (London, 1591), sig. G2.

logs, he wonders "Why might not a woman as well be Pope, as Popes made by women?"[19]

On the stage, which adeptly mobilized misogyny, deploying the visual associations between Catholicism and female bodies, popes were often depicted as women or as allied with women. In these plays, theatricality was a weapon mobilized against Catholicism, despite the fact that theatricality and Catholicism were often associated, at least from the perspective of their detractors. Indeed, vilifications of Catholicism may have enabled dramatists to dissociate themselves from the rituals and spectacles of Catholicism, to prove that the theater could be a resource for rather than an obstacle to Protestant proselytizing. Theatrical representations of Catholicism divide roughly into three kinds: stories set in a Catholic country, such as Italy or Spain, to convey pervasive vice; overt attacks on the Catholic church's history of corruption and conspiracy, especially as it was seen to threaten English monarchs and English peace; and topical references to recent events or controversies. The stage refers to the Gunpowder Plot only through allusion, indirection, and displacement. On the stage, for the most part, Catholics are from someplace else; their most fiendish schemes are devised elsewhere and imported; they are also frequently women, or men obscenely and degradingly coupled with them.

Both Thomas Dekker's *Whore of Babylon* (1606–7) and Barnabe Barnes's *Devil's Charter* (1607) depict the world of Catholicism, whether "Babylon" or Rome, as unremittingly vicious, by focusing on the pope as the source of corruption. Why should the pope become a central figure in responses to an apparently home-grown plot? In part because anti-Catholicism had always targeted a pope, in whom, as Carol Z. Wiener puts it, "all popes became one arch-villain—the Pope."[20] Common parlance dwelt on the supposed centrality of the pope in "Roman" Catholicism, blaming him for the assumed disloyalty of Catholic subjects and labeling the religion "popery" and its adherents "papists." The Gunpowder Plot brought antipapal feeling to the fore because Pope Paul V was widely blamed for promoting treason by licensing Catholic subjects not to obey a heretical (that is, a non-Catholic) sovereign and by granting pardons for crimes committed for the Roman cause. In his remarks at the conspirators' trials, as presented in *A True and Perfect Relation,* Edward Coke insists again and again that the pope and the Jesuits seek to depose kings and discourage subjects from obedience.

19. Andrew Willet, *Synopsis Papismi, That Is, a Generall View of Papistrie* (London, 1614), sigs. Z6v–Aa.

20. Carol Z. Wiener, "The Beleaguered Isle: A Study of Elizabethan and Early Jacobean Anti-Catholicism," *Past & Present* 51 (1971): 30.

Plays often depict papal power as outrageous, presumptuous, and usurped by putting it in women's hands. Most strikingly, in *The Whore of Babylon* the pope is "that bad woman, Babylon's proud queen."[21] The Empress of Babylon faces off with Titania, queen of fairyland. According to Jean Howard, one effect of this "debate structure" is "to undermine the absolute distinction between [Titania] and her Satanic double, the empress."[22] Undermining that distinction was often the project of Catholic writers such as William Allen, who pointed out that if any church inappropriately empowered women, it was the Church of England, which removed authority from the pope "to invest a woman [Elizabeth] (which is against nature) in his supremacy and spiritual charge over all her subjects' souls."[23] As Dekker's oppositions blur, the play reveals the difficulties of distinguishing a virgin queen from her feminized celibate clerical counterpart—even when the beloved patron of Protestantism is dead. For Titania, like Elizabeth, challenges gender conventions and hierarchies as much as the Empress does. The play further muddies the ideological waters because Titania stands not only for Elizabeth, seen, once safely dead, with nostalgic reverence, but also, at moments, for James.[24] In the showdown between the "rival queens," *The Whore of Babylon* shores up the gender hierarchy threatened by Catholicism by masculinizing the winning queen. Titania boasts of her "manliness" in the field—"I'm born a soldier by the father's side!" (5.6.26). The ruler who stands up to the Empress, warning her that there are limits to her power over other rulers, is not Titania but a king who, pushed too far, threatens to make her his slave, and even to put a ring through her nose.

In other forms of anti-Catholic polemic, as in *The Whore of Babylon*, both Catholicism and its opposite, the reformed religion that such texts defend and celebrate, are represented as female.[25] Either England or Protestantism can suddenly, disturbingly become feminized. In *Mischeefes Mysterie; or,*

21. Thomas Dekker, *The Whore of Babylon*, ed. Marianne Gateson Riely (New York: Garland, 1980), 1.2.9. Subsequent references appear in the text. Thomas Middleton's *A Game at Chess* (1624) similarly dramatizes the conflict between Protestantism and Catholicism, England and Spain, as that between a good (white) queen and a bad (black) one.

22. Jean E. Howard, *The Stage and Social Struggle* (New York: Routledge, 1994), p. 54.

23. Allen, *True, Sincere, and Modest Defense*, p. 213; see also p. 249.

24. Gasper, *Dragon and the Dove*, p. 97 and chap. 3 passim.

25. On these face-offs between "good" and "bad" women, see ibid., chap. 3; Helen Hackett, *Virgin Mother, Maiden Queen: Elizabeth I and the Cult of the Virgin Mary* (Houndmills, Basingstoke, Hampshire: Macmillan, 1995), pp. 69–70, 76–77, 130–36; Kim F. Hall, *Things of Darkness: Economies of Race and Gender in Early Modern England* (Ithaca: Cornell University Press, 1995), chap. 4; and Claire McEachern, "'A Whore at the First Blush Seemeth Only a Woman': John Bale's *Image of Both Churches* and the Terms of Religious Difference in the Early English Reformation," *Journal of Medieval and Renaissance Studies* 25.2 (1995): 245–69.

Treasons Master-peece, the Powder-Plot (1617), for instance, the pope and the Roman church are represented not only as the Whore of Babylon but also as a *"step-dame,* nay a *Strumpet mother."* Yet the Commonwealth endangered by the Gunpowder Plot is also a mother, pleading with her Catholic subjects: "O childe unnaturall, oh Sonne ingrate,/ Who too too long hast sucked from my brest,/ The milke of peace and plenty fortunate"; the traitors imitate "vile *Nero . . . /* In ripping up [their] *mothers* wombe"; the earth of "th'illustrious *Capitoll,"* whose "intrals" the explosives threatened to "puffe and penetrate," is "the *Gran-dame* of us all,/And our kind *Nurce."*[26] Describing the betrayed country as feminine works here to emphasize how affectionate England has been to her Catholic subjects, and how viciously they have betrayed that trust. The imagery questions England's judgment in tolerating Catholics at the same time that it censures them for their ingratitude.

While other plays that respond to the Gunpowder Plot also contrast good and bad women, they domesticate the gender disorder and female conspiracy threatened by Catholicism. These plays associate Catholic conspiracy with the intimate rebellion of a wife within the household rather than with the invasion of a rival foreign power, such as the Empress of Babylon. Vivid depictions of female treachery and vice suggest that the problem with Catholicism is that it can so thoroughly empower and corrupt women; they also suggest that Catholics hurt those who are closest to them, who harbor and trust them. *The Devil's Charter,* for instance, offers the "history" of Pope Alexander VI, who commits incest with his daughter, Lucretia, sodomizes captive boys, invokes devils, and employs a gifted poisoner on his staff; as his son summarizes: "This is infallible, that many crimes/ Lurke underneath the robes of Holinesse."[27] Some of the play's most memorable scenes depict the sin and downfall of Alexander's daughter and lover, Lucretia Borgia. In the scene in which we first meet her, she entraps and murders her husband—binding him to a chair, gagging him, forcing him to sign a paper (which she will later present as a suicide note), then stabbing him. In a later scene, we watch as Lucretia inadvertently poisons herself with a cosmetic "tincture" her father sends her, which spots her and afflicts her with a "strange leoprosie" (4.3.2259). In Lucretia the family (and the corrupt papacy) finds explicitly feminine representation in the shape of the murderous wife or petty traitor, and then of the vain

26. Francis Herring, *Mischeefes Mysterie; or, Treasons Master-peece, the Powder-Plot,* trans. John Vicars (London, 1617), sigs. K2v, Kv, K2.

27. Barnabe Barnes, *The Devil's Charter,* ed. Jim C. Pogue (New York: Garland, 1980), 3.5.1822–23.

woman who rapidly fulfills Hamlet's threat that the woman who "paints an inch thick" will soon "come to this," a death's-head. She simultaneously overturns gender hierarchy in her extraordinary and murderous mastery of her husband and succumbs horribly to gender convention. Her death, then, is not unlike the shaming end to which Pope Joan comes. It is Lucretia's femininity, finally, that reasserts itself and finishes her humiliatingly, as she withers, screaming, from the "tincture" she could not resist.

Ben Jonson's *Catiline* (1611) ties its references to the Gunpowder Plot to a story that more explicitly resembles the conspiracy than others I have discussed, for in it men conspire against other men. However, Jonson also grants women a more central role in planning, executing, and discovering conspiracy than these other plays or his own classical sources do. Indeed, he devotes all of Act II to women's machinations. In Jonson's play, the threat of those who literally undermine the commonwealth from within or below, rather than invading it from without, can best be conveyed as the work of women.

In *Catiline*, a world in which conspiracy occurs is also a world in which gender is turned upside down. At the end of Act I, the Chorus attributes the conspiracy in part to Roman men's effeminacy. They are

> More kemb'd and bath'd and rub'd and trim'd,
> More sleek'd, more soft, and slacker limb'd,
> As prostitute; so much that kind
> May seek itself there and not find.[28]

These men who are almost indistinguishable from prostitutes also depend on them. Catiline's first step in his plot is to appeal to his wife, Aurelia, to help him by enticing the conspirators with "freedom and community": "Get thee store and change of women/As I have boys, and give 'em time and place/And all connivance" (1.171–73). The two other women involved in the conspiracy are prostitutes: Fulvia, who reveals the conspiracy to Cicero, and Sempronia, who remains a stalwart coconspirator to the end. All three of the female characters gain information and participate in public life through sexual activity. Sempronia claims that "There are of us [women] can be as exquisite traitors/As e'er a male-conspirator of you all" (4.5.17–18) and is baffled

28. Ben Jonson, *Catiline*, ed. W. F. Bolton and Jane F. Gardner (Lincoln: University of Nebraska Press, 1973), 1.561–64. The play does not seem to have been popular when it was first produced, but it was revived in the 1630s and 1660s and republished in 1635, 1669, and 1674.

> That states and commonwealths employ not women
> To be ambassadors sometimes. We should
> Do as good public service, and could make
> As honorable spies . . .
>
> (4.5.9–12)

Yet the play suggests that women's contribution is distinctly different from men's. For one thing, only in a society in crisis would men be forced to depend on women, as both Cicero and Catiline remark. Cicero praises Fulvia for revealing the secret to him and thereby saving his life and regime, yet behind her back he laments that he needs "so vile a thing" (3.2.216–17). Similarly, Catiline muses:

> What ministers men must for practice use!
> The rash, th'ambitious, needy, desperate,
> Foolish and wretched, ev'n the dregs of mankind,
> To whores and women.
>
> (3.3.225–28)

Thus the significant role of women in the play stands, both for Catiline, the leader of the conspiracy, and Cicero, the man against whom he conspires, as evidence of a decline in Roman manhood that infects both sides. *Catiline* also suggests that there is no Titania to counter the Empress, that, just as all men in Rome are effeminate and dependent on "whores and women," all women are untrustworthy. The play repeatedly links the conspiracy to wives' disloyalty. As Jonathan Goldberg points out, in this play "corruption begins at home."[29] Traitors emerge from within Rome, rather than invading it from without; the untrustworthy wife stands as the figure for this kind of treason, all the more threatening because of its intimacy. Catiline urges his wife, Aurelia, to approach her female "confederates"

> About the drawing as many of their husbands
> Into the plot as can; if not, to rid 'em.
> That'll be the easier practice unto some
> Who have been tir'd with 'em long.
>
> (3.3.45–48)

Later he reflects on his dependence on "domestic traitors, bosom thieves / Whom custom hath call'd wives, the readiest helps / To betray

---

29. Jonathan Goldberg, *James I and the Politics of Literature: Jonson, Shakespeare, Donne, and Their Contemporaries* (Baltimore: Johns Hopkins University Press, 1983), p. 194.

heady husbands, rob the easy . . . " (3.3.238–40). Finally Cethegus, in response to Sempronia's boast that women can perform as valuable "public service" as men, scoffs that women are good only at "smock treason" (4.5.19). Furthermore, he insists that women absolutely cannot be trusted. The play bears out this contention. Neither the state nor their husbands can trust women not to betray them; the conspirators cannot trust women either, for Fulvia betrays them.

Just as murderous wives were compared to traitors and their crime was construed as "petty treason," traitors were understood by analogy to rebellious wives. Many texts written about Catholic subjects, for instance, drew disturbing parallels between a Catholic wife of a Protestant husband and a Catholic subject within a Protestant nation; in both cases, it was feared that Catholicism released subordinates from their duty to obey. Thomas Morton cautions that when the papacy brands Protestants as heretics, it licenses all kinds of inversion, rebellion, and disorder by freeing servants, parents, and children from obligations. "Wives are not bound to render due benevolence unto their husbands, if heretiques. . . . Heretikes may not bee termed either Children or Kinred; but according to the old law, Thy hand must be against them to spill their blood." Catholicism is a religion "which dissolveth the dutie of Servants, Subjects, Debtors, and strangleth the vitall spirits of humane societie; and by not acknowledgement of naturall duties of Wedlocke, naturall Parents, naturall Children, naturall Countrie, doth bowell up nature."[30] A later text attributes to one Julius Caesar Vaninus, "a Doctor of both their Laws, the Civil and Canon," the claim that "a Catholick Wife is not obliged not to defraud her Husband, because by the Husbands Heresy the Wife is free from that Duty," although not freed from the marriage itself.[31] Similarly, on the stage, whether in *The Devil's Charter* or *Catiline*, murderous wives or domestic traitors are the perfect figures for the threat a tolerated Catholicism might offer.

Although *Catiline* suggests that "domestic traitors, bosom thieves," and "smock treason" pervade Roman culture, the counterpoint to its sleek, soft, slack-limbed men, and that these "domestic traitors" can cause real damage, it also retreats from punishing them. Regarding Sempronia, Cicero announces: "A state's anger/Should not take knowledge either of fools or women" (4.6.34–35). Jonson's depiction of female traitors is as uncertain as his own shifting and irrecoverable relationship to Catholicism. The women in *Catiline* are woven into the treason and its discovery, into house-

---

30. Thomas Morton, *An Exact Discoverie of Romish Doctrine in the Case of Conspiracie and Rebellion, by Pregnant Observations* (London, 1605), sigs. B3–4.

31. *Jesuits Assassins; or, The Popish Plot Further Declared* [supposedly extracted out of Dr. Israel Tonge's papers] (London, 1680), sig. D2v.

holds and communities. They are knowledgeable, active, yet, in the end, negligible. Their femininity seems to make them both more threatening and less so. The play repeats and feeds the familiar fear of "domestic traitors" and "smock treason" yet avoids plumbing the reasons why women might be so ready to be rid of their husbands, the reasons women might indeed be as good spies as men. In this respect the play resembles both other discourses about petty treason and representations of the Gunpowder Plot, which demonize rather than explore the traitors' motives. Perhaps Jonson imposed so much distance from the treason that is his subject because he was already too closely associated with Catholic conspiracy for his own safety, as Barbara De Luna, for instance, avers. (Jonson supposedly informed against the conspirators.)[32] But Jonson's distance and his reluctance to imagine the dilemma of the Catholic subject or the domestic traitor from within are more typical of representations of the Gunpowder Plot and of Catholicism more generally than they are unique to his situation.

As the fears of "smock treason" dramatized in *Catiline* suggest, the power attributed to women in fantasies of gender inversion at home and in the state is power over men. Just as social order was often figured in terms of the couple, the man on top and woman subordinate, social disorder was often figured as the inversion of that hierarchy. Diverse discussions—of the relationships between the soul and the body and between spiritual and temporal powers; of religious diversity and tolerance, the unification of the kingdom, political alliances, and legal reform—all return to marriage as the model for relationships in which one party dominates the other. Thus the paradoxical project of denouncing a church run by powerful, celibate men by associating it with the feminine turned to marriage to describe the coexistence of Protestants and Catholics in England both positively (Protestants/men on top) and negatively (Catholics/women on top).

Whatever changes may or may not have been occurring in the lived experience of early modern spouses or in the ideals or prescriptions for marriage found in sermons and conduct books, writers who use marriage as a figure for other relationships rarely understand it as the yoking of equal partners; again and again they refer to the legal conception of coverture, the process by which two unequal partners become "one flesh" and one legal subject, a corporate entity in which the dominant partner (the husband) represents the union and raises its voice.[33] While coverture assumed

---

32. B. N. De Luna, *Jonson's Romish Plot: A Study of "Catiline" in Its Historical Context* (Oxford: Clarendon, 1967).

33. Amy Louise Erickson points out that coverture was unique to England, and was not the only available way of construing married women's legal status in early modern Europe. See her *Women and Property in Early Modern England* (London: Routledge, 1993), pp. 233–35.

that the "husband" could subsume the "wife," becoming through this engrossment a larger, more powerful or important version of himself, deployments of the image of marriage to describe other unions often disclose an anxiety that this process might be inverted or reversed, that the feminized category, here the Catholic, might subsume the masculinized one, here the Protestant, should they unite. Although Protestant polemicists assert Englishness as the dominant and justifiably superior category, they constantly worry about its integrity and its ability to keep its subordinates down. Some feared, for instance, that should the English and Scottish legal systems be combined as part of the unification of Great Britain, English law would become "covert"; that is, subsumed or lost. From the English point of view, such a marriage of the two legal systems would be acceptable only if English law were the husband, superseding Scottish law. As James famously reassured Parliament in 1607: "Must they not be subjected to the Lawes of England . . .? you are to be the husband, they the wife: you conquerours, they as conquered, though not by the sword, but by the sweet and sure bond."[34] In the feared phenomenon of inverse coverture, this process is reversed, and the supposedly lesser party subjects the greater. In this inversion, the woman, or whatever group is playing her part, does not simply clamber "on top" but also undertakes the husbandly function of absorbing, subsuming, or covering.

JACOBEAN PENAL LAWS AND THE PROBLEM OF THE RECUSANT WIFE

Just as polemic and drama often figured Catholicism in the abstract as an insubordinate, even treasonous wife, penal laws, especially those enacted by James after the Gunpowder Plot, target Catholic wives as particularly troublesome. But not because they are "women on top." What makes Catholic wives a legal problem is not that they invert the process of coverture, subsuming their husbands, but that coverture shelters them, making them legally inaccessible. Penal legislation thus faces the challenge of controlling women and profiting from their recusancy without wrenching them so far out from under the shelter of coverture as to damage this crucial fiction—a bulwark against the gender inversion feared in Catholicism—beyond repair. The resulting compromise, which required the state to confer significance on wives' beliefs and practices but not to reconceive marriage as a result, was extremely sticky to manage, and resulted in con-

34. James I, *The Political Works of James I* (1616), ed. Charles Howard McIlwain (Cambridge: Harvard University Press, 1918), p. 294.

fusion about the exact extent of married women's accountability for their recusancy under the law.

One might expect, instead, attacks on Catholic women for withholding themselves from marriage and overvaluing their own virginity. Many Catholic women remained unmarried, as did many Protestant women as well.[35] Some still became nuns, although, for the most part, they had to go abroad to do so. According to Rowlands, seventeen houses of English women belonging to eight orders were established on the Continent between 1597 and 1642, and at least three hundred young women went to join these communities; J. C. H. Aveling puts the number of English convents founded in those years as high as forty.[36] Several English gentlewomen, such as Mary Ward and Lucy Knatchbull, played important roles in founding English orders or houses and in educating other women. Although Catholicism was widely attacked for prizing virginity over marriage, unmarried women were as marginalized in anti-Catholic polemic and penal statutes as they were more generally in early modern discourses. Female popes, nuns, virgin mothers, and virgin martyrs, who resided safely in the past, were favorite satirical targets, of course. But the "problem" of English Catholic women was most often defined as the problem of recusant wives.

The law did not hold either husbands or wives accountable for their consciences or for "internal mental reservation"; rather, the issue was how their consciences became manifest in public action. In refusing to conform, were recusant wives conscientious, autonomous individuals who should be held accountable for their actions, as arguments for women's spiritual equality might suggest, or were they extensions of their husbands? If the latter, should husbands bear responsibility for their wives' actions whether they approved or disapproved, had licensed or prohibited them? Thus the problem of the recusant wife was inseparable from the problem of the recusant couple.

In the lengthiest account of the trials of the alleged Gunpowder Plot conspirators, *A True and Perfect Relation of the Whole Proceedings against the Late Most Barbarous Traitors* (London, 1606), Sir Everard Digby, one of the accused, explains that Catholics were motivated by resentment of penal laws and fear of harsher ones to come, particularly fear of greater accountability for their wives: "They generally feared harder Lawes from this Parliament against Recusants, as that Recusants wives, and women should bee

35. Erickson, *Women and Property*, pp. 83, 96, 195.
36. Rowlands, "Recusant Women," p. 167; J. C. H. Aveling, *The Handle and the Ax: The Catholic Recusants in England from Reformation to Emancipation* (London: Blond & Briggs, 1976), p. 90.

lyable to the mulct [or fines] as well as their husbands, and men."[37] Surely men's legal, social, and financial privileges would seem to offer more plausible grounds for grievance or motives for treason. Yet *A True and Perfect Relation* attributes to Digby a Catholic point of view, from which the recusant wife is a limit case. When the law reaches for her, it reaches too deeply into Catholic domestic privacy, male privilege and authority, men's pockets. *A True and Perfect Relation* suggests that Catholic men were suspected of wanting desperately to limit their wives' liability, and thereby their own. If extending the law to wives was too great an incursion, then this was, of course, what the king and Parliament should do if they wished to discourage recusancy. This text, then, offers one contemporary explanation of why Jacobean penal legislation included among its emphases an attempt to increase the legal accountability of recusant wives: it attributes the concern with wives to English Catholics themselves, depicting the law as responding to their own sense of their vulnerabilities.

Another compelling explanation of why the recusant wife emerged as a problem in legal discourse is not that she was the focus of Catholic fears but that she revealed the problems inherent in the legal construction of the wife. Although men who were convicted of recusancy might be stripped of most of the rights and privileges of their gender, as well as financially penalized, even ruined, recusant wives had few rights or privileges to lose. Paradoxically, their conformity was thus more difficult to secure. If they refused to swear the oath of allegiance to James, they could be indicted for high treason and, in principle, executed; a few women were executed under Elizabeth in connection with harboring priests.[38] Women were imprisoned for recusancy, sometimes for many years; some even died of the hard usage they endured there. Women were not, however, subject to the penalties for praemunire, an offense against the ecclesiastical supremacy of the sovereign (forfeiture of goods and estate and loss of liberty for life) or to being forced to abjure the realm (a banishment and concommitant forfeiture of property, which resulted in "civil death").[39] Coverture pro-

37. *True and Perfect Relation*, sig. L2v.
38. William Cawley, *The Laws of Q. Elizabeth, K. James, and K. Charles the First. Concerning Jesuites, Seminary Priests, Recusants, &c.* (London, 1680), sig. Cc2 (on 3 and 4 Jac. I, cap. 5). Throughout, I have checked Cawley against *Statutes of the Realm. Printed by Command of His Majesty King George the Third* (1819). On women who were executed, see *A Relation of Sixtene Martyrs: Glorified in England in Twelve Monethes* (Douai, 1601), sigs. C8, F5v–6, and the discussion of executions in Chapter 1.
39. On praemunire see Cawley, *Laws . . . Concerning . . . Recusants*, sig. Z4 (3 Jac. I, cap. 4); on abjuration, see *Statutes of the Realm*, vol. 4, pt. 2, p. 846 (35 Eliz., cap. 2). Editions of Michael Dalton's *Countrey Justice* in 1618 and after claim that "no woman covert (or maried woman) shall be forced to abjure [the realm], by vertue of this statute" (p. 92). Cawley mis-

tected married women from these punishments because they did not really have anything to seize, nor were they independent agents who could
be banished. Thus married women were protected from the harshest
penalties meted out under penal legislation because including them
would require too far-reaching a revision of married women's legal and
political status, too violent an assault on married men's prerogatives.

The greatest controversy regarding recusant wives' legal accountability
focused on whether they could be fined—whether, that is, they were "lyable
to the mulct as well as their husbands, and men." Those jurists who commented on penal laws, such as Michael Dalton, Edward Coke, and William
Cawley, tended to emphasize that women had always been liable under
even the earliest penal statutes. In his response to Digby, Attorney General
Edward Coke predicted the direction of Jacobean penal legislation:

> Concerning wives that were Recusants, if they were knowen so to bee be-
> fore their husbands (though they were good Protestants) tooke them, and
> yet for outward and worldly respects whatsoever, any would match with
> such, great reason there is, that he or they should pay for it, as knowing the
> penaltie and burthen before. . . . No man receives injury in that, to which
> hee willingly and knowingly agreeth and consenteth. But if shee were no
> Recusant at the time of mariage, and yet afterwards he suffer her to bee
> corrupted and seduced, by admitting Priests and Romanists into his house,
> good reason likewise that hee, be he Papist or Protestant, should pay for
> his negligence and misgovernment.[40]

In other words, the husband was accountable for his wife's recusancy and
had to pay her fines, whether she was a recusant before they married or became one thereafter, whether he was a papist or a Protestant. Even in his
magnification of the problem of recusant wives, Coke stayed safely within
the conceptual horizons of coverture—no matter what, the husband bore
responsibility for his wife's conduct. Yet he underestimated the difficulty of
fining wives and oversimplified the operations of coverture.[41]

---

reads Dalton, claiming that his exemption of married women is more sweeping than it is.
"In the late additions to *Dalton, cap. 81. tit. Recusants, Sect. 7*, 'tis said, that no married
Woman is punishable by this Statute, but are thereout excepted; whereas in truth they are
no where excepted throughout this Statute, save only that they shall not be compelled or
bound to abjure" (Cawley, *Laws . . . Concerning . . . Recusants*, sig. R2v).

Warnicke argues that there was also reluctance to prosecute married women because "it
seemed improper to deprive law-abiding gentlemen of conjugal rights by imprisoning their
wives" (*Women of the English Renaissance and Reformation*, p. 171). This is an intriguing suggestion, with bearing, too, on why wives were not forced to abjure the realm, but I have
found no direct evidence for it.

40. *True and Perfect Relation*, sigs. L3r–v.

41. Elsewhere Coke claimed that while a feme covert was "within" earlier Elizabethan
statutes, "before the Statute of 35. *Eliz.* if a Feme Covert had been indicted of recusancy, the

As William Cawley explained in codifying and commenting on penal laws in 1680, a wife "can have no Goods or Lands during the Husbands life which may be seized for non-payment of the penalty"; furthermore, "'tis a general rule, that his Goods or Lands cannot be seized for the forfeiture or penalty, where the Wife only is Indicted and Convicted of the Offence."[42] Cawley's discussion demonstrates that coverture was designed to maximize the husband's authority while limiting his responsibility. One consequence, however, was that the wife's status was contradictory: she was simultaneously constructed as incapable of holding "goods or lands" in her own name and as capable of committing offenses independent of her husband. Although married women managed to gain some control over property through a range of ingenious strategies, in the case of recusancy, it was precisely their lack of control over marital property—at the level of theory—that shielded them.[43] Despite every effort to secure the accountability of recusant wives, loopholes remained, and they opened up largely around husbands' prerogatives. Considering coverture from married women's perspective, we have tended, understandably, to concentrate on all that it denied wives. That perspective is also relevant here. Yet seeing the wife from the perspective of penal laws suggests the complexities of her status—not just in the gulf between prescription and practice but within prescription itself. Conceptually eclipsed and subsumed, recusant wives might evade legal scrutiny; they might find an advantage in "covert" operation. Catholic wives might thus play one set of legal disabilities against another, the "feme covert" against the recusant, sometimes defining a status for themselves as legal untouchables.

Some contemporaries contended that the difference between the legal vulnerability of husbands and wives prompted some Catholic couples to make a deal: the husband would conform outwardly, attending church to protect property and maintain access to office, while the wife would oversee Catholic practice in the home and maintain the family's identity as Catholic at lower cost to their resources. This scenario suggests that Catholic wives were participating in setting the agenda for religious identity and observance. A Catholic wife might be the only open nonconformist in a conforming family, risking imprisonment and fines to maintain the fam-

---

forfeiture should not have been levyed of the goods of the Husband, because he was not a party thereunto" (*An Abridgement in English of the Eleven Books of Reports of the Learned Sir Edward Coke, Knight*, composed by Sir Thomas Ireland [London, 1650], pp. 430–31). Rowlands offers an especially detailed chronology of debates over and changes in legislation affecting recusant women ("Recusant Women," pp. 150–60).

42. Cawley, *Laws . . . Concerning . . . Recusants,* sig. Y4 (discussing 3 Jac. I, cap. 4).

43. See, for instance, Erickson, *Women and Property;* and Susan Staves, *Married Women's Separate Property in England, 1660–1833* (Cambridge: Harvard University Press, 1990).

ily's connection to Catholic practice and to a public Catholic identity at cut rates, since the fine for a wife's recusancy was half that for a husband's; she might act as a de facto widow if her husband had abjured the realm or been imprisoned; she might engage in clandestine or even illegal activity to exert some control over her children's education, as I will discuss in the next chapter. Not all "church papists," or those who engaged in occasional and strategic conformity, had consistently nonconforming wives. Yet occasional conformity is often represented as a spousal agreement to disagree.

This supposed spousal conspiracy is most famously depicted in John Earle's character of a "church papist" who "loves Popery well, but is loath to lose by it"; he conforms to avoid paying fines, but "his wife is more zealous, and therefore more costly, and he bates her in tyres, what she stands him in Religion."[44] Earle's character trivializes the nature of the bargain as well as the motives for entering into it. He presents the wife's fines as parallel to a clothing allowance, another kind of female consumerism and self-indulgence. While the husband shares the love of popery, her refusal to conform emerges out of her own extravagance rather than shared convictions. Earle concedes that when a husband conforms and a wife recuses herself, the motives and consequences are, at least in part, financial. Yet, in Earle's view, the two do not conspire to register the family's love of popery while limiting financial losses. Instead, each succumbs to his or her particular vice: he is too greedy, she is too spendthrift.

While historians disagree on how long or how widely couples engaged in what Alexandra Walsham calls "division of labour in the management of dissent," many agree with Janet Halley that such disagreement could be strategic, helping Catholicism to survive through "a constantly adaptive and even opportunistic strategy of passive resistance."[45] Outward conformity could enable (upper-class) Catholic men to preserve their access to public office or their control over their estates; that is, their privileges as men. There was considerable reluctance to interfere in the property rights of men who were not themselves convicted recusants. For instance, Cawley discussed the awkward situation of searching for prohibited Catholic books

44. John Earle, *Microcosmographie; or, A Peece of the World Discovered; in Essayes and Characters* (London, 1628), sigs. C9, C10.
45. Alexandra Walsham, *Church Papists: Catholicism, Conformity, and Confessional Polemic in Early Modern England,* Royal Historical Society Studies in History no. 68 (Rochester, N.Y.: Boydell, 1993), p. 81; Janet E. Halley, "Equivocation and the Legal Conflict over Religious Identity in Early Modern England," *Yale Journal of Law and the Humanities* 3.1 (Winter 1991): 51. On the prevalence and persistence of such arrangements, see Aveling, *Handle and the Ax,* p. 187; John Bossy, *The English Catholic Community, 1570–1850* (New York: Oxford University Press, 1976), pp. 155–59; and Caroline Hibbard, "Early Stuart Catholicism: Revisions and Re-Revisions," *Journal of Modern History* 52.1 (1980): 1–34, esp. 16–19.

in a house in which the wife was a recusant but the husband was not. A Jacobean law (3 and 4 Jac. I, cap. 5, sec. 23), he advised, did not intend that justices of the peace "should seize, burn or deface any Books of the Husbands though Popish, unless such whereby the Wife might be aided or confirmed in her Superstition: so that in this Case Books, written in a Language or Stile unintelligible to the Wife, are not within the meaning of this Act, nor ought by colour thereof to be taken from the Husband, who is no Popish Recusant."[46] In such a case, the husband's conformity might protect even otherwise prohibited books when they could be assumed to belong to him and to be "unintelligible" to his wife.

Yet a strategic agreement to disagree about religious conformity would have required husbands to transact a complex bargain with their wives, and to depend on their wives to maintain the family's religious identity and practices. What did this strategy say about gendered relations among Catholics? One might wonder whether circumstances forced Catholic spouses to collaborate and strategize together. Contemporaries, however, assumed that, even in disorderly Catholic households, hierarchy prevailed. Either the man was on top and could be held accountable or the woman was on top, thus signaling what was wrong with Catholicism. Both alternatives were tidy and familiar, conforming to gender conventions. Penal laws tended to favor the former alternative. Even if Catholicism was often associated with an enlarged and egregious femininity, such associations did not inform legal attempts to expand Catholic accountability and accessibility. Rather than separate the wife from the husband, these statutes attempted to expand his responsibility for her.

The strong terms in which one anti-Catholic writer, John Baxter, denounces this legal emphasis on the husband reveal how coverture could be seen to protect and exempt women. According to Baxter, priests seek to

> seduce poore simple women, that they may intise their husbands, as *Eva* did *Adam*. Madame must be recusant, and Mounsire a monthly church-hant [church-haunter]. The meane gentlewoman or yeomans wife forsweares the Church, and faceth out the force of our lawes; the good man of the house peepes into the Church for feare of a fine, setting more by his dames *pater noster* in her closet, then any Christian exercise in the congregation: as if our lawes were made to rule men, and not women, husbands, and not wives.[47]

In Baxter's interpretation of penal laws and their enforcement, women and wives stood outside of the law, empowered not only by their husbands' con-

---

46. Cawley, *Laws . . . Concerning . . . Recusants,* sigs. Hh2v–3.
47. John Baxter, *A Toile for Two-Legged Foxes* (London, 1600), sig. D5.

fidence in their closet prayers but by the operations of coverture. As Baxter feared, penal laws did indeed focus on men, even as they attempted to rule women.

One strategy for extending the law to wives without undermining coverture was to construe fines as a kind of debt, thus justifying a suit against a husband for their payment. In general, a husband was not liable for his wife's fines, since he was not fully accountable for her conduct. As Cawley explains, the husband "shall never be charged for the Act or default of his Wife, but where he may be made party to the Action or Suit, as in an Action of Debt, Trespass, Action of the Case or scandalous words by the Wife, &c. but not upon an Indictment."[48] Since a husband was liable for his wife's debts, according to a law enacted under Elizabeth (35 Eliz., cap. 1, secs. 8–9), recusancy fines could be recovered "as by the ordinary course of the Common Laws of this Realm, any other Debt due by any such person in any other Case should or may be recovered or levied."[49] Before that statute was enacted, Elizabeth was in a worse position than the informer who brought the charge against the recusants and who stood to profit from a percentage of the fine. Only by placing herself in the position of an informer or a creditor did the queen enable herself, and future sovereigns, to profit from women's recusancy. To do so, she had also to treat women's recusancy not as a crime under indictment but as a financial excess, an unpaid debt to be pursued.

Although later Elizabethan and Jacobean statutes tried to ensure that married women recusants could incur financial penalties, they still held husbands accountable for their wives' conduct and its consequences. Penal laws threatened husbands with progressively stiffer penalties if they did not ensure the conformity of their dependents, especially their wives and children, for whose religious observance they were held directly responsible. A 1593 act threatened men with the forfeiture of all property and goods for life if their wives and children did not conform; a 1606 statute made a wife's refusal to conform grounds for denying her husband civil promotion and appointment.[50] The later statute put into action the misogynous assumption, articulated by John Knox, that "men subject to the coun-

---

48. Cawley, *Laws . . . Concerning . . . Recusants*, sigs. Rv–2. See also Margot Finn, "Women, Consumption, and Coverture in England, c. 1760–1860," *Historical Journal* 39.3 (1996): 703–22.

49. Cawley, *Laws . . . Concerning . . . Recusants*, sig. Q4v. According to John Miller, a husband did not become fully liable for his wife's recusancy until 1610, with 7 and 8 Jac. I, cap. 6, despite the possibility, set out under 35 Eliz., cap. 1, of proceeding against husband and wife by an action for debt (*Popery and Politics in England, 1660–1668* [Cambridge: Cambridge University Press, 1973], p. 54).

50. Martin Havran, *The Catholics of Caroline England* (Stanford: Stanford University Press, 1962), chaps. 1 and 6, esp. pp. 9–10; Walsham, *Church Papists*, p. 80.

sel or empire of their wyves were unworthie of all publike office."[51] A man
could regain access to office if he and his servants and children received
the sacrament at Church of England services at least once a month; this
would demonstrate that the husband represented or determined the family's religious identity and that the wife was the aberration (3 and 4 Jac. I,
cap. 4, "Proviso for Offences of Wives").[52] A statute of 1610 (7 and 8 Jac. I,
cap. 6) stipulated that a married woman who did not conform and receive
the sacrament within three months after her last conviction could be committed to prison without bail or mainprize (that is, without allowing either
a sum of money or another person to stand surety for her) until she conformed or her husband undertook to pay a monthly fine of £10 (half what
he would pay for his own recusancy) as long as she did not conform; her
husband was also liable to the forfeiture of one-third of his property.

Thus the law attempted to close what A. C. F. Beales has called the "feminine loophole" by maintaining its focus on the spouse it recognized as a
legal subject, the husband.[53] The law also used various penalties to moti-
vate and coerce husbands to compel their wives to conform. Respectful of
coverture, this approach foreclosed direct address to women. Jacobean
penal laws also attempted to catch women at the moment they emerged
from coverture—that is, when their husbands died—or at least to use the
threat of impoverishment as widows to control their conduct as wives. Recusant widows who would not conform might lose two-thirds of their
dower and of their jointure, and all of their husbands' goods.[54]

None of these "solutions" really addressed the problem, nor is it clear
how effective any of them was. Michael C. Questier has found evidence
that financial pressures compelled some married women to conform.[55]
There is also evidence that Catholics worked to minimize penalties by
strategizing within and around these increasingly stringent laws.[56] Considering how Catholics might maneuver around the law—through occasional

51. John Knox, *The First Blast of the Trumpet against the Monstruous Regiment of Women*
(Geneva, 1558), sig. B2.
52. *Statutes of the Realm*, pp. 1076–77.
53. A. C. F. Beales, *Education under Penalty: English Catholic Education from the Reformation
to the Fall of James II, 1547–1689* (London: Athlone, 1963), p. 198.
54. Cawley, *Laws . . . Concerning . . . Recusants*, sigs. Ee2v–3, regarding 3 and 4 Jac. I,
cap. 5. See also J. A. Williams, "English Catholicism under Charles II: The Legal Position,"
Recusant History 7.1 (1963): 123–43, esp. 125–26.
55. According to Questier, "thirty-two of the 114 women whose conformities were registered in the lord treasurer's remembrancer's office were married," and widows and unmarried women made up almost 10 percent of "those who certified their conformities to
the exchequer" (*Conversion, Politics, and Religion in England, 1580–1625* [Cambridge: Cambridge University Press, 1996], p. 147).
56. Rowlands, "Recusant Women," p. 159; see also Cawley, *Laws . . . Concerning . . . Recusants*, sigs. Ee3r–v.

conformity, a spousal division of the labor of recusancy, or conveyances—
brings back into view the specters haunting the statutes themselves: the
complicit wife and the conniving couple. Yet anti-Catholic discourses more
frequently describe the recusant wife not as her husband's coconspirator
but in the more comfortingly familiar terms of the unruly woman, thought-
lessly ruining her husband to satisfy her own imperiously silly conscience.
In an epistle "To All Romish Collapsed Ladies, of Great Britanie" (1609),
Edward Hoby writes:

> "Why should you be so respectlesse of those worthy Gentlemen, your hus-
> bands, as to cause their honors to be eclipsed, their loyalty suspected, and
> their advancement hindred, by your recusancie? How do you think he
> should be reputed wise, who can no better order his owne house? How
> should he be held fit for government in the State, who cannot bring those
> that are so neere him to the conformitie of the Church?"[57]

Here, as so often, the convention of the disorderly or shrewish wife affords
an easy way to articulate the disorder in and of the recusant family, yet it
evades the possibility of spousal conspiracy. Conventional gender figurations—wives who obey or disobey their husbands or boss them around—
obscure the negotiations that seem more interesting: Catholic spouses conspiring together to survive; an accountability shared between husband and
wife, rather than lodged in one or the other.

Constant emphasis on coverture and inverse coverture, a gendered
marital hierarchy either right side up or upside down, makes it difficult to
imagine alternatives, even from the retrospect of centuries. For instance,
neither A. L. Rowse nor John Bossy can resist the pull of this way of understanding gender relations and female influence in the early modern
period. Following Rowse, Bossy considers whether the recusant community was, in its early days, "in effect a matriarchy." Bossy praises Rowse's view
that "English Catholicism was founded not in legitimate decisions made by
responsible men but in a series of conjugal *coups d'état* mounted by aggressive wives, and allowed to take root because of the feeble resistance offered to their spouses by too many henpecked husbands"; Bossy even goes
so far as to call this scenario "a comic invention of some power" at the same
time that he concludes that it is "to a large degree true."[58] Bossy is widely

57. Edward Hoby, *A Letter to Mr. T. H. Late Minister: Now Fugitive* (London, 1609),
sigs. A4r–v.
58. Bossy, *English Catholic Community*, p. 153; see also 154–55. Rowse claims, for instance,
that "the earls of Northumberland, Westmorland and Arundel all owed their troubles to being under the thumbs of their women: more fools they for listening to them." He also suggests that Catholic wives could recklessly insist on recusancy because they didn't have to pay
the consequences themselves; "they did not have to go to prison," he claims, although in

respected as *the* historian of the "English Catholic community"; Rowse is widely dismissed. Yet here Bossy endorses Rowse's interpretation at the same time that he observes its connection to a long-standing comic tradition of aggressive wives and henpecked husbands; whether or not Catholic women were unusually independent or authoritative, seventeenth-century polemic and some historians present their power in terms of a comic tradition of "women on top."

If anyone in the seventeenth century could escape these already tired conceptual and representational options, you might think that it would be Protestants. I do not mean to imply that Protestants invented the ideal of the companionate marriage. Pre-Christian and pre-Reformation writers had often praised marriage in terms strikingly similar to those so widely disseminated with the help of both Protestantism and print.[59] Just as many women continued to live unwed even after the Reformation foreclosed the alternative of the convent, so many members of the laity had married before the Reformation, and many English recusants continued to marry thereafter. Furthermore, the ideal of a hierarchical relation between spouses continued to coexist with the ideal of greater equality and intimacy between the two. Still, Protestantism and print conjoined to raise the visibility and prestige of marriage and to increase the expectations many brides and grooms brought to the institution. As Mary Beth Rose has argued, post-Reformation texts about personal conduct in England brought to the discussion of marriage an "emphasis, elaboration, and wide distribution" that were "completely new."[60] Yet if the ideal of companionship, mutuality, and equality within marriage was broadly discussed and busily inculcated, it was not unambivalently espoused. As is well known, the inconsistencies inherent in the dominant conceptualizations of marriage center on the wife: should she be equal or subordinate?[61] For all of their excesses and divergences, anti-Catholic constructions of the recusant wife cannot think their way out of coverture, whether right side up or inverted. Some texts dimly recognize the frightening prospect of Catholic couples in ca-

fact some of them did (A. L. Rowse, *The England of Elizabeth: The Structure of Society* [New York: Macmillan, 1951], pp. 454, 456).

59. Kathleen M. Davies, "Continuity and Change in Literary Advice on Marriage," in *Marriage and Society: Studies in the Social History of Marriage*, ed. R. B. Outhwaite (New York: St. Martin's Press, 1981); Todd, *Christian Humanism;* and Valerie Wayne, "Introduction" to Edmund Tilney, *The Flower of Friendship: A Renaissance Dialogue Contesting Marriage*, ed. Wayne (Ithaca: Cornell University Press, 1992).

60. Mary Beth Rose, *The Expense of Spirit: Love and Sexuality in English Renaissance Drama* (Ithaca: Cornell University Press, 1988), p. 119.

61. Ibid., pp. 126–31; Catherine Belsey, *The Subject of Tragedy: Identity and Difference in Renaissance Drama* (London: Methuen, 1985), pp. 149–60.

hoots, yet they return to familiar figurations of men who are accountable under the law and women who are rebelliously on top. From the unlikely angle of Protestant constructions of their opposites and enemies, we can see that hierarchy remained more familiar than equality throughout the seventeenth century. Perhaps Protestant polemicists displaced anxieties about the increasing prestige and influence of wives in their own culture onto recusant wives. The ambiguities and failures of imagination that bedeviled constructions of Catholic couples provide further evidence that the wife, whether or not she was a recusant, was always a problem.

The "Homme Covert," Divided Duty, and the Place of the Catholic Man

Penal laws attempted to punish and control Catholic men through two contradictory strategies: first, the laws attempted to extend men's responsibility for their wives' and dependents' conduct, as we have just seen; second, they stripped men of those rights and privileges that distinguished them as men and as gentlemen. Under an early Jacobean statute, passed in 1606, a man who was found guilty of recusancy and excommunicated by an ecclesiastical court could not plead in a court of law or transact legal business. He could not serve on a jury, testify as a witness, bring an action to recover property owed him, or serve as an executor or as the guardian of a child. He could not come to court, except at the king's command; he could not practice a profession or hold an office. If a priest rather than an Anglican minister married him, the marriage would not be valid in law, nor would any transfer of land that it involved.[62] A Catholic was not allowed to possess any of the accoutrements of manhood, Catholic books or devotional articles, or arms and munitions.

As these laws were not necessarily enforced, they worked more as a threat than as an omnipresent and insurmountable obstacle. At least at the level of prescription, however, these newly stringent restrictions redressed the recognition that a Catholic husband might perceive his interests as different from those of the sovereign, rather than as both analogous to and interdependent with them. The breakdown of that analogy between householder and sovereign rendered Catholic manhood particularly precarious and contingent. If enforced, these laws threatened to reduce Catholic

---

62. J. A. Williams, "English Catholicism under Charles II," esp. p. 130; Miller, *Popery and Politics*, pp. 52, 55.

men's legal rights to those of the average *married* woman. While, according to Amy Erickson, "no man underwent anything like the disabilities of coverture—unless he was convicted of treason," the male recusant, at least at the level of theory, was an homme covert.[63] Unlike the "corruption of the blood" that extended some of the financial and social consequences of a treason conviction to the traitor's heirs, recusancy, like coverture, was confined to the individual; its penalties extended to the recusant's heirs only if they, too, were recusants. Furthermore, this status was reversible. A recusant man could regain his privileges by conforming, just as a feme covert could regain some legal autonomy through her husband's death. Unlike the feme covert, however, the recusant man did not have a husband to represent him legally in property transactions and in court. In addition, the recusant man or homme covert retained legal responsibility for his dependents, which a married woman did not have: he could be fined if his children and servants did not conform; as we have seen, attempts were made to hold him accountable for his wife's recusancy.

However erratic their enforcement, penal laws had one relatively consistent consequence. Since candidates for university degrees, mayors and other royal officials, judges, and those elected to the House of Commons were required to take the oath of supremacy, conformity was the only way for men to hold office.[64] A harsher clerical attitude toward compromise conspired with Jacobean penal legislation to limit the option of being a "church papist," to force many men to choose, and thus to push Catholic men out of public life while simultaneously pushing them into public notice.[65] Obviously, some Catholic men did achieve office and influence, especially at court, but they had to do so through patronage, personal influence, and deception. Thus, while penal laws addressed the problem of Catholics' widely suspected sneakiness and "cunning," the laws also forced Catholic men to be as "covert" as their wives, both by excluding them from official public action and by making secrecy and duplicity the only available avenues for action. This survival strategy, the only alternative for maintaining some political influence, might itself be viewed as feminizing Catholic men.

63. Erickson, *Women and Property*, p. 229.
64. Williams, "English Catholicism under Charles II," p. 129; see also J. P. Kenyon, *The Popish Plot* (London: Heinemann, 1972), p. 7.
65. See John Bossy, "The Character of Elizabethan Catholicism," *Past & Present* 21 (1962): 39–59, esp. 45; Halley, "Equivocation and the Legal Conflict," p. 51; Hibbard, "Early Stuart Catholicism," pp. 18–19; and Peter Holmes, *Resistance and Compromise: The Political Thought of the Elizabethan Catholics* (Cambridge: Cambridge University Press, 1982), esp. chaps. 6 and 7.

According to the oft-quoted Marquis of Halifax, the "pleasure of a lazy unmanly life" could not compensate for exclusion from public office.[66] An assumption that exclusion from public life set off a chain reaction of laziness and "unmanly" pleasure leading to excess informs even the work of twentieth-century historians. John Miller, for instance, mentions the Earl of Castlehaven, executed for sodomy and rape, as an extreme example of what could happen when a Catholic gentleman was not allowed appropriate employment. "Few were as spectacularly sinful as the second earl of Castlehaven," he concedes, but "many" fell into the trap. Miller similarly reproduces the early modern assumption that indolence and domestication led priests to go "spectacularly off the rails."[67] Miller accepts that "coverture" for men—exclusion from public life, the need for secrecy—produced transgressive behavior corresponding to an early modern definition of "effeminacy."

In early modern discourses, Catholic men were not feminized in the concretely visible ways that James Shapiro has identified in representations of Jewish men; they did not ooze fluids associated with female bodies (menstrual blood, breast milk) or perform biological or social functions associated with the female body (for the most part). Furthermore, I take Richard Rambuss's point that a male body does not have to be feminized to be penetrable or "leaky"; indeed, these designations might be considered as appropriate to male bodies as to female ones.[68] While not corporeal, the effeminacy attributed to Catholic men was material. "Effeminacy" described their relationships: their alliances with Catholic women and their differences from Protestant men. It also described their place in a cultural and theological structure, a place they were seen to share with

66. George Savile, Marquis of Halifax, *Complete Works*, ed. J. P. Kenyon (Harmondsworth: Penguin, 1969), p. 84.

67. Miller, *Popery and Politics*, pp. 18, 41. Miller's sources include Miles Prance, *The Whore of Babylon's Pockey Priest* (London, 1679/80). Prance, a former Catholic who provided crucial evidence against Catholics accused in the Popish Plot and the Meal Tub Plot (discussed in Chapter 4), announces his prejudices in his title; his scurrilous anti-Catholic polemic is a highly unreliable source.

68. James Shapiro, *Shakespeare and the Jews* (New York: Columbia University Press, 1996), pp. 37–39; and Richard Rambuss, "Pleasure and Devotion: The Body of Jesus and Seventeenth-Century Religious Lyric," in *Queering the Renaissance*, ed. Jonathan Goldberg (Durham, N.C.: Duke University Press, 1994), pp. 253–79. On early modern meanings of effeminacy, see also Anthony Fletcher, *Gender, Sex, and Subordination in England, 1500–1800* (New Haven: Yale University Press, 1995), chaps. 5 and 16; Michael McKeon, "Historicizing Patriarchy: The Emergence of Gender Difference in England, 1660–1760," *Eighteenth-Century Studies* 28.3 (1995): 295–322; Stephen Orgel, *Impersonations: The Performance of Gender in Shakespeare's England* (Cambridge: Cambridge University Press, 1996), esp. p. 26; and Bruce Smith, *Homosexual Desire in Shakespeare's England* (Chicago: University of Chicago Press, 1991), esp. pp. 196–97.

women. Catholic men were feminized not by sharing qualities or characteristics, physical or otherwise, usually attributed to women, but rather by occupying a position constructed as appropriate to women. This position was one of subordination, dependence, and divided allegiance, which might be understood in sexual terms but also in social ones. It was a matter of class and status as well as gender. Catholic men did not necessarily choose or prefer it, but they were thrust into it by law, then censured for taking so unmanly a part. When penal laws pushed men into this position, they promoted rather than resolved the gender confusions associated with Catholicism.

Other discourses, too, associated Catholicism with disturbing relationships between men and women. Two of Shakespeare's plays produced shortly after the Gunpowder Plot—*Macbeth* (1606), which has long been seen as referring to the plot, and *Antony and Cleopatra* (1606–8), which rarely has—join with anti-Catholic discourses in exploring the threat of heterosociality and the feminized position of the man who perceives his allegiance as divided. The topicality of both plays, like that of *Catiline*, is complex, shifting, ultimately indeterminate; all three of these plays respond to and rewrite Scottish or classical history as well as recent English history. Neither Lady Macbeth nor Cleopatra can "represent" Catholicism as, for instance, the Empress of Babylon and the Borgia family obviously do. But I would like to suggest one more way of thinking about the rich relationship between these plays and other contemporary discourses and controversies.

Shakespeare, whose body of work has become central to discussions of the construction of racial and religious difference in early modern England, did not write Italianate tragedies, like John Webster's or Thomas Middleton's, in which the whole casts are sinisterly Catholic, and their use of crucifixes and rosary beads as murder weapons reminds the audience that the relationship between their religion and nationality on the one hand and their villainy on the other is causal, not coincidental. Nor does he create a Catholic equivalent of Othello or Shylock, whose difference and resulting doomedness are made central to the play's concerns; there is no Catholic of Rome (or, God knows, of Yorkshire) to match the Jew or the Moor of Venice. This absence of Catholic protagonists testifies to the fact that it was not yet possible in England to construe local Catholics as recognizably and unremittingly "other," or even to define precisely who they were. It also testifies to the extent to which the demonization of Catholicism was the demonization of collectivity. Catholic malice was construed as conspiratorial and collaborative; it was not the work of individual villains but the result of individuals' slavish submission to a corrupting com-

munity. Alexander VI and the Empress of Babylon surround themselves
with those who do their bidding, follow their bad example, but, mercifully,
go down with them.

Although Shakespeare did not devote a play to exploring anti-Catholicism, as he explored racism, anti-Semitism, and colonialism, he did place
the phenomenon of inverse coverture at the center of *Macbeth* and *Antony
and Cleopatra,* as it was at the center of so many anti-Catholic discourses.
To a certain extent, he feminized the threat to order and manhood, as
anti-Catholic discourses did. In both plays the female characters wield sexual and occult power, but they also absorb manhood into themselves,
whether by invoking spirits to "unsex" them or by appropriating and wearing a "sword Phillipan"; as if there were only a limited amount of masculinity to go around, their male consorts are swordless, in need of help to
screw their courage to the sticking place or to define what it means to "be
a man." Both Macbeth and Antony experience a conflict of "divided duty"
that Shakespeare elsewhere presents as a female one: Macbeth is torn between loyalty to kinsman, guest, and king on the one hand and the ambition he shares with his wife on the other; Antony is torn between his re-
sponsibilities as a member of the triumvirate and his "gaudy nights" with
Cleopatra. In both plays the female "dearest partner in greatness" represents the temptation that the play suggests the hero should resist, just as,
in the conflict between pope and sovereign, the seductive yet treacherous
pope is often female. The male characters' dependence on female advice
and direction in these plays, as in *Catiline* and *The Whore of Babylon,* is at the
root of their tragic conflict. If the dyad—the bossy woman and the dependent man—is the shape that Jacobean nightmares of Catholic triumph took, the triangle—the man torn between that bossy woman and
the male leader, whether Octavius Caesar or Duncan or James I—is the
prior configuration, the conflict to which submission to the Whore of
Babylon is the wrong solution. While choosing the woman—that is, marrying—resolves conflict in many comedies, in these tragedies the male-
female dyad is neither a given nor an answer. To choose the woman, even
if choosing her does not mean submitting to her, is misguided. Whether
or not parallels between the tragic heroes and Catholic subjects are inten-
tional, these configurations mark, for me, the most interesting connection
between these plays and Jacobean anti-Catholic polemic and legislation—
not, say, the Porter's references to equivocation.

The connections between *Macbeth* and the Gunpowder Plot have been
widely discussed.[69] What has not been discussed is why and to what end the

---

69. On topicality, see Leah S. Marcus, *Puzzling Shakespeare: Local Reading and Its Discontents* (Berkeley: University of California Press, 1988), esp. chap. 1. On the topicality of

play, produced just after the Gunpowder Plot was "discovered," dramatizes treason not as a conspiracy among men but as a collusion between husband and wife. Numerous critics have commented on Lady Macbeth's resemblance to and alliance with the witches. She is also allied, however subtly, with those other figures of female disorderliness, Catholic wives. Her connection to Catholic belief and practice intensifies as the play unfolds. Since the Lady Macbeth of Act II seems, for the most part, to renounce superstition and reverence, she seems at first more skeptical of Catholic belief and practice than enmeshed in them. For instance, her contempt for Macbeth's hesitation echoes the conventional critiques of Catholic idolatry:

> The sleeping, and the dead,
> Are but as pictures; 'tis the eye of childhood
> That fears a painted devil.[70]

While Lady Macbeth's early contempt for "pictures" would seem to ally her with iconoclasm, her belief that she can wash away not only the evidence of the murder but the guilt seems like a parody of Catholic confidence in sacraments. Macbeth cannot believe in the efficacy of a purification ritual: "Will all great Neptune's ocean wash this blood/Clean from my hand?" (2.2.59–60). But Lady Macbeth insists that "A little water clears us of this deed:/How easy is it then!" (2.2.66–67). Protestant polemicists similarly claimed that the Gunpowder Plot conspirators operated on the promise of absolution. Knowing that the pope licensed their treason and that confession would subsequently "clear them of this deed," the plotters could say they were innocent and mean it. This concern about the Catholic confidence in sacraments accompanied the concern about equivocation and how it might vitiate testimony; while equivocation might enable Catholic suspects to deny their guilt, to perjure themselves, the participation of priests in the plot might lead them to believe their protestations of innocence, to think themselves genuinely guiltless. Whereas Catholicism is now popularly associated with guilt, what bothered the Jacobean opponents of Catholicism was that Catholics did *not* feel guilty. Repeatedly, official accounts of the plot and the trials dwell on how remorseless the conspirators seem. The accusation that they had celebrated mass together became a fo-

---

Macbeth, see Leeds Barroll, *Politics, Plague, and Shakespeare's Theater* (Ithaca: Cornell University Press, 1991), pp. 135–52; Karin S. Coddon, "'Unreal Mockery': Unreason and the Problem of Spectacle in *Macbeth,*" *ELH* 56.3 (1989): 485–501; and Garry Wills, *Witches and Jesuits: Shakespeare's "Macbeth"* (New York: Oxford University Press, 1995).

70. William Shakespeare, *Macbeth,* ed. Kenneth Muir (London: Methuen, 1951), 2.2.52–54.

cus for this conviction that Catholics viewed their treason as an enactment of rather than a transgression against their faith.

The "mad scene," which is Lady Macbeth's last, depicts her as plagued by the very guilt she earlier disclaimed. The scene simultaneously attributes guilt to her, by depicting her search for exonerating and reassuring rituals, and suggests that these rituals are symptoms of rather than solutions to her distress. In her nightly vigil, Lady Macbeth employs paraphernalia that could be associated with Catholic as well as occult ritual: the phantom water from which she hopes for purification, like holy water used in exorcism, baptism, and blessings; the candle; the talismanic writings. The Doctor who observes her concludes:

> infected minds
> To their deaf pillows will discharge their secrets.
> More needs she the divine than the physician.
> (5.1.69–71)

From a Protestant perspective, this "discharge" is a symptom of the infection, not a cure. Yet there is a "Roman" and, the play suggests, a deranged optimism in Lady Macbeth's nightly confession, which is both deeply private and performed for an audience; she seeks relief or forgiveness. Lady Macbeth seems to operate here on what might be called a "purgatorial hypothesis": that there is something she can do that will exonerate her, that she can somehow work her way out of her guilt. Just as Catholic prayers and rituals are frequently described as empty and repetitive, the scene dwells on reenactment. Every night she does the same thing; on any given night she repeats her frantic washing; but no matter how much she repeats, the rituals fail her. Only suicide can release her from this doomed liturgical cycle of repetition. Lady Macbeth's conviction that she can be so easily absolved reveals both her sinister ruthlessness at the beginning of the play and her madness at the end. Her hand-washing, like Pilate's, cannot clear her of the deed. Thus, in a displaced and incomplete way, in Macbeth's sleeplessness and the apparitions that haunt him, as well as in Lady Macbeth's sleepwalking and insanity, *Macbeth* explores the interiority of traitors, as other depictions of the Gunpowder Plot were very reluctant to do. It also suggests that their sense of remorse is unbearable and maddening, and that their search for rituals of ablution and absolution—rituals widely associated with Catholic practice—is incriminating, hopeless, and deranged.

Antony and Cleopatra has an even more oblique relationship to the Gunpowder Plot and to Jacobean anti-Catholic discourses. Yet Antony's much-discussed oscillation between Rome and Egypt, Octavius and Cleopatra, can be read as a dramatization of divided allegiance for which the most pressing cultural analogue was the Catholic subject torn between his king in England and his pope in Rome. Here the dilemma is explored sympathetically, although it ends in death. There is no solution to divided allegiance in these plays, "no midway," as Octavia complains, "'Twixt these extremes at all."[71]

From a Catholic perspective, the dilemma of divided allegiance arose when Henry VIII declared himself supreme head of the Church of England in 1536. Formerly, most English subjects had divided their allegiance between their sovereign in England and the pope in Rome; hereafter, Henry declared, his subjects owed him religious as well as political allegiance. His successors all, with the notable exception of Mary, followed Henry's lead in declaring themselves head of the church; they took the view that, in combining spiritual and temporal leadership, they had resolved rather than created a dilemma of divided allegiance. But those English subjects who chose to remain Catholic found their loyalty more conflicted, contested, and suspected than it had been before the Reformation. Henry VIII had created a unique situation. As Peter Holmes states, "there was no other country in Europe where the problem existed as it did in England, where Catholicism was proscribed and yet there survived a sizeable minority willing to express resistance to a Protestant settlement."[72] This minority was too "sizeable" to ignore, yet not large enough to rebel without the help of a foreign invasion (or an ambitious and successful internal conspiracy like the Gunpowder Plot).

From a Protestant and nationalist point of view, the turning point was not 1536 but 1570, when Pope Pius V issued a bull, *Regnans in excelsis*, declaring Elizabeth to be a usurper. This bull, which attracted more rather than less attention as time went on, raised many troubling questions, most of which were not confronted immediately. If the pope excommunicated a ruler or pronounced him or her a heretic, did he simultaneously justify Catholic subjects not only in disobedience but in violent rebellion? Were Catholic subjects licensed and encouraged to assassinate a Protestant monarch? Anti-Catholic polemicists tended to take the darkest possible view: the pope encouraged (and would even reward) assassination and rebellion. Catholic apologists, conversely, either denied or downplayed so-called papal deposing power, tending to advocate nonresistance in hopes

---

71. William Shakespeare, *Antony and Cleopatra*, ed. M. R. Ridley (Cambridge: Harvard University Press, 1954), 3.4.19–20.
72. Holmes, *Resistance and Compromise*, p. 82.

of gaining acceptance and ameliorating persecution in non-Catholic countries.

Concern about the capacity of Catholics to be loyal subjects became especially acute just after the Gunpowder Plot. Although James at first distinguished between the conspirators and other, loyal Catholic subjects, uncertainty about how to recognize the difference rapidly led him to require, in May 1606, that his subjects swear an oath of allegiance solely to him; the oath was enacted as part of the new penal legislation. In this oath, which was required of men and women (including married women), and ultimately even of nobles, the pledge of loyalty to the sovereign coexisted with a strongly worded repudiation of papal deposing power (crudely conceived). The oath juxtaposed acknowledgment of James as "lawful and rightful King" with an acknowledgment that "the Pope neither of himself nor by any authority of Church or See of Rome, or by any means with any other, has any power or authority to depose the King." It went even further, requiring the oath-giver to swear: "I do from my heart abhor, detest, and abjure, as impious and heretical, this damnable doctrine and position, that princes which be excommunicated or deprived by the Pope may be deposed and murdered by their subjects or by any other whatsoever."[73] Many English Catholics had reservations about papal deposing power, its reach and its binding force; as a result, many were inclined to swear the oath to prove conclusively that they could be both Catholics and loyal subjects. But the wording of the oath so directly impugned papal authority that Pope Paul V condemned it. Controversy over the oath thus not only exacerbated the dilemma for English Catholics but ignited an international as well as a fiercely nationalist debate about the rights of kings in which

73. On the oath of allegiance and the ensuing controversy, see Thomas Clancy, S.J., "English Catholics and the Papal Deposing Power, 1570–1640," pt. 1, "The Elizabethan Period," *Recusant History* 6 (1961): 114–41; pt. 2, "The Stuarts," ibid. 6.5 (1962): 205–27; pt. 3, "The Stuarts (continued)," ibid. 7.1 (1963): 2–10; idem, *Papist Pamphleteers: The Allen-Persons Party and the Political Thought of the Counter-Reformation in England, 1572–1615* (Chicago: Loyola University Press, 1964), chaps. 4 and 5; Maurus Lunn, "English Benedictines and the Oath of Allegiance, 1606–1647," *Recusant History* 10 (1969–70): 146–63; Charles Howard McIlwaine, "Introduction," in *Political Works of James I*, pp. li–lxxx; Peter Milward, *Religious Controversies of the Jacobean Age: A Survey of Printed Sources* (Lincoln: University of Nebraska Press, 1986), pp. 94–131; Clarence J. Ryan, "The Jacobean Oath of Allegiance and English Lay Catholics," *Catholic Historical Review* 28.2 (1942): 159–83; and J. H. M. Salmon, "Catholic Resistance Theory, Ultramontanism, and the Royalist Response, 1580–1620," in *The Cambridge History of Political Thought, 1450–1700*, ed. J. H. Burns (Cambridge: Cambridge University Press, 1991), pp. 219–53.

The oath appears here as quoted in both Lunn, "English Benedictines and the Oath of Allegiance," pp. 146–47, and Clancy, "English Catholics and the Papal Deposing Power," pt. 2, p. 209. Ryan suggests that married women often refused to take the oath, and offers evidence of their resulting hardships ("Jacobean Oath of Allegiance," pp. 178–80).

James had a strong voice.[74] Rulers such as James I defended and extended their authority in the face of papal incursions on it; defenders of Catholic resistance strenuously questioned absolutism and affirmed that subjects were not bound to obey a king who did not rule in their interests.

In *Antony and Cleopatra,* a fragmentation linked both to a female character and to a feminizing dilemma draws resonance from these debates. Shakespeare's most discussed dramatizations of the dilemma of "divided duty" explore the conflict of the young woman torn between love for and loyalty to her father and to her husband; in choosing to subordinate filial devotion to wifely hope and love, in leaving her father's house to enter into adulthood, marriage, and her own future, the daughter comes into conflict with both her father's jealousy and possessiveness (in both *Othello* and *Lear*) and her husband's inability to trust that a woman who could deceive and reject a father can be loyal to a husband (*Othello*). Various critics have assessed how the wedding ceremony, which is often reenacted in comedies but, tellingly, not in tragedies, works to resolve the potentially tragic dilemma of divided duty by ritualizing the transfer of the woman from father to husband and enforcing celebration of rather than resistance to exogamy.[75] Mario DiGangi has shown how comedies such as *As You Like It* depict the strained process by which both prospective spouses repudiate homoerotic attachments in the service of their marital bond.[76] Comedies enact a fantasy of how marriage works to create and support an erotic and procreative bond between a man and a woman, distinguishing it from and privileging it over a web of other relations. Tragedies imagine the consequences when marriage fails in this cultural task.

The marriage ceremony suggests that the resolution of divided duty requires that one duty be given priority and the other subordinated; the daughter moves from one duty to the other, the young man or woman moves from a same-sex relationship to a cross-sex one. Thus the process of marrying offers an analogy only for hierarchizing or shifting duties, but not for holding allegiance to two equal powers in tension. There was no

74. James I, "Apologie for the Oath of Allegiance" (1607), "A Premonition to All Christian Monarches" (1609), and "Remonstrance for the Right of Kings" (1616), in *Political Works of James I.*

75. On the marriage ceremony and the exchange of women, see Lynda Boose, "The Father and the Bride in Shakespeare," *PMLA* 97 (1982): 325–47; Claire McEachern, "Fathering Herself: A Source Study of Shakespeare's Feminism," *Shakespeare Quarterly* 39.3 (1988): 269–90; and Carol Thomas Neely, *Broken Nuptials in Shakespeare's Plays* (New Haven: Yale University Press, 1985). On "divided duty," see *Othello* (1.3.183) and *King Lear* (1.1.95–104).

76. Mario DiGangi, *The Homoerotics of Early Modern Drama* (Cambridge: Cambridge University Press, 1997), chap. 2.

ceremony for resolving the conflict between a Catholic subject's loyalty to
the pope and to his (or her) sovereign, although converts to the Church
of England might participate in elaborate rituals, and James offered the
oath of allegiance as an occasion, like the marriage ceremony, on which to
forsake former allegiances, pledging monogamous devotion only to one.

Antony and Cleopatra explores the conflicts and repercussions when the
divided subject is unable to choose between or transfer loyalties, because
"Equality of two domestic powers / Breed scrupulous faction" (1.3.47–48;
my emphasis). The play explores this conflict, as *Othello* and *King Lear* do,
as the conflict of the marriageable woman; in this case, the woman, Octavia, is unable to transfer her allegiance. Her brother and her husband
both require her loyalty, and each expects her to act as an intermediary
with the other. Octavia clearly articulates the dilemma at the play's center:
"Ay me most wretched, / That have my heart parted betwixt two friends, /
That does afflict each other!" (3.6.76–78). The play offers Octavia a solution, although Antony, whose dilemma is similar, cannot find one. Unable
to establish a midway 'twixt these extremes, she returns to the protection
of her brother.

The play also dramatizes Antony's dilemma in sexual and domestic
terms. He is torn between wife (first Fulvia, then Octavia) and mistress, between duty and pleasure. But, as has been widely noticed, Cleopatra's rival
for Antony's attention and allegiance is Octavius Caesar more than his sister, Octavia. Furthermore, Cleopatra is an abstraction as well as a beloved
woman. As "Egypt," queen and goddess, she stands not just as a diversion
from duty and devotion but as an alternative object of worship or reverence.
The descriptions of Cleopatra—exotic, theatrical, seductive, a bejeweled
idol—link her to the widely disseminated representations of the Whore of
Babylon.[77] Whether or not Cleopatra can be compared to Duessa, the Empress of Babylon, or the Whore of Babylon as a feminized figure for the
Catholic menace, *Antony and Cleopatra* is certainly structured around
Antony's inability to reconcile his dueling allegiances and the disastrous
consequences for him and for others. Antony's untenable yet irreconcilable position as sojourner, as, in Linda Charnes's words, "one who exists
between places, unembedded, without the firmness of identity provided by
unwavering allegiance to a particular place," resembles not only the divided duty of female characters but the dilemma of Catholic subjects in a
Protestant country, torn between actively hostile rival powers.[78] These are

77. Mary Nyquist, "'Profuse, Proud Cleopatra': 'Barbarism' and Female Rule in Early
Modern English Republicanism," *Women's Studies* 24.1–2 (1994): 85–130, esp. 92.

78. Linda Charnes, *Notorious Identity: Materializing the Subject in Shakespeare* (Cambridge:
Harvard University Press, 1993), p. 113. See also Laura Levine, *Men in Women's Clothing:
Anti-Theatricality and Effeminization, 1579–1642* (Cambridge: Cambridge University Press,

not the only kinds of divided duty imaginable in seventeenth-century England, but they are the most discussed. They are linked conceptually and structurally, suggesting that to be "feminized" is to stand in the woman's place, in this case between two uncompromising and irreconcilable authorities.

Antony and Cleopatra explores Antony's dilemma exhaustively and, most of the time, sympathetically. But it also depicts Cleopatra's influence as bewitching and unmanning, as numerous critics have noted. Antony progressively loses his ability to resist or even to choose consciously. After Actium, for instance, when Cleopatra refuses responsibility for Antony's retreat ("I little thought / You would have followed"), he, in turn, projects his agency and accountability onto her:

> Egypt, thou knew'st too well
> My heart was to thy rudder tied by the strings,
> And thou shouldst tow me after. O'er my spirit
> Thy full supremacy thou knew'st, and that
> Thy beck might from the bidding of the gods
> Command me.
>
> (3.11.56–61)

Obviously, assumptions about gender informing popular discourses, such as those about shrews and shrew-taming, provide one way of reading exchanges like this one. Cleopatra has gained inappropriate "supremacy" over Antony, usurping his sword and his manhood, with the result that he is disarmed, fragmented, dissolved. This vision of gender inversion and disorder also corresponds to and supports denunciations of papal supremacy as whimsical, arbitrary, senselessly demanding, and destructive. Dividing the subject between two places and two leaders, Catholicism strands him at sea.[79] The more he tries to pursue both, the less he can attain either. Antony is feminized, then, by his structural position, a position in which the oath of allegiance—not the Whore of Babylon—placed many men. The play does not depict Antony as a Catholic man, but rather explores the dilemmas arising from a position of divided duty that Catholic men in England shared with marriageable women, especially after the Gunpowder Plot.

Various critics have seen early modern English drama as a kind of shell game, which explores some fears while diverting attention from others. Such analyses suggest that it is worth scrutinizing the processes used to dis-

---

1994), pp. 65, 69. Both Charnes and Levine link Antony's dilemma to Renaissance attitudes toward theatricality, which are inseparable from attitudes toward Catholicism.

79. Charnes, *Notorious Identity*, also discusses the significance of Antony's landing "at sea."

tract our attention from the shells while keeping the shells in our periph-
eral vision. Both contrasting the drama to other representations (such as
prescriptive literature or legal statutes or court records) and attending to
internal evidence can help to reveal these theatrical sleights of hand. Lisa
Jardine, for instance, has argued that the drama emphasizes the threat
posed by "female autonomy in choice of marriage partner" rather than
"hidden undertakings between men" because the former were, "given the
constraints on women's behaviour in general," "likely to be less really socially and politically disruptive."[80] That is, the stage displaces the blame
from male networks more likely to have "real political consequences" onto
unruly women, or, as Dympna Callaghan insists, men's fantasies of unruly
women, as enacted by boys.[81]

I am reluctant to point toward a "real problem" that can be documented
outside the theater and that the theater ignores or obscures. Instead, I
want to argue that the location of threat is always an imaginative and representational process, whether we trace it in legal statutes, in court records, or on the stage. For in early modern culture, as in the shell game, it
is almost impossible to know for sure which shell hides the pea, what exactly the pea is, or, indeed, if there is anything there at all. What I am
testing, then, is not the "real" threat—of Catholic female power, for instance—against the theatrical representation, but one group of representations against another, or the hypothesis that one kind of evidence will
support against another. Although lengthy and widely publicized trials and
executions construed and redressed the Gunpowder Plot as a hidden un-
dertaking among men, the story rapidly evolved, shifting the focus toward
the threat of gender disorder, morphing the crowd of men with explosives
into the troublesome Catholic couple.

Jacobean anti-Catholicism tends to focus on the scandal of heterosociality more than the scandal of same-sex attachments, the man allied to
a woman rather than to another man. Does this mean that the commanding or companionable (rather than submissive) woman is more or less
threatening than the desired man? There is no sure answer. But writers'

---

80. Lisa Jardine, "Companionate Marriage versus Male Friendship: Anxiety for the Lin-
eal Family in Jacobean Drama," in *Political Culture and Cultural Politics in Early Modern En-
gland: Essays Presented to David Underdown,* ed. Susan D. Amussen and Mark A. Kishlansky
(Manchester: Manchester University Press, 1995), p. 250. For the "shell game" approach,
see also my *Dangerous Familiars: Representations of Domestic Crime in England, 1550–1700*
(Ithaca: Cornell University Press, 1994), and Lynda Boose, "*The Taming of the Shrew,* Good
Husbandry, and Enclosure," in *Shakespeare Reread: The Texts in New Contexts,* ed. Russ
McDonald (Ithaca: Cornell University Press, 1994), pp. 193–225.

81. Dympna C. Callaghan, *Shakespeare without Women: Representing Gender and Race on the
Renaissance Stage* (London: Routledge, forthcoming).

retreat to the well-worn figuration of danger and disorder as inverse coverture does not mean that powerful women were not considered "really" threatening; instead, it confirms that depicting a threat as feminine was a quick and dirty way to invest it with a whole range of qualities, to insist on it as simultaneously familiar and apocalyptic, and to place it within an even broader sense of anxiety about the gender order. Furthermore, these fictions of inverse coverture had real consequences, shaping responses to Catholic men and women and setting limits on their opportunities. By associating the threat of Catholicism with other threats from within or below, the language of gender described the consequences of national conversion in concrete, imaginable terms. These terms made the threat more vivid, but they also confirmed very conventional definitions of order and laid out familiar and manageable avenues for attacking the problem.

PRIESTS AND THE SCANDAL OF HETEROSOCIALITY

The Catholic men most consistently described as effeminate were priests. Their vows of celibacy and poverty made them the exact opposite of "married, property-owning men," who, according to Susan Amussen, were the only ones who were recognized as "'real' men."[82] Even more than lay Catholic men in England, they found that their position allied them to women, especially wives. In a particularly striking articulation of this structural similarity between priests and wives, James I, in a letter written to Robert Cecil shortly before he acceded to the throne of England, explained that Jesuits were "like married women or minors whose vows are ever subject to the controlment of their husbands and tutors, their consciences must ever be commanded and overruled by their Romish god as it pleases him to allow or revoke their conclusions."[83] For James, the parallel lay in being commanded and overruled, and therefore not having a conscience of one's own. Thus James assumed that coverture invariably succeeded in subsuming its subordinates; this assumption enabled him to maintain his focus on his rival, the pope, who called the shots and deserved the blame. Being commanded and overruled is not, in itself, a bad thing; obviously, James would have liked to command and overrule his own subjects without any competition from the pope. Indeed, monarchy, as James himself would

82. Susan Amussen, "'The Part of a Christian Man': The Cultural Politics of Manhood in Early Modern England," in Amussen and Kishlansky, *Political Culture and Cultural Politics*, p. 223; see also Fletcher, *Gender, Sex, and Subordination*, p. 97.

83. *Letters of King James VI and I*, ed. G. P. V. Akrigg (Berkeley: University of California Press, 1984), p. 205. I am grateful to Megan Matchinske for this reference.

come to define it, positioned all of its loyal subjects as subordinated wives. Catholics were uniquely troublesome not in being like wives but in having two husbands. Since Jesuits bent their consciences to a second, foreign husband, "their Romish god," James concluded that their coverture marked them as "the more to be distrusted."

Many critiques of the clergy similarly depict priests as parallel to, allied with, and even dependent on women. Of course, priests were often accused of sodomy and of seducing boys; long before the reformation, attacks on the clergy dwelt on these offenses; even within the church, sodomy was "considered a specifically clerical vice," according to Bruce Smith.[84] Furthermore, the definition of sodomy as a crime under Henry VIII may have been part of the complex process of denigrating the clergy and justifying the suppression of the monasteries.[85] Yet priests were always accused of both cross-sex and same-sex relations, and the many sexual sins of which they were accused were not grouped neatly by the genders of the parties involved. Adultery and sodomy had long been associated as sexual transgressions. Alan Stewart argues that, for early reformers such as John Bale, clerical celibacy meant not abstention from sexual activity but contempt for marriage; thus adultery and sodomy were two manifestations of "celibacy," or the refusal to confine one's sexuality within marriage. Similarly, Mario DiGangi suggests that, since adultery and sodomy were both viewed as disorderly sexual behaviors, in the early modern period sexual morality may have been judged more by "a distinction between orderly and disorderly behaviors" than by a distinction "between heteroerotic and homoerotic behaviors."[86]

Stewart's interpretation of the 1536 visitation of monasteries and convents bears out this suggestion. Assessors dispatched by Cromwell to catalog the income and possessions of monasteries in preparation for suppressing them reported at least as much about sexual transgressions as they did about economic resources. Stewart argues that their reports distinguish between same-sex and cross-sex transgressions largely in terms of space. In the reports, incontinence—that is, any kind of sexual congress with women—"refers to a lack of respect to being contained by boundaries, in this case the monastery walls. Incontinence is a literal *transgression*

---

84. Smith, *Homosexual Desire in Shakespeare's England*, p. 44. See also John Boswell, *Christianity, Social Tolerance, and Homosexuality* (Chicago: University of Chicago Press, 1980), pp. 187–93; Alan Bray, *Homosexuality in Renaissance England*, 2d ed. (New York: Columbia University Press, 1995), pp. 19–21, 26–27, 49; and Alan Stewart, *Close Readers: Humanism and Sodomy in Early Modern England* (Princeton: Princeton University Press, 1997), p. 54.

85. Smith, *Homosexual Desire in Shakespeare's England*, pp. 43–46.

86. DiGangi, *Homoerotics of Early Modern Drama*, p. 18.

of those walls, a going beyond the bounds of the monastic institution." Such incontinence required priests to leave the monastery to visit a convent or to meet with local women, or to admit women into the monastery. Sometimes it produced illegitimate offspring, who might either be clandestinely killed or become burdens on the local community. "Sodomy, in sharp contrast, is literally *embedded* within the institution, dependent on the organizational requirements whereby men share sleeping quarters and are forced into intimate situations with boys." According to Stewart, the injunctions issued as a result of the visitation of monasteries and convents focused on reinforcing the walls; that is, stopping traffic in and out: "These injunctions do not attempt to tackle the practice of embedded sodomy, preferring to concentrate on the transgressive acts of sex between men and women which breach the walls of the monastery."[87]

The suppression of the monasteries, however, literally broke down those walls, forcing priests out of their all-male communities. Stewart argues that, as a consequence, sodomy ceased to be seen as synonymous with the clergy and came to be suspected in all relations between men, especially those involving cohabitation and collaboration, relations that were central to humanism. If, in leaving monasteries, priests brought "sodomy" as a conceptual category with them into households, disseminating suspicion and hostility toward male-male intimacy, they also brought "incontinence." The concern about priests' relations with women that had always been there spread and intensified as priests' locations and relationships changed.

Denunciations of Catholicism as fostering a range of alliances between men and women, alliances in which women might be authoritative leaders or equal partners, respond, in part, to the dramatically altered circumstances of Catholics in post-Reformation England. In flight from everharsher penalties, priests abandoned the clerical dress that would have marked them out for prosecution (and for death), thus confirming the common association of Catholicism with disguise and deception. In addition, they scattered, divided from one another, and sought refuge in the homes of well-to-do Catholic sympathizers. By the seventeenth century, priests were no longer the nomads they had at first been after the Reformation, and were becoming instead, as Caroline Hibbard says, "domesticated (with ambiguous consequences for their spiritual authority) in aristocratic homes."[88] Priests' hosts took enormous risks to harbor them, and deferred to their spiritual authority and leadership in maintaining Catholicism in England. Yet the shelter they provided often reduced priests' op-

87. Stewart, *Close Readers*, pp. 44–52, esp. 51, 52.
88. Hibbard, "Early Stuart Catholicism," p. 2.

portunities to proselytize, limiting them to roles as domestic chaplains and narrowing their mission to what Bossy terms "household reformation."[89] In Christopher Haigh's view, many priests abandoned their obligations to poorer Catholics in order to live in greater comfort and security in gentry homes; through devotional works addressed to the gentry family, they then "fostered a brand of piety which created a demand for domestic chaplains, and the pattern of intense family religion."[90] This piety isolated families and exacerbated the domestication of priests; so did danger: "Wealthy Catholics would not permit their chaplains to attend the poor for fear of provoking the government." Furthermore, according to Miller, priests' "dependence on their host might prove embarrassing or even humiliating."[91] To justify and disguise their presence in the household, they might serve as stewards or as tutors for their hosts' children, and thus find it increasingly difficult to assert their difference from and authority over other servants, and, indeed, the household governors themselves.[92] While it is difficult to pin down the social position of the hunted priest within the recusant household, he was, in many ways, a dependent who needed not only material support but protection from the law.

Anti-Catholic polemic reflects priests' altered circumstances by describing them as insubordinate servants, or as interlopers who violate the household. John Gee, for instance, whose text repudiating Catholicism, after his brief flirtation with it, became hugely popular, informs his readers that "the Priests and Jesuites in their bookes pretend that they are servants to those over whom indeed they lord it. . . . While they pretend, that they are forced to creepe into private houses for feare of persecution, they carry more dominion over the Family, then any Parish-Priest doth in those Countries where Popish Religion publikely prevaileth."[93] Thus these domesticated priests are not servile enough; they challenge the authority of the husband and father in ways that are perceived as threatening the patriarchal family even outside of the "Catholic community."

89. John Bossy, "The English Catholic Community, 1603–1625," in *The Reign of James VI and I*, ed. Alan G. R. Smith (New York: Macmillan, 1973), p. 103; see also Kenyon, *Popish Plot*, p. 23.

90. Christopher Haigh, "From Monopoly to Minority: Catholicism in Early Modern England," *Transactions of the Royal Historical Society*, 5th ser., 31 (1981): 138.

91. Ibid., p. 145; Miller, *Popery and Politics*, p. 35.

92. On the social status of priests, see Bossy, "Character of Elizabethan Catholicism," p. 51; and Haigh, "From Monopoly to Minority," p. 139.

93. John Gee, *The Foot Out of the Snare: With a Detection of Sundry Late Practices and Impostures of the Priests and Jesuits in England* (London, 1624), sigs. M, L2r–v. Gee's work went through four editions in 1624 alone. See Michael C. Questier, "John Gee, Archbishop Abbot, and the Use of Converts from Rome in Jacobean Anti-Catholicism," *Recusant History* 21.3 (1993): 347–60.

They do so both because they stand as rivals to their male hosts and because they are allied to women. Because of their new circumstances, more priests lived with secular women than had ever done so before. In double monasteries, some priests had shared a roof with nuns; many convents needed to employ a priest to administer the sacraments. Some aristocratic households had employed priests in residence. But in seventeenth-century England, it became the norm for priests to live in households that might include, or even be run by, secular women.[94] As a consequence, Richard Sheldon laments, priests and Jesuits "feeding here in England daintily, arrayed gallantly, lodging softly," are "very domestically and privily conversant with Ladies, Dames, Matrones, Maids of all sorts."[95] Thomas Becon warns that priests have "shamelesse, smooth, smirking faces" and "lustie broad, bald, shaven crownes" that become signs legible to "such nice Nymphs as know your secret subtilties, and jolly juglings that yee are beasts of that marke that will never faile Lady *Venus*." Priests are enabled to "play *Priapus* part" by their idleness, on which Becon harps: "They of the labour of other mens hands, and the sweate of other mens browes may live an idle & voluptuous life, as Epicures and belly beasts, borne onely to consume the good fruits of the earth."[96]

Such texts not only compare priests to the privileged women with whom they lodged (fastidious, beardless, idle consumers), they also couple them; they accuse priests of committing the most outrageous transgression against a host or master short of murder: seducing the wife and daughters in the household. Adultery supplants sodomy as priests' particular vice, yet adultery becomes a clerical transgression that does not require them to breach the walls, since the priests have already been welcomed in as household members. For Becon, for instance, sodomy, with all its complex meanings, quickly gives way to a variety of sexual depredations with women: "Yee stinking Sodomites, ye deceitfull Deflowrers of mayds, yee devilish defilers of mens wives yee cankred corrupters of widowes, and yee lecherous locusts, may lie with your whores and harlots all night, and the next day after goe to Masse."[97] Samuel Harsnett, in his famously vitriolic *Declaration of Egregious Popish Impostures* (1603), contrasts priests' dalliances with women to actors' dalliances with boys: just as "it is the fashion of vagabond players, that coast from Towne to Towne with a trusse and a cast of fiddles, to carry

94. Robin Clifton, "The Popular Fear of Catholics during the English Revolution," *Past & Present* 52 (1971): 23–55, esp. 48.

95. Sheldon, *Survey of the Miracles*, sig. S4.

96. Thomas Becon, *The Displaying of the Popish Masse* (London, 1637), pp. 74–75, 272; see also pp. 90–91, 135, 245–46, 297.

97. Ibid., p. 157–58.

in theyr consort, broken queanes and *Ganimedes,* as well for their night pleasance, as their dayes pastime," so "every priest" involved in an exorcism "departed . . . suted with his wench after the same good custome."[98] Toward the end of the century, anticlerical pornography similarly dwelt on priests' transgressions with women, although it also salaciously imagined same-sex couplings in monasteries and convents.[99]

Men's sexual exploitation of women in households was probably not uncommon; most of the time, it was not much lamented. When priests seduce women, however, they debauch soul as well as body. Anti-Catholic polemic often speculated that priests tempted women to convert for the same reasons that Satan began by tempting Eve, or devils lured women into witchcraft more frequently than men: women were more gullible, more vulnerable, more malleable. The weaker sex, Edward Hoby writes, "by reason of [their] lesse abilitie of judgement, is soonest inveigled with their wiles."[100] As a consequence, Catholics tend to be, as Lord Chief Justice William Scroggs remarked in 1679, "silly women, or weaker men." One writer complained in the 1630s: "Our great women fall away every day."[101] The spiritual seduction of these fallen women was simultaneously depicted as sexual. Gee warns that "the Emissaries of Rome" "steale away *the hearts of the weaker sort:* and secretly do they creep into houses, *leading captive simple women loaden with sinnes, and led away with diverse lusts.*"[102]

The charge that priests invariably seduced the penitents who confessed to them worked to discredit priests, women, and the intimacies between them. In the sixteenth century, the martyr Margaret Clitherow was accused of harboring priests not for religion but for "harlotry," and of sharing with priests "delicate cheer, when she would set her husband with bread and butter and a red herring."[103] Anne Vaux's relationship with Fr. Henry Garnet, who was ultimately executed for complicity in the Gunpowder Plot, was similarly slandered. Vaux had a twenty-year friendship with Garnet, during which she protected him, traveled with him posing as his sister, and

---

98. Samuel Harsnett, *A Declaration of Egregious Popish Impostures* (London, 1603), sig. V3.

99. Roger Thompson, *Unfit for Modest Ears: A Study of Pornographic, Obscene, and Bawdy Works Written or Published in England in the Second Half of the Seventeenth Century* (Totowa, N.J.: Rowman & Littlefield, 1979), chap. 8.

100. Hoby, *Letter to Mr. T. H. Late Minister,* sig. A2v.

101. Scroggs's comment is recorded in *The Tryals of Sir George Wakeman [et al.] for High Treason for Conspiring the Death of the King* (London, 1679), p. 78; the following lament is quoted by Caroline Hibbard, *Charles I and the Popish Plot* (Chapel Hill: University of North Carolina Press, 1983), p. 55. See also David Underdown, *A Freeborn People: Politics and the Nation in Seventeenth-Century England* (Oxford: Clarendon, 1996), esp. pp. 63–64.

102. Gee, *Foot Out of the Snare,* sig. B2.

103. Fr. John Mush, "Life of Margaret Clitherow," in *The Troubles of Our Catholic Forefathers Related by Themselves,* ed. John Morris, 3 vols. (London: Burns & Oates, 1877), 3: 414, 427.

helped him to provide safe houses and meeting places for priests. As one observer remarked, "Mrs. Anne Vaux doth usually goe with him whithersoever he goethe." Antonia Fraser concludes that "without Anne Vaux's continuous, energetic, thoughtful loyalty Father Garnet could never have carried out his ministry in England for so many years without capture." Whereas this relationship might be considered a "partnership," as Fraser insists, it was widely slandered, in court, in gossip, and in print, as sexual.[104] In the 1630s, attempts to discredit Mary Ward, founder of the Institute of the Blessed Virgin Mary, commonly known as the "Jesuitesses," included the allegation that she engaged in unseemly intimacies with her Jesuit confessor. Such accusations ridiculed and debased the alliances between men and women that Jo Ann McNamara sees as the most positive legacy of the Catholic clerical tradition. McNamara calls this syneisactism, "religious men and women living together in chastity, recognizing equal spiritual capacities."[105] In anti-Catholic polemic, it appears simply as fornication. This polemic thus participates in the larger phenomenon in early modern culture that Jeffrey Masten has identified as "the uneasiness (in both senses) of imagining the possibility of an equitable conversation between the heterosexes—as well as the ostensible problem of effeminization through heterosexual practices." This uneasiness leads to and is fostered by the "pejorative portrayal of the impossibilities and dangers of cross-sex communication."[106]

Yet this polemic does obliquely register the interdependence and mutual respect of relationships between women and their confessors in the special circumstances of post-Reformation England. While confessors obviously have spiritual authority over their charges, English women often harbored the priests who heard their confessions, feeding them, sheltering them, and protecting them from the law. Furthermore, women were themselves most vulnerable when they acted to harbor priests, since to do so was a felony punishable by death. Under such conditions, each party is dependent on the other, and each wields some power. Either could "undo" the other, in any number of ways. Consider, for a moment, the popular image of a priest discovered in a woman's bed. As Overbury writes in his char-

104. *Calendar of State Papers, Domestic Series*, ed. F. H. Blackburne Daniell (1921) (Nedeln, Liechtenstein: Kraus Reprints, 1968),1603–10, p. 263; Fraser, *Faith and Treason*, p. 238.

105. Jo Ann Kay McNamara, *Sisters in Arms: Catholic Nuns through Two Millennia* (Cambridge: Harvard University Press, 1996), pp. 463, 5.

106. Jeffrey Masten, "Playwrighting: Authorship and Collaboration," in *A New History of Early English Drama*, ed. John D. Cox and David Scott Kastan (New York: Columbia University Press, 1997), pp. 359–60; see also Masten, *Textual Intercourse: Collaboration, Authorship, and Sexualities in Renaissance Drama* (Cambridge: Cambridge University Press, 1997).

acter of "A Jesuite": "No place in our Climate hides him so securely as a Ladyes Chamber; the modestie of the *Pursevant* [pursuivant; that is, warrant
officer] hath only forborne the bed, & so mist him."[107] Nor is this text unusual in its assumption that hunted priests "runne into the bed where one
of your faire *Females* lay, so to avoyde the search," as Sheldon similarly
claims. *A Letter from a Catholick Gentleman to His Popish Friends* echoes: "His
safest *Kennel* was a *Ladies Chamber;* the modesty of the *Messenger* left the *Bed
unsearch'd,* and so he *miss'd* him."[108] What the priest is doing in the bed, of
course, is hiding from laws that made it a felony to be a priest. In this image
the woman, whether or not she is having sex with him, is protecting him.
The priest enters the bed to evade the law as much as to pursue desire.

For James I, "searching the bed" is a Protestant activity since it requires
skepticism regarding the priest's motives and actions. James claims that "in
the time of the greatest blindnesse in Popery, though a man should find
his wife or his daughter lying a bed in her Confessors armes; yet was it not
lawfull for him so much as to suspect that the Frier had any errand there,
but to Confesse and instruct her."[109] Penal laws make suspicion "lawfull";
they also make confessing and instructing a wife or daughter as transgressive as having sex with her. Men may be free to suspect lascivious friars, but
wives and daughters have new reasons for sheltering priests in their beds.
The laws thus promote clandestine alliances between women and priests
more than they expose them. The vivid fantasies of couplings between
priests and their *dévotes* articulate the fear that Catholicism promotes unseemly intimacies between men and women, whether confessional, sexual,
or both. These fantasies attempt to disparage collaboration by recasting it
as sexual exploitation.

The "private" space of the Catholic house, with its pockets of even
greater privacy—its curtained beds, priest holes, and portable altars—was
open to scrutiny from within and without; its inhabitants, including
women and especially priests, were liable to be hauled out and fined, imprisoned, even executed. In both anti-Catholic polemic and penal legislation, then, Catholic privacy—whether that meant the household as site of
worship and resistance or the unknowable hearts and minds of Catholic
subjects—was political, contested, public, and presided over by women.[110]

107. Thomas Overbury, *New and Choise Characters, of Severall Authors* (London, 1615),
sig. M5v.
108. Sheldon, *Survey of the Miracles,* sig. S3v; *A Letter from a Catholick Gentleman to His
Popish Friends, Now to Be Exil'd from London* (London, 1678), p. 4.
109. James I, "A Premonition to All Christian Monarches," in *Political Works of James I,*
p. 155. This passage is reproduced in *Whore of Babylon's Pockey Priest,* sig. D.
110. On Catholics' unknowable hearts and minds, see Lowell Gallagher, *Medusa's Gaze:
Casuistry and Conscience in the Renaissance* (Stanford: Stanford University Press, 1991),
pp. 63–93; Halley, "Equivocation and the Legal Conflict"; Elizabeth Hanson, "Torture and

Whereas some critics have claimed that prayer closets in Protestant households were segregated by gender into "his" and "hers," in the secret spaces of the Catholic house, men and women were together, "very domestically and privily conversant," up to no good.[111] Priests administered sacraments to women; women delivered food to priests in their hiding places and secreted them in their own beds. Viewed with suspicion from without, the Catholic household was a space of gender inversion, gender integration, and gender leveling; the attempts to penetrate and regulate it only exacerbated that gender disorder and extended its reach. Catholic privacy may have been violated, as well as constituted, by being so obsessively fantasized and represented; it was also made central to a Protestant imaginary, an imaginary that routinely eschewed modesty to search the bed.

On the discursive landscapes of early modern England, as we survey them through the lenses of gender and sexuality, we have tended to see, on the one hand, marriage, as the dominant institutionalization of male-female relations, and adultery or fornication, the transgressive margins of heterosexuality; and, on the other hand, an increasingly diverse range of homosocial and homoerotic possibilities in friendships, military service, master-servant relationships, court circles, monasteries, and convents.[112] Obviously, these two spheres were not distinct, and many, even most people would have crossed between the two, or have experienced them as overlapping. What I want to stress here is that, just as there was a wide range of same-sex attachments and relations for which "sodomy" cannot account, to which Mario DiGangi refers as "nonsodomitical or nonsubversive homoerotic relations," so there was a whole range of relations between the sexes for which marriage and heterosex cannot account.[113] In early modern England, fantasies of and attacks on Catholic belief and practice often dwelt on these relationships: whether between male confessors and female penitents or fugitive priests and their female protectors; between mothers and sons or sisters and brothers; between friends and correspondents.

Truth in Renaissance England," *Representations* 34 (1991): 53–84; and Katharine Eisaman Maus, *Inwardness and Theater in the English Renaissance* (Chicago: University of Chicago Press, 1995), chaps. 1 and 4.

111. On the gendering of closets, see Stewart, *Close Readers*, chap. 5; and Richard Rambuss, *Closet Devotions* (Durham, N.C.: Duke University Press, 1998). Lena Cowen Orlin challenges the idea in "Gertrude's Closet," *Shakespeare Jahrbuch* 134 (1998): 44–67.

112. See Gregory W. Bredbeck, *Sodomy and Interpretation: Marlowe to Milton* (Ithaca: Cornell University Press, 1991); DiGangi, *Homoerotics of Early Modern Drama*; Jonathan Goldberg, *Sodometries: Renaissance Texts, Modern Sexualities* (Stanford: Stanford University Press, 1992), and *Queering the Renaissance*; Smith, *Homosexual Desire in Shakespeare's England*; and Valerie Traub, "The (In)significance of 'Lesbian' Desire in Early Modern England," in *Erotic Politics: Desire on the Renaissance Stage*, ed. Susan Zimmerman (New York: Routledge, 1992), pp. 150–69.

113. DiGangi, *Homoerotics of Early Modern Drama*, p. 9.

Fear of Catholicism seems to have mobilized anxieties about how men and women organize their relationships, anxieties that take subtler forms than shaming rituals, jokes, and ballads might suggest. We have more to learn about same-sex relationships in the early modern period; in addition, this important work in progress opens up more interesting and supple approaches to constructions of heterosocial relations and identities. What forms did the privy conversations between men and women take? Where and when were they possible? That popular couple—Protestantism and marriage—has too long dominated our understanding of the contested histories of relationships between men and women.

I turn next to precisely how, in the 1630s and '40s, critics of Catholicism and of Stuart monarchy drew on anxieties about men's attachment to and dependence on women to associate and attack Catholic theology, Charles's marriage and court, and Catholic households in England.

CHAPTER THREE

The Command of Mary:
Marian Devotion, Henrietta Maria's
Intercessions, and Catholic Motherhood

James I's relationship with Catholicism, like that of his next two successors, was as unstable as the status and prospects of Catholics themselves. The lingering suspicion that James was "soft" on Catholicism reached a crisis in the final years of his reign (in the early 1620s). In support of diplomatic relations with Spain and in pursuit of a marriage between his son, Charles, and the Spanish infanta, James advised judges to suspend prosecutions and to release recusant prisoners. On the possibility that Charles would turn Catholic if he married the infanta, conversions became fashionable at court.[1] Most scandalously, both the mother and the wife of James's favorite, George Villiers, Duke of Buckingham, converted to Catholicism in 1622.[2]

If Catholicism was gaining ground, as some contemporaries feared, it was doing so, in part, through women: the new bride anticipated for the future king; the conversions of influential court ladies. Although much recent scholarship has focused on what Jonathan Goldberg has described as

---

1. Michael C. Questier, "John Gee, Archbishop Abbot, and the Use of Converts from Rome in Jacobean Anti-Catholicism," *Recusant History* 21.3 (1993): 347–60, esp. 349, 348; Alexandra Walsham, "'The Fatall Vesper': Providentialism and Anti-Popery in Late Jacobean London," *Past & Present* 144 (August 1994): 36–87, esp. 43–44.

2. Timothy H. Wadkins, "The Percy-'Fisher' Controversies and the Ecclesiastical Politics of Jacobean Anti-Catholicism, 1622–1625," *Church History* 57 (1988): 153–69, discusses the debates organized to persuade the countess to reconvert; see also David Underdown, *A Freeborn People: Politics and the Nation in Seventeenth-Century England* (Oxford: Clarendon, 1996), pp. 33–35.

the "open secret" of James's erotic and emotional attachments to his male favorites, contemporaries often criticized the distributions of power and intimacy in the courts of Stuart kings for empowering wives or mothers rather than male lovers. Thus women's power in the traditional roles of wives and mothers was also an "open secret." Certainly a great deal of hostility was directed at Buckingham and his influence over James, and later over Charles; the hostility was so great that Buckingham was assassinated in 1628. But contemporaries rarely accused James of sexual impropriety with his male favorites (at least in print). Instead, they argued that the problem was maternal influence, despite the fact that James so carefully distanced himself from his mother, as well as from his wife (both Catholic).[3] Even texts that retrospectively censure James's dependence on Buckingham point over Buckingham's shoulder to his Catholic mother. In *The Popish Royall Favourite* (1643), William Prynne explained that James was influenced by "the first *Grand Favourite,*" the Duke of Buckingham, who was, in turn, "swayed wholly by his Jesuited Mother, and Dutchesse, professed Papists, and their Cabinet counsell of Jesuits."[4] Another text, *The English Pope,* similarly warned that three kingdoms were under the subjection of one prince, "who is under the subjection of one lustfull, rash, young Favourite, and that Favourite solely at the devotion of his vitious, opprobrious, mischievous mother, and that mother a meere Votaresse to Rome, utterly forfeited, resigned, and sold to the commands of Jesuites."[5] In these texts, censure rapidly moves beyond the male favorite to the Jesuited mother and her Jesuit counselors. When, like the salacious pursuivants who must overcome modesty to search women's beds for the priests hiding there, anti-Catholic polemicists pry into the "open secret" of James's Privy Chamber, they find not a scandalous sodomy but an equally scandalous heterosociality: the dominating wife and mother and the Jesuits with whom they consort.

3. Jonathan Goldberg, *Sodometries: Renaissance Texts, Modern Sexualities* (Stanford: Stanford University Press, 1992), p. 70. On Anne's conversion to Catholicism, see Albert J. Loomie, "King James I's Catholic Consort," *Huntington Library Quarterly* 34.4 (1971): 303–16; and Ethel Carleton Williams, *Anne of Denmark: Wife of James VI of Scotland, James I of England* (Harlow: Longmans, 1970), pp. 109–13. For James's attempts to downplay his mother's "superstition" and to insist that he himself was no "Apostate," see James I, "A Premonition to All Christian Monarches," in *The Political Works of James I,* ed. Charles Howard McIlwain (Cambridge: Harvard University Press, 1918), p. 122.

4. William Prynne, *The Popish Royall Favourite* (London, 1643), sig. G4v.

5. *The English Pope; or, A Discourse Wherein the Late Mysticall Intelligence betwixt the Court of England, and the Court of Rome Is in Part Discovered* (London, 1643), sig. B4. See also *Vindiciae Caroli Regis; or, A Loyall Vindication of the King, in Answer to the Popish Royall Favourite* (London, 1645), which denounces the claim that James was "wholly swayed by [Buckingham's] Jesuited Mother and Dutches" (sig. H).

The shocking discovery of women's domestic influence is an even more extreme version of the fear of female power that surfaces so often in anti-Catholic discourses. Here the accusation is not that Catholic men seduce and dally with women, or even conspire with and depend on them. The accusation is that Catholic men worship women as goddesses and submit themselves to women's advice or rule. These are fantasies not of the seducing priest who invades the home and family, preying on its most vulnerable members, or of women who stray outside the home into adultery, but of women's empowerment within the household as wives and mothers, and of women as the conduits of priestly influence. Although these fantasies take the familiar shape of inversion, they reveal that coverture, a husband who shelters and absorbs his wife, and its inverse, the woman who subsumes a man, cannot account for the complex relationships between men and women or the perceived threat of Catholicism.

Like attacks on Buckingham and his mother, many attacks on Charles I and his wife, Henrietta Maria, discover and lament the scandal of heterosexuality. In the controversies regarding the proposed Spanish marriage and the fashionable court conversions, anxiety focused on the power of a Catholic queen consort to transform the religious identity of king and country. Although these fears were briefly assuaged when the Spanish marriage fell through, they found a new form only a few years later, when another foreign alliance was transacted: Charles's "French marriage" to Henrietta Maria in 1625. In the escalating attacks on Charles and his rule, the bed that is obsessively imagined and discursively searched is the marriage bed; the scandal discovered therein is his wife.

That Henrietta Maria provoked suspicion and criticism is hardly surprising. She may not have been the much maligned Spanish infanta, but she was, as Caroline Hibbard points out, "the first foreign royal consort to arrive in England since Philip II—an entirely unfortunate precedent."[6] Simply by being the daughter of one French king and the sister of another, Henrietta Maria was suspect. The "articles" outlining the conditions of the marriage, versions of which were published in 1625, at the time of the marriage, then again in 1642 (with quite different aims and consequences, no doubt), fueled suspicions. These articles guaranteed Henrietta Maria free exercise of her religion, a chapel, a large clerical staff, and her own French Catholic household servants (most of whom Charles banished before the

---

6. Caroline Hibbard, "The Role of a Queen Consort: The Household and Court of Henrietta Maria, 1625–1642," in *Princes, Patronage, and the Nobility: The Court at the Beginning of the Modern Age, c. 1450–1650*, ed. Ronald G. Asch and Adolf M. Birke (London: Oxford University Press, 1991), p. 403.

couple had cohabited for a year, but who were long remembered). Henrietta Maria was also to control her children's education and religious allegiance until they were thirteen.

Many English people viewed the articles as shockingly one-sided. Article 9, for instance, promised that "his said Majestie of great Brittaine is by oath not to endeavour by any meanes at all to have his said Lady and Queene, to forsake or renounce her said Catholique Apostollicall, and Romane Religion: Nor compell her to doe any thing that is contrary to the same."[7] As William Prynne later summarized, she "is left free, by all meanes and arts that may be, to withdraw the King from the Protestant Religion to her owne, and his children too: Wee have great cause to feare (if *Adams, Solomons,* or *Ahabs* seducements by their wives be duly pondered)" that the king will be seduced into his wife's religion. This suspicion was so widespread that even in the 1640s Charles routinely denied that his wife had ever tried to convert him.[8] The official marriage articles, which Charles honored only irregularly, remained a focus of controversy nonetheless. They were supplemented by an even more incriminating secret treaty to which both James, who died before the marriage was celebrated by proxy, and Charles subscribed. This "secret" treaty, about which there was speculation from the start, promised toleration for English Catholics; in the course of his reign, Charles delivered this toleration erratically and usually unofficially as his political interests dictated.

Distrust of Henrietta Maria as a Catholic agent went hand in hand with distaste for her perceived willfulness. As she acknowledged herself, she was viewed as "the popish brat" who always got her own way.[9] Several notorious incidents early in her marriage contributed to this English construction of the queen, who was only fifteen when she arrived in England. Henrietta Maria refused to attend, let alone participate in, Charles's coronation, since

7. *A True Relation of the Treaty and Ratification of the Marriage Concluded and Agreed Upon betweene Our Soveraigne Lord Charles . . . and the Lady Henrietta Maria* (London, 1642), p. 5. See also *A True Discourse of All the Royal Passages, Tryumphs and Ceremonies, Observed at the Contract and Mariage of the High and Mighty* CHARLES, *King of Great Britaine, and . . . the Lady* HENRIETTA MARIA *of Burbon* (London, 1625); and *A Relation of the Glorious Triumphs and Order of the Ceremonies, Observed in the Marriage of the High and Mighty Charles, King of Great Brittaine, and the Ladie Henrietta Maria* (London, 1625).

8. Prynne, *Popish Royall Favourite,* sig. H2. Charles repeatedly swore that he was not a Catholic and "neither did my Queen ever to my knowledge so much as perswade me once to alter my Religion" (*The Queens Letter from Holland: Directed to the Kings Most Excellent Majesty* [London, 1642], p. 6). See also Dagmar Freist, "The King's Crown Is the Whore of Babylon: Politics, Gender, and Communication in Mid-Seventeenth-Century England," *Gender & History* 7.3 (1995): 457–81, esp. 466; and Caroline Hibbard, *Charles I and the Popish Plot* (Chapel Hill: University of North Carolina Press, 1983), pp. 39–42, 51–60, 230.

9. Carola Oman, *Henrietta Maria* (London: Hodder & Stoughton, 1936), p. 138.

it was a Church of England ceremony and she did not want to receive her crown from a heretic or to attend a heretical service. As a result, she was an uncrowned consort, the first in English history. She maintained two chapels in London, at which not only her own circle but other Londoners could openly attend mass. So many people attended that the chapels, at St. James's and Somerset House, could not accommodate the crowds; in 1636 the queen's new, very elaborate chapel on the grounds of Somerset House was opened to the public. Inigo Jones designed this new chapel, as he had the one at St. James's.[10] Although purposefully unremarkable from the outside, these internally splendid chapels and the "great resort" to them became a focus for Parliament's hostility toward the queen and extravagant, unapologetic court Catholicism.[11] Because of these chapels and those of foreign ambassadors, Catholicism was more visible and international in London than it was anywhere else in England.

Henrietta Maria also notoriously engaged in theatrical performances, taking speaking parts, perhaps even dressed as a man, and presenting works she had written and directed.[12] Her performances reinforced associations among women, theatricality, the foreign, and the Catholic.[13] Furthermore, Henrietta Maria's entertainments were indistinguishable from her devotions, both because of a long tradition of attacking Catholicism for its the-

10. Cyprien of Gamache, "Memoirs of the Mission in England of the Capuchin Fathers (1630–1669)," in *The Court and Times of Charles the First*, ed. Thomas Birch, 2 vols. (London: Henry Colburn, 1848), 2: 306–16; John Harris, Stephen Orgel, and Roy Strong, *The King's Arcadia: Inigo Jones and the Stuart Court* (London: Lund Humphries, 1973), pp. 123–24, 138, 148–49, 152–54; Martin Havran, *The Catholics in Caroline England* (Stanford: Stanford University Press, 1962), p. 59; Hibbard, *Charles I and the Popish Plot*, pp. 56–58; and Bryan Little, *Catholic Churches since 1623: A Study of Roman Catholic Churches in England and Wales from Penal Times to the Present Decade* (London: Robert Hale, 1966), pp. 21–23.

11. "A Message sent from the Queenes Majesty to the House of Commons," in *A Coppy of 1. the Letter* (London, 1641), pp. 11–12. On how fashionable attendance at these chapels became and how the new Somerset House chapel boosted conversions, see Gordon Albion, *Charles I and the Court of Rome: A Study in Seventeenth-Century Diplomacy* (London: Burnes Oates & Washbourne, 1935), pp. 104, 196–97, and chap. 8, "Converts at Court," passim; and Robin Clifton, "Fear of Popery," in *The Origins of the English Civil War*, ed. Conrad Russell (London: Macmillan, 1973), pp. 144–167, esp. 152–53. According to Hibbard and Smuts, Henrietta Maria's Catholicism became more public and controversial after 1637 (Hibbard, "Role of a Queen Consort," p. 412; R. M. Smuts, "The Puritan Followers of Henrietta Maria in the 1630s," *English Historical Review* 93.366 [January 1978]: 26–45, esp. 43, 26).

12. On Henrietta Maria's performances, see Alfred Harbage, *Cavalier Drama* (New York: MLA, 1936), pp. 10–21, esp. 12; and Sophie Tomlinson, "She That Plays the King': Henrietta Maria and the Threat of the Actress in Caroline Culture," in *The Politics of Tragicomedy: Shakespeare and After*, ed. Gordon McMullan and Jonathan Hope (London and New York: Routledge, 1992), pp. 189–207.

13. Stephen Orgel, *Impersonations: The Performance of Gender in Shakespeare's England* (Cambridge: Cambridge University Press, 1996), p. 11.

atricality and because of practices that did indeed blur the distinction between liturgy and performance. Court Catholicism, like Stuart sovereignty,
self-consciously employed theatricality to attract attention, impose reverence, and win converts. At Somerset House, theatricality went as far as a
literal deus ex machina, a contraption for elevating and illuminating the
Eucharist.[14] Furthermore, Henrietta Maria acted out her Catholicism in
offensively public ways: refusing to attend the coronation, chatting and
giggling with her ladies through a Westminster Abbey service, or, perhaps
most scandalously, enacting her notorious if apocryphal "penances."

The most infamous of what contemporaries censured as her "unhand-
some and unbecoming," "ridiculous and absurd" penances involved an alleged pilgrimage to Tyburn.[15] Did the queen and some of her followers,
while strolling through the parks around St. James's Palace, just happen to
stop at the Tyburn gallows to say a spontaneous prayer for the Catholics
who had died there? Or did the queen set out at the head of a public procession with that demonstration in mind (which she denied)? Various
sources elaborated even on this second, far more incriminating scenario:
the queen walked barefoot while her confessor rode in a carriage, and then,
at the gallows, she dropped to her knees with a rosary in her hands.[16] Kneeling before the gallows, at least in the escalating accounts of this incident,
the queen licensed treason, conferring the status of martyr on those the
state had condemned as traitors. Such a public performance seemed to
announce that she would act as a spokesperson for English Catholics, con-
veying disturbing Catholic revisions of English law, custom, and history to
the king. Just as her chapels offered English Catholics a community center
as well as a locus for worship, her intercessions could give them a visibility
and influence they had not yet had. If this prospect seemed threatening in
1626, early in the marriage when relations between husband and wife

14. Erica Veevers similarly argues that "Henrietta herself made no great distinction between entertainments and 'devotions'" (*Images of Love and Religion: Queen Henrietta Maria
and Court Entertainments* [Cambridge: Cambridge University Press, 1989], p. 2). On the theatrical machinery at the Somerset House chapel, see Cyprien of Gamache, "Memoirs,"
pp. 311–12.

15. John Dauncey, *The History of the Thrice Illustrious Princess Henrietta Maria de Bourbon,
Queen of England* (London, 1660), sig. C9r–v; John Pory to Rev. Joseph Mead, July 1, 1626,
in Birch, *Court and Times of Charles the First*, 1: 119–23, esp. 121. Pory's account is often used
as a source for the most incriminating version of the story in circulation.

16. Even Royalist Restoration biographers describe the queen as progressing barefoot to
Tyburn "to pray for those of her own Religion that had been executed there for Treason":
John Verney, *The Life and Death of That Matchless Mirrour of Magnanimity* (London, 1669),
p. 16. Published in celebration of James II's coronation, Verney's biography reprints much
of Dauncey's earlier one. Contrast Havran's description of the "harmless and quite acci-
dental visit to Tyburn" (*Catholics in Caroline England*, pp. 43–44).

were still strained, it would become even more disturbing once Buckingham was dead, the queen's closest French servants had been banished, and the royal spouses, bereft of their confidants, moved into greater intimacy.

Representations of Henrietta Maria responded as much to a history of anti-Catholicism, and to its rhetorical conventions, as they did to anything the queen herself purportedly did. She was compromised even by her name. According to Lucy Hutchinson, "some kind of fatality, too, the English imagined to be in her name of Marie."[17] Post-Reformation suspicion of Mariolatry conjoined with a historical association of the name Mary with Catholic female rule. The "monstrous regiment of women" that John Knox maligned was exemplified for him in the reigns of Mary Tudor and Mary Stuart, whom he called "our mischevous Maryes."[18] A return to Catholicism would be a return to "Marian times": "*Maries* times are English staines, and who gave the dye, but that Romish red Dragon, bloudy beast, and whore of *Babylon?*" wrote William Leigh in 1606; "The Lord in mercie deliver his Church from such *Marian* times," prayed Andrew Willet in 1602.[19] From this perspective, all of the commanding "Maryes" run together: queens of heaven and earth, of Scotland and England, of the past and the present, queens regnant and queens consort.

During Henrietta Maria's years as the queen consort, debates over Marian devotion are not neatly separable from debates about the queen's influence over her husband and sons. In the 1630s, attacks on Marian devotion intertwined with and enabled attacks on Henrietta Maria, as Erica Veevers and Danielle Clark have also noted.[20] However, the "command of Mary" was not described only by its detractors, who used it to evoke vividly the horrifying prospect of an England and a church in which Catholics regained ascendancy, and consequently women dominated. Catholic writers defended "the command of Mary" in their ritual lives, in history and in the court, in their own households. Whereas anti-Catholic polemic linked and

17. Lucy Hutchinson, *Memoirs of the Life of Colonel Hutchinson* (London: George Bell, 1905), p. 89.

18. John Knox, *The First Blast of the Trumpet against the Monstruous Regiment of Women* (Geneva, 1558), sig. Fv.

19. William Leigh, *Great Britaines Great Deliverance, from the Great Danger of Popish Powder* (London, 1606), sig. B3; Andrew Willet, *A Catholicon, That Is, a Generall Preservative or Remedie against the Pseudocatholike Religion* (Cambridge, 1602), sig. A3.

20. Veevers, *Images of Love and Religion;* and Danielle Clark, "The Iconography of the Blush: Marian Literature of the 1630s," in *Voicing Women: Gender and Sexuality in Early Modern Writing*, ed. Kate Chedgzoy, Melanie Hansen, and Suzanne Trill (Pittsburgh: Duquesne University Press, 1997), pp. 111–28. In contrast to Clark and Veevers, I focus on Mary and Henrietta Maria as mothers as well as objects of romantic desire, and consider this connection in the context of larger debates over Catholicism and female authority and across a longer span of years and a wider variety of locations than the court.

deplored the "monstrous regiment" of queens named Mary, devotion to the Virgin Mary, and "the Whore of Babylon," Catholic apologists viewed a genealogy of female rule with satisfaction. For them, the prospect of women intervening on their behalf was encouraging rather than terrifying. When Catholic writers responded to attacks on their queens of heaven and of England, they justified and celebrated women's authority and influence. Their texts thus challenge the assumption that Catholicism is inevitably associated with repressive attitudes toward women, and that Catholicism in seventeenth-century England was conservative and backward. They also complicate the map of attitudes toward women and gender in early modern English discourses. Yet until recently Catholic texts have been largely forgotten, just as the sites on which Catholic women's command and community centered in England, such as Henrietta Maria's Somerset House chapel, have been razed. In this chapter I excavate the evidence that, in the years when Henrietta Maria was queen consort, some Catholics were able to advocate, perhaps even experience, women's command and women's community, however briefly. In ignoring their writings, we have oversimplified the conceptual and discursive options for representing wives and mothers in the period.

MARIAN DEVOTION

In his history of "popery and politics" in seventeenth-century England, John Miller asserts that there was "something distinctively English about English Catholicism. It escaped the baroque extravagances of continental spirituality, especially those that grew around the cult of the Virgin Mary."[21] On the Continent, these "baroque extravagances" might have included professing oneself Mary's "captive and Bond-slave," and, in token thereof, wearing "a little Chayne of iron, brasse, or other metall" around the waist, neck, or arm, "as the badge of a Slave." The risks of so openly practicing one's Catholicism foreclosed such ostentatious subservience in England, although the text describing this cult, *The Devotion of Bondage*, was translated into English.[22] Unlike Miller, however, many seventeenth-century English writers, Protestant and Catholic, male and female, could not so comfortably dismiss Marian devotion, especially men's abasement before their dominatrix, as a "continental" extravagance. Instead, they defended or at-

21. John Miller, *Popery and Politics in England, 1660–1668* (Cambridge: Cambridge University Press, 1973), p. 19.
22. Martin Couvreur, *The Devotion of Bondage*, trans. John Wilson (St. Omer, 1634), sigs. A6v, B5v.

tacked Mariolatry as a central practice in English Catholicism, as a para-
digmatic example of where Catholics invested power and directed adoration, and as a telling analogy to the distribution of power in the Caroline
court and in recusant households. In devotion to the Virgin Mary, Protestants saw a radical and blasphemous reorientation: Catholics, explains
Richard Sheldon, "yeeld unto her attributes befitting a Goddesse, to redeeme, to save, to protect, to defend, to rule, to command all earthly crea-
tures."[23] In their "Lady's Psalter," objects William Crashaw in a widely repeated formulation, they "turne the Psalmes from *Dominus* to *Domina*, from
God to our Ladie."[24]

Although even the earliest reformers condemned Marian devotion, in
England attacks on and defenses of it (with roughly equal numbers of texts
on the two sides) seem to have proliferated first in the years of James's
reign, just after the Gunpowder Plot, when he enacted new penal laws and
when seventeenth-century prosecutions seem to have peaked, and then in
the 1620s and '30s, the years when the Spanish marriage was debated, the
French marriage was transacted, and Henrietta Maria became a fertile,
influential queen and a focal point for English Catholics and their opponents. Devotional treatises in English followed this same trajectory—they
were Jacobean and Caroline rather than Elizabethan, building to a peak in
the 1630s. Debate over Mariolatry proliferated again during James II's
brief reign in the 1680s, when hopes for a Catholic succession focused on
the fecundity of his wife, Mary.

The Madonna who stands at the center of these debates, while powerful
and controversial, does not stand alone. Her relationships, to God the father and especially to Jesus, are at issue. As described by attackers and defenders alike, she cradles an infant Jesus in her arms, and she stands between believers and their God. The redemptive couple, Mary and Jesus,
counter the lapsarian couple, Adam and Eve; mother and son restored

23. Richard Sheldon, *A Survey of the Miracles of the Church of Rome* (London, 1616),
sig. X2.
24. William Crashaw, *The Sermon Preached at the Crosse, Feb. xiiii, 1607* (London, 1608),
sig. H4v; compare *The Jesuites Gospell. Written by Themselves. Discovered and Published by
W. Crashaw* (London, 1621), sig. O3. This William Crashaw was the father of the poet Richard Crashaw, a convert to Catholicism famous for his adoration of the Virgin in religious
poetry such as "Blessed Be the Paps." In the 1640s, Henrietta Maria helped the younger
Crashaw find a place in the entourage of Cardinal Palotta of Rome. See also James I, "Premonition to All Christian Monarches," p. 137. For a "Ladies Psalter," see Bonaventure, *The
Psalter of the B. Virgin Mary,* translated from the French by R. F. (n.p., 1624); on *The Primer,
or Office of the Blessed Virgin* in English and Latin (with English rubrics), see A. F. Allison and
D. M. Rogers, *Contemporary Printed Literature of the English Counter-Reformation between 1558
and 1640,* vol. 2 (Brookfield, Vt.: Gower, 1994), items 688–94. For a celebration of Mary's
status as "*Domina,* Lady, or Mistresse," see John Sweetnam, *The Paradise of Delights; or, The B.
Virgins Garden of Loreto* (Douai, 1620), sigs. A5–6v.

what husband and wife lost. While no one on either side questions the role of Eve in the fall, conflict centers on how important Mary was to the redemption. The Protestant Andrew Willet, for instance, asks: "Was shee crucified for us? did she create, or redeeme us? or are we baptized into her name?" Willet is certain of the answer—no. "Wherefore shee is not to be praied unto, or trusted in, or praise and glorie to be yeelded to her."[25] Mary should be humble, William Fleetwood insists, "but *Papism* has made Her a very pattern of Pride and Ambition, always aiming at Divine Honours; angry with all that pay them not, severely Punishing those that offend Her, and Recompensing amply all that are peculiarly devoted to Her, and working Miracles perpetually, for nothing but to acquire Adoration, and Honour to Her self."[26]

From this Protestant perspective, Catholic constructions of Mary inappropriately elevate her by putting "a *Sceptre* into the hands of this *Handmaid of the Lord,* as she calls her self."[27] By inviting Mary into the limelight of devotion, Catholics encourage her to elbow aside or upstage both the Father and the Son, becoming a kind of "pope *Mary,*" as the Catholic apologist John Floyd jokingly sums up the Protestant case.[28]

Catholic apologists for Marian devotion do indeed confer power and preeminence on Mary, but they insist that she deserves it. While Protestant writers tend to assume that women should be humble handmaidens, and that a woman elevated to the Virgin Mary's position in Catholic worship is of necessity proud, ambitious, vengeful, and bossy, Catholic writers are less resistant to the very idea of female power. "Great is the force undoubtedly of the mother of God; who not only was and is able to combate with the devil, but to crush him, & domineere over him, as over a poor worme," writes Robert Chambers.[29] Chambers also interprets Mary's response to the Annunciation, "Fiat," or "Let it be," not as submission but as an assertion of agency equal to God's creation of the world: "By his *Fiat,* he made the world and man, by her Fiat, God entred into the world, and became man."[30]

25. Willet, *Catholicon,* sig. N8v. Willet here applies to Mary the questions Paul asked of himself (1 Cor. 1:13), downplaying his own significance.
26. William Fleetwood, *An Account of the Life and Death of the Blessed Virgin, According to Romish Writers* (London, 1687), sig. D2v.
27. [John Patrick], *The Virgin Mary Misrepresented by the Roman Church* (London, 1688), sig. Bv. In Adam Widenfeldt's *Wholsome Advices from the Blessed Virgin to Her Indiscreet Worshippers* (London, 1687), Mary pleads with her followers: "These excessive praises displease me, and I am griev'd with these your foolish Flatteries" (sig. C4v).
28. John Floyd, *Purgatories Triumph over Hell, Maugre the Barking of Cerberus in Syr Edward Hobyes Counter-Snarle* (St. Omer, 1613), sig. X3v.
29. Robert Chambers, "Epistle Dedicatorie" to Philippe Numan, *Miracles Lately Wrought by the Intercession of the Glorious Virgin Marie, at Mont-aigu,* trans. Chambers (Antwerp, 1606), sig. C4.
30. Ibid., sig. C4v.

These debates over Mary's merits, like the medieval and early Reformation discussions that anticipated them and have received more attention, had mixed results for women. Members of Mary's cult amplified her power and exalted her status, but they did so by distinguishing her from other women. With the author of *The Widdowes Mite*, a devotional treatise, they insisted that she did not deliver Jesus "after the same laborious, vulgar, and uncomly manner to which other women are subject by their descendence from Eve."[31] Indeed, many joined Thomas Price in condemning any assertion "that Mary the Mother of Christ is no better than other women."[32] Protestant writers seeking to deflate her status insisted that while she may have been "advanced . . . above all other women," as Andrew Willet conceded, she remained a woman like other women in most respects.[33] They repeatedly pointed to the paucity of scriptural references to Mary, and particularly to the lack of any scriptural foundation for Mary's "immaculate conception" (which would have distinguished her as the only human conceived after the fall without original sin) or for her "assumption" (which would have distinguished her as the only human assumed directly into heaven, without undergoing corporeal decay or a separation of soul from body, perhaps without undergoing bodily death).[34] Both sides in the debate, then, viewed Mary's resemblance to other women as a disparagement, a "foule comparison," as John Floyd said, which served Protestant but not Catholic purposes.[35]

Mary therefore offered an unattainable ideal to other women. As Marina Warner, for instance, asserts, "every facet of the Virgin had been systematically developed to diminish, not increase, her likeness to the female condition. Her freedom from sex, painful delivery, age, death, and all sin exalted her *ipso facto* above ordinary women and showed them up as inferior."[36]

31. A. G., *The Widdowes Mite. Cast into the Treasure-house of the Prerogatives, and Prayses of our B. Lady*, including a prayer attributed to Sir Tobie Matthew (St. Omer, 1619), sig. Fv.

32. Thomas Price in his translator's preface to Orazio Torsellino, *The History of Our B. Lady of Loreto* (St. Omer, 1608), sig. **4. A. G. complains that Protestants are "so wisely zealous of the Sonnes honour, as that they cannot forbeare to be carping at his Mother upon all occasions . . . as if our Lady were no better then one of us" (*Widdowes Mite*, sig. E7).

33. Andrew Willet, *Synopsis Papismi, That Is, a Generall View of Papistrie* (London, 1614), sig. Zz3v.

34. Elizabeth's "immaculate conception" of Mary, which should be distinguished from Mary's "virgin birth" of Jesus, did not become dogma until 1854; the assumption did not become dogma until 1950.

35. John Floyd, *Overthrow of the Protestants Pulpit-Babels* (St. Omer, 1612), sig. D2v.

36. Marina Warner, *Alone of All Her Sex: The Myth and the Cult of the Virgin Mary* (New York: Knopf, 1976), p. 153. On the persistence of contests over Mariolatry, see Jaroslav Pelikan, *Mary through the Centuries: Her Place in the History of Culture* (New Haven: Yale University Press, 1996). Some women converts from or critics of Catholicism attacked Marian devotion; see Anne Gargill, *A Brief Discovery of That Which Is Called the Popish Religion* (London,

With their emphasis on breast milk, virginity, original sin, and bodily decay, debates over Mary drew on and fueled a visceral, corporeal misogyny
that recoiled from yet was fascinated by porous, leaking female bodies.
Dévots, however, might find in the Virgin Mary a model of a life lived outside of biological determinism and male domination, although still within
the roles of wife and mother.³⁷ Mothers might find in the Virgin a model
of their own importance and influence, if not of their bodily experience of
intercourse, pregnancy, and labor; they might also turn to her for succor
in childbed.³⁸

Whether or not Mary was viewed as a remarkable exception, the sustained
and passionate public debate over her status in seventeenth-century England did not take place in a vacuum, remote from other contests over
women's authority and agency or from historical women. Because many
writers weighed in both pro and con, and over many decades, this debate
offered one popular discursive site for a more general discussion of female
authority and influence. The stature of Mary in Catholic belief and practice, proof of the excessive power Catholics were willing to invest in women,
served as a starting point for attacks on actual Catholic women, such as
Henrietta Maria; it also informed Protestant, mainstream assumptions
about and responses to Catholic women, especially mothers.

The fear of, fascination with, and hostility toward maternal power in
early modern English culture motivated attempts to understand and control, even repudiate it in medical treatises about reproduction, prescriptive writings on breast-feeding and other maternal conduct, legal constructions of infanticide, and witchcraft discourses and prosecutions. These
discursive contests never corresponded neatly with women's actual experience of maternity or their lived opportunities to exercise maternal authority. Nor were the constructions of maternal power consistent, even at
a given site. Instead, across a strikingly wide range of locations and genres,

---

1656), sigs. B3v, C3v; and Helen Livingston, *The Confession and Conversion of the Right Honorable, Most Illustrious and Elect Lady, My Lady C. of L.* (Edinburgh, 1629), pp. 7–8.

37. Ruth Vanita, *Sappho and the Virgin Mary: Same-Sex Love and the English Literary Imagination* (New York: Columbia University Press, 1996), esp. chap. 1.

38. On the positive values assigned to motherhood and to Mary in the medieval period,
see Caroline Walker Bynum, *Jesus as Mother: Studies in the Spirituality of the High Middle Ages*
(Berkeley: University of California Press, 1982), chap. 4; and Merry Wiesner, "Luther and
Women: The Death of Two Marys," in *Disciplines of Faith: Studies in Religion, Politics, and Patriarchy*, ed. Jim Obelkevich, Lyndal Roper, and Raphael Samuel (London and New York:
Routledge & Kegan Paul, 1987), pp. 295–308, esp. 303. Patricia Crawford observes "the
high esteem of maternity in Catholic popular culture" (*Women and Religion in England, 1500–
1720* [London and New York: Routledge, 1993], pp. 47, 61). Even some Protestant women
writers revere the Virgin Mary, as Elaine Beilin shows in *Redeeming Eve: Women Writers of the
English Renaissance* (Princeton: Princeton University Press, 1987), pp. 197–99, 278–79.

early modern English culture fiercely debated the extent and value of maternal authority. The varied perspectives available demonstrate that, as Mary Beth Rose has argued, in sixteenth- and seventeenth-century England, "motherhood was very slowly beginning to be construed as a problematic status, and . . . the perceived conflicts center on parental power and authority."[39] Discussions of the Virgin Mary's apparently exceptional status participated in this more widespread construction of maternal power as a problem.

Addressing three crucial and controversial stages in a mother's relationship with her child—pregnancy, lactation, and adulthood (the most troublesome)—attacks on and defenses of Mary suggest that the problems began in her blessedly fruitful womb. Certainly Mary's situation is extraordinary; during her miraculous pregnancy, conceived without sexual intercourse, she contained and nurtured within her body "him whome Heaven cannot containe." According to *The Widdowes Mite,* Mary is not only the woman clothed by the sun "but [she] didst also cloath the Sunne of Justice, whilest [her] immaculate flesh and bloud was imparted to the Sonne of [her] womb."[40] Three-dimensional images of Mary that opened to reveal an infant or a crucifix or the Trinity in their bellies reflect the frank Catholic acceptance of Mary's role as corporeal enclosure and Jesus' status as son "covert."[41] Yet Mary's pregnancy, however unusual, reveals that motherhood always embodies "coverture" at its most literal; the mother of a son, let alone the son of God, inverts the expected operations of coverture in particularly threatening ways. Whereas *The Lawes Resolutions of Womens Rights* describes a wife or *feme covert* as "veiled, as it were, clouded and overshadowed," *The Widdowes Mite* explains that during Mary's conception and gestation of her son, "the vertue or power of the most High was to environe, and overshaddow her, whereby she might be enabled to enclose, and as it were again to overshaddow the Sonne of God."[42] Thus, during pregnancy, Mary, like other mothers, "overshadows," covers, or subsumes her fetal son. The Holy Spirit must first "overshadow" her to empower her to do so, as a wife must submit to her husband before she gains her

---

39. Mary Beth Rose, "Where Are the Mothers in Shakespeare? Options for Gender Representation in the English Renaissance," *Shakespeare Quarterly* 42.3 (Fall 1991): 290–314, esp. 296. Motherhood continued to be viewed as a problem into the eighteenth century (Toni Bowers, *The Politics of Motherhood: British Writing and Culture, 1680–1760* [Cambridge: Cambridge University Press, 1996]).

40. A. G., *Widdowes Mite,* sigs. B8v, L3.

41. Michael Camille, *The Gothic Idol: Ideology and Image-Making in Medieval Art* (Cambridge: Cambridge University Press, 1989), p. 232.

42. T. E., *The Lawes Resolutions of Womens Rights* (London, 1632), sig. I7; A. G., *Widdowes Mite,* sig. B5.

status as wife and mother. Yet under the cover of these enabling, to a large
extent conceptual subsumptions, the mother then engages in a concrete
subsumption of the unborn son that reverses and undermines the gender
hierarchy on which marriage (and Christian theology) depend.

When Mary's attackers describe the errors of Marian devotion, they use
quite similar imagery, although they interpret it differently. From their
perspective, Mary also "overshadows" Jesus, but the result is an apocalyptic eclipse. As *The Widdowes Mite* presents this Protestant view, Mary "sinned
by exceeding her boundes, and by intruding her selfe so far, as that she
might chance to have obscured the glory of Christ thereby."[43] William
Crashaw suggests that *The Widdowes Mite* does not overstate the case when
he warns that "wee must take heede we so inlarge not the excellencie of
the Mother, that wee diminish the glorie of the sonne."[44] Here, as in so
many prescriptions for household order and marital harmony, mother
and son, like husband and wife or master and servant, compete for a finite
amount of power; as a consequence, to enlarge the mother is, of necessity,
to diminish the son. Descriptions of Mary as a vessel attempt to redress this
maternal empowerment and inverse coverture. If Mary encloses and overshadows Jesus, she does so only temporarily, serving rather than subordi-
nating him. When he exits her body, he leaves no residue of the divine. As
The Widdowes Mite complains, such arguments treat the Virgin as "a saffron
bagge" that is of no value once its precious contents are gone.[45] This argument counters a more disturbing possibility: that Mary is not a vessel but
a parthenogenetic mother who does not need a human inseminator. As
Anthony Stafford marvels in *The Femall Glory*, "it is a miracle that in the
forming of such, and so great an issue [Jesus] the aide of man should be
utterly excluded, and that as he was man, he was onely made of the pure
bloud of the Virgin."[46]

Such opposing interpretations of Mary's contribution to Jesus' incarnation—as "saffron bagge" or sole human creator—participate in discussions of whether Mary is a vessel or an efficient cause. The subtle distinctions between Catholic and Protestant positions on this issue reveal that
both sides operate within the same theological logic—which subordinates

43. A. G., *Widdowes Mite*, sig. Fv.
44. Crashaw, *Sermon Preached at the Crosse*, sig. H4v, quoting Bonaventure.
45. A. G., *Widdowes Mite*, sig. F; cf. Samuel Harsnett, *A Declaration of Egregious Popish Impostures* (London, 1603), sig. V2.
46. Anthony Stafford, *The Femall Glory* (London, 1635), p. 87. Because this was an Anglican text, it was highly controversial. See Maureen Sabine's introduction to her facsimile
edition of Stafford (Delmar, N.Y.: Scholars' Facsimiles ae Reprints, 1988); and Anthony
Milton, *Catholic and Reformed: The Roman and Protestant Churches in English Protestant Thought,
1600–1640* (Cambridge: Cambridge University Press, 1995), pp. 67–68.

human initiative to divine providence—and the same ideological logic—which particularly constrains women's capacity for effectively and positively intervening in history. Yet there is a crucial difference. In however qualified a way, Catholic writers attribute efficacy to Mary, while Protestant writers vehemently deny it. Protestant attacks on Mariolatry insist that Mary simply cannot contribute as well as submit to the processes of incarnation and redemption, because, as Willet declares, "Christ onelie was the efficient cause and meritorious worker of our redemption, the Virgin *Marie* was a chosen vessell and instrument only of his holy incarnation."[47] George Hickes concurs that Mary is "a chosen vessel, but nevertheless a woman, who hath not changed her nature."[48] Since she is like other women, a fallen creature, she does not deserve to be worshiped as a creator, an "efficient cause," a goddess.

Obviously, those Catholic writers who exalt Mary's power always emphasize that God confers it on her, that it is a reward to her for her service, and that she acts as God's agent. But they emphasize the operation of Mary's will and the extent of her powers rather than her humility. Answering the Protestant charge that Mary may be praised only "as an instrument . . . not . . . as an agent," Catholic defenders of Mary concede her instrumentality while yet attempting to infuse it with agency.[49] *The Widdowes Mite* explains that God "is the fountaine, she is the streame; he is the great Artificer and primary cause, and she a most elevated Instrument; he is the Sunne, and she the Beame, whereby he hath communicated his light, and heat to this darke & frozen world of ours."[50] The imagery here resembles explanations of the relationship between husband and wife, in which the husband is the *primus motor* and the wife the tributary who submerges herself in the larger river, thus losing her separate identity.[51] This passage also offers a variation on the sun and moon analogy so prevalent in prescriptions for marriage. Here Mary is not the moon, borrowing her light from the sun, but a part of the sun itself, its beam. By describing Mary as a beam and an "elevated Instrument," this text can confer some efficacy on her without positioning her as God's equal or rival.

Furthermore, Mary's defenders insist that she deserves credit for her role in Christ's incarnation because she freely consented to serve. According to *The Widdowes Mite*, "our B. Lady did whatsoever she did with perfect

---

47. Willet, *Synopsis Papismi*, sig. Zz5.
48. George Hickes, *Speculum Beatae Virginis: A Discourse of the Due Praise and Honour of the Virgin Mary* (London, 1686), sig. F.
49. Willet, *Synopsis Papismi*, sig. Zz5.
50. A. G., *Widdowes Mite*, sigs. G6r–v.
51. T. E., *Lawes Resolutions of Womens Rights*, sigs. O6v, I6v–I7.

liberty of will, though prevented [i.e., anticipated] and assisted by the rich grace of God, to the very last point whereof, she did most eminently co-operate as a most elevated, active, and lively instrument; and was not of no more use unto her selfe then a very stocke, or stone could be."[52] According to this Catholic view, although Mary may be represented by "a very stocke, or stone," she is an "active and lively instrument"—that is, both agent and instrument, cause and vessel—in the processes of incarnation and redemption. As a consequence, according to Catholic belief, the images of Mary may borrow some of this efficacy, channeling Mary's own power in order to work miracles in the contemporary world.

Descriptions of miracles enacted by images of Mary, such as those at Halle and Montaigu, seem to have inspired many of the most vitupera-tive denunciations of Mariolatry.[53] In accounts of these miracles, Mary's statuses as symbolic representation and effective agent conjoin disturb-ingly, for, in the miracle-working images, symbolic preeminence becomes agency. Images of Mary made of "stock or stone" reinforce her connection to materiality, the flesh, the mortal, the transient; for most Protestant writ-ers, these associations conjoin with feminine gender to disparage Mary, proving that she is a human creature of the earth, not a goddess or creator in heaven; that she is associated with the lowly flesh, not the transcendent spirit. But images that are simultaneously passive matter and miraculously endowed with agency confuse that neat hierarchy. Associated with the ma-terial world, these images may yet intervene in and change it. "Mari-onettes" seem to have derived their name from the "little Mary" or auto-mated figure of Mary in crèche scenes, suggesting how closely connected Mary was to animate images that disturbed the distinction between passiv-ity and action, body and spirit.[54]

Protestant attacks on Mary's miraculous images draw on a tradition, fully developed and widely deployed in early modern England, that denigrated women's agency by associating or conflating it with violence. One particu-larly virulent attack on Marian devotion, William Crashaw's *Jesuites Gospell*

---

52. A. G., *Widdowes Mite*, sig. C7.

53. One of the most discussed accounts of the Virgin Mary's miraculous powers is Justus Lipsius's *J. Lipsii Diva Virgo Hallensis* (1604). Lipsius's text was not translated into English until 1688, when it appeared as *Miracles of the B. Virgin; or, An Historical Account of the Origi-nal, and Stupendious Performances of the Image, Entituled Our Blessed Lady of Halle* (London, 1688). In a preface, the translator claims to offer the text as "an Antidote against their Er-rors, to expose some of these pretended Miracles to the view of the World" (sig. A2). Yet the text itself is offered without interruption or gloss. On Lipsius, see Questier, "John Gee, Archbishop Abbot," pp. 356–57.

54. Scott Cutler Shershow, *Puppets and "Popular" Culture* (Ithaca: Cornell University Press, 1995), pp. 40–42.

(published in 1610 and 1621, then in 1641 as *The Bespotted Jesuite*), insists that Catholics believe that "all the miracles must be wrought by her, and at her picture, as though either he [Jesus] could not, or in his mothers presence would not" work miracles himself. In response, John Floyd jested that Crashaw "might add with as great truth, that we say that he [Jesus] dare not, for shee being a *shrew*, would rappe him on the fingers, did he stretch out his hand to do any Myracle before her."[55] Floyd's joke—that Crashaw depicts the "commanding mother" Mary as a "shrew"—is an astute one. As in the vast range of depictions of shrews in medieval and early modern discourses, Crashaw's ridicule of Marian devotion assumes that women's exercise of power is invariably presumptuous, arbitrary, and laughable. There is something funny about a bossy woman, even when she is God's mother. As Floyd intuits, this comic tradition for exaggerating, censuring, and mocking women's exercise of authority also links their self-assertions to violence. The Virgin tenderly nursing her baby might "rappe him on the fingers" at any moment.

One of Crashaw's defenders, Sir Edward Hoby, shares this assumption that female authority erupts into violence. Hoby describes Heresy—that is, the Roman Church—as a woman who, discontent at her dwindling retinue and resources, "flieth abroad like a shrewish distracted malecontent, in her frantique mood, pulling, haling, spurning, scratching, and tearing al that stand in her way." No matter who her opponents are, "she will be sure they do not passe, without a broken head, or a black eye."[56] Catholic claims that Mary takes revenge on those who neglect her or desecrate her image played into Hoby's parodic portrait of a shrew-goddess. In Hoby's dialogue *A Curry-Combe for a Coxe-Combe*, one interlocutor, a minister, refers to Our Lady of Halle, a purportedly vengeful image, as "a hard-hearted Saint." Remarking on the claim that the Virgin Mary repaid iconoclasts with the same mutilations they inflicted on her, he scoffs: "I never heard before that a milde Ladie did cut off so manie Gentlemen's noses." If images are so vengeful (and powerful), he wonders, how did it come to pass "when Popish Idols were suppressed in *England*, that no man lost his nose, nor received any harme, though many such woodden Ladies then lost their heades?"[57] In Hoby's analysis, as in depictions of a shrew's vio-

55. Crashaw, *Jesuites Gospell*, sig. E4; Floyd, *Purgatories Triumph*, sig. X3.
56. Sir Edward Hoby, *A Counter-Snarle for Ishmael Rabshacheh, a Cecropidan Lycaonite* (London, 1613), sig. Bv.
57. Sir Edward Hoby, *A Curry-Combe for a Coxe-Combe; or, Purgatories Knell* (London, 1615), sigs. Ee2v, Gg3v. For the claim that those who neglect or dishonor the Virgin fall into "poverty, misery, and disreputation, and confusion" see A. G., *Widdowes Mite*, sig. K5v. On Mary as an inspiration for or patron of violence, consider the claim that one of the Gunpowder Plot conspirators, Thomas Percy, "pretended with a colour of devotion to kisse the

lence in ballads, jokes, and other popular discourses, the woman's violence reveals that she does not deserve power, and that she will abuse whatever power she usurps; her violence does little lasting damage to anything other than her own credibility and authority.

While women's violence was usually depicted in these terms, it might also be understood positively. Mothers, for instance, could legitimately administer punishment. In addition, children might appeal to their mothers, and the faithful, by analogy, might appeal to the Virgin Mary, for protection against paternal violence. "Having then a Mother in heaven so powerful as she," wrote Alexis de Salo, "let us have recourse to her, as children to . . . their Mothers when they fly their Fathers wrath."[58] Like the anxious jokes about the shrew who is also a mother, Salo's appeal offers a reminder of mothers' perceived power both to inflict harm and to defend against it.

Representations of Mary as a nursing mother, cradling or suckling an infant Jesus, became another focus both for Catholic reverence for and defenses of Mary's power and for Protestant attacks on it. Although Marina Warner, for instance, argues that "the image of the Virgin suckling Christ represented women's humility in accepting the full human condition," seventeenth-century English debates over Mariolatry constructed the suckling mother as a very powerful figure, whether in negative or in positive terms.[59] Infants' dependence on and symbiosis with their lactating mothers provoked controversy in other discursive registers in seventeenth-century England. On the one hand, a range of medical and moral texts sought to persuade elite women that they should nurse their own infants rather than farm them out to wetnurses; identifying maternity with lactation, such texts also, it has been argued, worked to identify women with mothers and with bodily needs, and to limit women's mobility and independence. Some also emphasized the erotic pleasure and intimate attachment mother and child might both derive from breast-feeding as an incentive. On the other hand, pamphlets, demonological treatises, and published trial narratives that describe witches suckling their familiars at displaced teats promote these same identifications—women = mothers = nursing—but only to demonize and criminalize women.[60] However great their differences, both

---

Image of the Blessed virgin, after he had plighted faith and promise to his complices, by blowing up the bodie of the State, to destroy the King, who is indeede the sacred Image of the eternall Sonne" (*A True and Perfect Relation of the Whole Proceedings against the Late Most Barbarous Traitors* [London, 1606], sig. Bbb3v).

58. Alexis de Salo, *An Admirable Method to Love, Serve, and Honour the B. Virgin Mary*, trans. R. F. (Rouen, 1639), p. 314.

59. Warner, *Alone of All Her Sex*, p. 204.

60. Gail Paster, *The Body Embarrassed: Drama and the Disciplines of Shame in Early Modern England* (Ithaca: Cornell University Press, 1993), chaps. 4 and 5; and Deborah Willis, *Malev-*

discourses participated in a larger movement to subordinate women and restrict them to a narrowly defined domestic sphere by promoting a maternity of service and criminalizing a maternity of power. Controversy over Mariolatry reveals that if mothers had been identified as a problem, the problem had not yet been resolved. For both Catholic and Protestant writers, the nursing Virgin, so confusingly combining service and power, nurture and eros, was not a humble figure but a threatening one.

Protestant writers censure the image of Mary as suckling mother for exaggerating her power and diminishing Jesus'. Most concretely, these images depict Mary as physically larger than Jesus. Crashaw, always the most colorfully virulent attacker of Mary, complains that Catholics infantilize Christ, dwelling on him as a "suckling child in his mothers armes," "an Infant governed, and an obedient child," "in *wardship* and under age"; "Nay that is nothing, they make him an underling to a woman."[61] Even after 1,600 years, Crashaw complains, Catholics refuse to allow Jesus to grow up. Mary "must still bee a commanding Mother, and must shew *her authority over him*, and he *must receive our prayers by her meanes*, and still she must beare him in her armes; or lead him in her hand, and her Picture must worke all the miracles, but his none; and she must be saluted as a Lady, a Queene, a Goddesse, and he as a Child."[62]

In Crashaw's view, to depict or imagine Christ as an infant is to degrade him; to confer command and authority on Mary is to wrench them away from both God the Father and his Son: "The *Christ* of God and of his Church, is God equall to the father, and can do all things himselfe: the Christ of the Romish Church is a child inferiour to his mother and may deny her nothing."[63] Floyd counters that to depict Jesus as an infant is not to diminish his majesty but to emphasize his humanity. The Christ who is a babe in arms, sucking on the Virgin's breasts, is "though not in bignes of body, yet in Majesty, power, wisdome, sanctity, both as God and man . . . equall to himself bleeding on the Crosse." Those who think of Jesus as a child do not imagine that he presently is one, but remember that he once was one.[64] Floyd presents this memory as a comfort, a reminder that even the Saviour shares human mortality and fragility.

Such a memory was not inevitably comforting, however. For many Protestant writers, this remembrance of infant dependency, Jesus' or their

---

olent Nurture: Witch-Hunting and Maternal Power in Early Modern England (Ithaca: Cornell University Press, 1995).

61. William Crashaw, *Jesuites Gospell*, sigs. A3, I3, I2, A3.
62. Ibid., sig. F2v.
63. Ibid., sig. K.
64. Floyd, *Overthrow of the Protestants*, sig. F.

own, announced the return of the repressed. One way to cope with this
memory, made so concrete in Catholic iconography, was to grow up and
away from the mother, to grow bigger and more powerful than she. Another strategy was to free Jesus and unmother Mary through iconoclasm,
wrenching the infant from her arms. John Stow, for instance, described
how a Virgin at the cross in west Cheap was "robbed of her son, and her
armes broken, by which she staid him on her knees"; repaired and sup-
plied with "a new misshapen son," who, "borne out of time, all naked was
laid in her armes," the statue was later "again defaced, by plucking off her
crowne, and almost her head, taking from her her naked child, & stabbing
her in the breast, &c."[65]

Catholic depictions of the relationship between Mary and Jesus were disturbing not only because they seemed to freeze Jesus in infancy or to compel him back into it, but also because they suggested that he remembered
his early dependency and revered his mother as a consequence, that her
early nurturance of him translated into later authority over him. Robert
Chambers, for instance, locates Mary's power not just in God's grace but in
her intimacy with her son. With Jesus, Mary "had not onely domestical fa-
miliaritie for many yeares, but had motherly authoritie over him, for he
was obedient unto her, yea subject unto her, yea subject to Joseph for her
sake, which truly was a power above all power, a miracle above all miracles,
to have in pious and reverend subjection the high Majestie of heaven, the
author and supreme worker of all miracles." This passage asserts not only
Mary's maternal authority but her precedence over her husband, Joseph.
Jesus is subject to Joseph only "for her sake"; obviously, her contribution is
much more important than Joseph's and therefore her power and prestige
are far greater. "In his life tyme," Jesus "alwaies yelded unto her authoritie."[66] As a consequence, according to *The Widdowes Mite,* "she cannot without blasphemy be denied to have beene for many yeares Superiour to the
true, only, & begotten Sonne of God, who is the Lord both of Saints and
Angells." Mary's power, then, stems from her maternal authority over Jesus: "it is infinitly a greater dignity to have God for her Son, and her subject, then to be the Superiour and Empresse of all things created."[67] This
genealogy of Mary's power assumes that mothers inevitably exercise authority over their offspring, not only in childhood but into adulthood.

Although Chambers claims that the reverence for mothers "is a law
meerely natural, & consequently indispensable," such reverence for moth-

---

65. John Stow, *A Survey of London* (1603), ed. Charles Lethbridge Kingsford, 2 vols. (Oxford: Clarendon, 1971), 1: 266, 267.

66. Chambers, preface to Numan, *Miracles Lately Wrought,* sig. C5; see also A. G., *Widdowes Mite,* sig. C3.

67. A. G., *Widdowes Mite,* sigs. C5 (mismarked A5), E4v.

ers was not at all a given in either medieval or early modern English culture, as many scholars have demonstrated.[68] Thus, while Catholic apologists base their defenses of the Virgin Mary's power on her authority as a
mother, those who question devotion to Mary begin by questioning that
premise. As Willet states, "it is great presumption to thinke, that the Vir-
gine *Mary* may commaund her Sonne in heaven, seeing she had no authoritie to commaund him upon earth, in any thing pertaining to his
office."[69] Many early modern political theorists refer to women's lack of
maternal authority, whether natural or cultural, to explain why they cannot and do not rule. John Knox, for instance, proposes that, just as men's
power as fathers is an analogy to or source of their power over other men
as rulers, so women's lack of authority as mothers, especially over their
sons, explains why they cannot rule: "those that will not permit a woman
to have power over her owne sonnes, will not permit her (I am assured) to
have rule over a realme."[70] Almost a century later, Thomas Hobbes offers
a more complicated version of the same argument. He claims that maternal and paternal power cannot be equal, as mothers' and fathers' mutual
participation in the act of generation and equal ability to kill might suggest, because "no man can obey two Masters." Hobbes here uses the phrase
frequently employed to describe the untenable position of Catholic subjects in a Protestant state to describe the dilemma of the child whose parents are equals; in his formulation, the mother who vies for power with the
father is analogous to the pope, who competes with the sovereign and divides the subject's allegiance. Hobbes resolves the child's dilemma by sub-
ordinating or excluding the mother. He concedes that, by "Nature," "Dominion is in the Mother," but goes on to insist that in a commonwealth
that has risen out of and above the state of nature, maternal power is subordinated to paternal power; through a generational contract with their
sons, men govern both the household and the commonwealth.[71] Knox
and Hobbes, then, represent the two alternatives that Rose has identified
in discourses that are more explicitly about sexual and familial life: "male-

68. Chambers, preface to Numan, *Miracles Lately Wrought,* sig. C5v. On ambivalence toward mothers in medieval and early modern culture, see Janet Adelman, *Suffocating Mothers: Fantasies of Maternal Origin in Shakespeare's Plays, "Hamlet" to "The Tempest"* (New York and
London: Routledge, 1992); Clarissa W. Atkinson, *The Oldest Vocation: Christian Motherhood in
the Middle Ages* (Ithaca: Cornell University Press, 1991); Valerie Fildes, ed., *Women as Mothers
in Pre-Industrial England* (London and New York: Routledge, 1990); and Jodi Mikalachki,
The Legacy of Boadicea: Gender and Nation in Early Modern England (London: Routledge,
1998), chap. 4.
69. Willet, *Synopsis Papismi,* sig. Zz3.
70. Knox, *First Blast of the Trumpet,* sigs. B4v–5.
71. Thomas Hobbes, *Leviathan,* ed. C. B. Macpherson (Harmondsworth: Penguin, 1983),
2.20.253–54. See Carole Pateman, *The Sexual Contract* (Stanford: Stanford University Press,
1988), pp. 44–50; and Mikalachki, *Legacy of Boadicea,* pp. 47–49.

authored sexual discourse either denies maternal authority altogether or acknowledges and then erases it."[72] Yet Catholic defenders of Marian devotion suggest a third possibility—a male-authored discourse that assumes and even extends maternal authority.

However misogynous their dismissals of "all other women," Catholic writers' zealous reverence for this one female figure countered the sweeping misogyny of Protestant writers, creating the possibility of a positive discussion of women's contributions. Furthermore, while Protestant writers compared Mary to "all other women" as the coup de grâce in their assaults on Mariolatry, Catholic writers repeatedly drew the connection between Mariolatry and other kinds of devotion to women, suggesting that it was not an unprecedented and bizarre practice, but part of a web of social relations in which women were, sometimes, valued. Jane Owen addressed a section of her *Antidote against Purgatory* (1634) to Catholic gentlewomen, especially widows, and urged the Virgin as an example: "Well (*Worthy Ladyes*) let a Woman once preach to women, and since you are Women, Imitate that *Blessed Woman* so much celebrated for her charity to others. . . . It is in your power (if your selves will) to enjoye the like felicity and retaliation, for your workes of charity, with her."[73] Many writers dedicated their devotional treatises to Catholic women, religious and lay.[74]

They also extended their engagements with Protestant writers beyond the Virgin Mary to ask under what conditions power might be conferred on a woman. Yes, such a woman would need to be an exception, but even Protestants had to admit that such exceptions did occur. For, however shocked and amused they were by Mariolatry, Protestants themselves sometimes adored women. Catholic writers drew attention to these occasions, because they proved that worshiping a woman was not unimaginable, even to benighted Protestants. Although they refused to worship pictures of Mary or of Christ, Protestants revered pictures of their mistresses. As John Floyd remarks, "before Images of *Venus* they can direct their humble duty and harty affection unto *Queanes*, which is nothing els but their relative honour of foule pictures."[75] Floyd goes so far as to suggest that William

72. Rose, "Where Are the Mothers in Shakespeare?" p. 312.

73. Jane Owen, *An Antidote against Purgatory* (St. Omer, 1634), pp. 186–87.

74. See, for example, the English translation of *The Psalter of the B. Virgin Mary* (1624), dedicated to Lady Cecily Compton; *The Patterne of All Pious Prayer* (Douai, 1636), dedicated to Viscountess "Baltemore"; Couvreur, *Devotion of Bondage*, dedicated to Lady M. C.; John Falconer, *The Mirrour of Created Perfection* (St. Omer, 1632), dedicated to Agnes Rosedale (Sr. Agnes of S. Albert); N. N., *Maria Triumphans; or, The B. Virgin Mary Her Triumph* (Douai, 1635), dedicated to Henrietta Maria; Alexis de Salo, *Admirable Method*, dedicated to Lady Audeley; and Stafford, *Femall Glory*, dedicated to Lady Theophila Coke.

75. Floyd, *Purgatories Triumph*, sig. Ev.

Crashaw's irreverence for the Virgin's breasts reveals more about his sexual fantasies than it does about her, "seeing her breasts in his conceipt are no better, & so no more to be honoured & respected, then those of other women, with which to play eyther imaginarily or indeed."[76] Floyd's attack on Crashaw is a particularly vivid version of the Catholic objection to Protestants' refusal to distinguish the Virgin Mary from other women. But it is also more than that. Attributing the passion of Crashaw's fulminations against Mary to uncontrolled (and unconsummated) desire, Floyd hints that women in general and Mary in particular exert power over Crashaw, no matter how much he resists. The cheap shot that Crashaw is a randy hypocrite implies a more serious charge, and one that Crashaw's obsessive and graphic text bears out: breasts, especially the Virgin Mary's, haunt Crashaw's imagination. To defend Mary, Floyd must also deny the potential eroticism of Marian devotion. Sternly distinguishing mothers and mistresses, pious devotion and sexual fantasy, the divine and secular, Floyd denies the fluid movement across those boundaries that helps to animate Mariolatry but also disturbs and arouses its critics.

Various Catholic writers observe that the cult of Elizabeth borrowed from the cult of Mary, raising the champion of Protestantism to the position of an idol. To prove Protestants' inconsistency and hypocrisy, Chambers turns to Stow's account of one Hacket, who in 1591 was executed for treason. Among his several offenses was an assault on "a certaine Picture of the Queenes Majestie"; into "that part of the sayd picture that did represent the breast and heart of the Queenes Majestie" he "did maliciouslie, and traiterouslie thrust an yron Instrument." Chambers points out that the harsh response to Hacket's crime reveals a close correspondence between the queen and her image. "They thought her Maiestie iniuried and disgraced; by the iniurie and disgrace which the said caitif offered unto her armes and image. Upon which consideration I would aske, what punishment they have merited, that have so dispitefully and barbarously thrown down mangled and trodden under their accursed sinful feet the Pictures of God himself, and of his blessed Mother, and of his holy Saincts?"[77] Such assaults on Elizabeth's image, which was reportedly "stabbed, stoned, burned, and hanged from gallows," might simply express opposition, as well as "a superstitious belief that damage to the Queen's image could actually do harm to her person," as Helen Hackett points out.[78] Yet Cham-

---

76. Floyd, *Overthrow of the Protestants Pulpit-Babels*, sig. G3v.

77. John Stow, *The Annales of England* (London, 1601), sig. Dddd2; Chambers, preface to Numan, *Miracles Lately Wrought*, sigs. D5v–6.

78. Helen Hackett, *Virgin Mother, Maiden Queen: Elizabeth I and the Cult of the Virgin Mary* (Houndmills, Basingstoke, Hampshire: Macmillan, 1995), p. 212.

bers takes these assaults, and especially the retaliation they sometimes provoke, as proof that Protestants revere some images of some women.

The author of *Maria Triumphans; or, The B. Virgin Mary Her Triumph*
(1635) reminds readers that

> some Poets in dedicating their Poems to their Prince, feare not for the
> tyme, to invest him, or her, with the Name of *God*, or *Goddesse*. I will insist
> in *Spencer*, the chiefest English Poet in this age. He dedicating his *Faery
> Queene*, to Queene *Elizabeth*, thus saluteth her.
>
> > 'O Goddesse heavenly bright,
> > Mirrour of grace, & Majesty divine,
> > Great Lady of the Greatest Ile.'
>
> Now, who carps at the *Poet* herein? Or what Man thinketh that the Poet did
> truly commit Idolatry to that Queene, in taking her (who was a mortall sin-
> full Woman) to be a *Goddesse* indeed?[79]

Since, even in Protestant discourses, women sometimes are apotheosized
into idols, the question becomes: What are the grounds on which women
are so transformed or elevated? For Protestants, it is particularly inappropriate to revere Mary, as opposed to Queen Elizabeth or one's mistress,
precisely because to do so confers on her a kind of divinity to which she is
not entitled. For Catholics, it is acceptable to revere Mary since she is more
than a woman, since she intervenes between the human and the divine.
Catholic writers explicitly connect debates over Mary to attitudes toward
real women, whether queans or a queen, to demonstrate the relatively large
number of exceptions, the resemblances among these exceptions, and a
custom of revering women. While they reject the idea that a minister's wife
might be "as good a Woman as *Mary*," they pursue this (usually Protestant)
skeptical strategy of comparison to forge connections between debates over
the Virgin Mary and men's attachment to and dependency on women.[80]

HENRIETTA MARIA'S INTERCESSIONS

If Catholic apologists had too completely divorced Mary from the world
of lived social relations, they would have been unable to explain her lasting power. Mary's popularity as an object of devotion depended not only
on her extraordinary intimacy with the divine during her own life on

79. N. N., *Maria Triumphans*, sig. D6.
80. Ibid., sig. M8.

earth—through her "immaculate conception," her role as Jesus' mother, her assumption directly into heaven—but on her continuing role as a liaison between the human and the divine. Her role as mediator between human supplicants and God was her most beloved and her most disputed because, in interceding for humans, Mary usurped a priestly, even a Christlike function.[81] Critics of Mariolatry articulate the power attributed to this role most vividly. Crashaw, for instance, argues that Catholics believe "that a man shall oftentimes bee sooner heard at Gods hands in the Meditation of *Mary*, then of Jesus Christ." Although Protestants, in contrast, honor Mary, "we dare not pray unto her, to make her our advocate or intercessor," according to Andrew Willet.[82] Protestants refrain both out of reverence for God and out of practicality. Why appeal to Mary, when she has no power to help? She is not the equal of either God or Jesus, and certainly does not have more power than either. Why not appeal directly to Jesus? The outrageous blasphemy of appealing to Mary as intercessor is most apparent, in Crashaw's view, when Mary is imagined presiding over a court of appeals. If, as some Catholics believe, Mary's court of mercy counters, even corrects, God's court of justice, then "shee and her Court are in this respect above God and his court." But how could God's court err? And how could Mary's court be of higher jurisdiction than his? "This is blasphemie of a high nature, that there needes a Chancerie to rectifie his proceedinges and mitigate his Judgements."[83] As God's rival and gatekeeper, Mary became, for many seventeenth-century Englishmen hostile to Catholicism, the embodiment of usurped, arbitrary power, the symbol of Catholics' misplaced obedience and reverence. The debate over Mary's authority as mother and mediator, particularly vehement in the 1630s, provided a vocabulary for, and was sometimes indistinguishable from, the controversy surrounding Henrietta Maria.

With time, what one of Henrietta Maria's Restoration biographers called her "*most prevalent mediation*" on behalf of English Catholics became her most controversial intervention in English political life.[84] What interests me is how attacks on Mariolatry enabled such attacks on Henrietta Maria. William Prynne, perhaps her most outspoken and indomitable critic, of-

81. Luisa Accati, "The Larceny of Desire: The Madonna in Seventeenth-Century Catholic Europe," in *Disciplines of Faith: Studies in Religion, Politics, and Patriarchy*, ed. Jim Obelkevich, Lyndal Roper, and Raphael Samuel (London and New York: Routledge & Kegan Paul, 1987), pp. 73–86, esp. 79–80.
82. Crashaw, *Jesuites Gospell*, sig. Bv; Willet, *Synopsis Papismi*, sig. Zz3v.
83. Crashaw, *Sermon Preached at the Crosse*, sigs. I–Iv. Catholic apologists countered that believers sought succor and support from Mary, not a different verdict; see Floyd, *Overthrow of the Protestants Pulpit-Babels*, sig. X3f.
84. Verney, *Life and Death of That Matchless Mirrour of Magnanimity*, p. 16.

fers an extended comparison of the queen and the Virgin Mary. According to Prynne, English Catholics have

> Queen Mary her selfe in the King's own bed and bosome for their most powerfull Mediatrix, of whom they might really affirme in reference to his Majesty, what some of their popish Doctors have most blasphemously written of the Virgin Mary in relation to God and Christ, That all things are subject to the command of Mary, even God himselfe: That she is the Empresse and Queen of Heaven, and of greatest Authority in the Kingdome of Heaven, where shee may not only impetrate [obtain by request] but command whatsoever shee pleaseth; That shee sitteth as Chauncellor in the Court of Heaven, and giveth Letters of Grace and Mercy to whom she pleaseth. . . . That if any (Roman Catholike) doth finde himselfe aggrieved in the Court of Gods (or the Kings) Justice, (for being prosecuted for his Recusancy or seducing the Kings people) he may safely appeale to Maries Court of mercy for reliefe, shee being the Throne of Grace.[85]

Here Prynne quotes directly from discussions of Mary, echoing charges such as those Crashaw, for instance, levels; distrust of female power serves to link and intensify attacks on Catholic belief and practice and on Charles's court. The problem with the command of Mary, in heaven or in Charles's court, is that it is an inversion and a usurpation.

Although one royalist writer claimed that Prynne's charge that she acted as the papists' "Mediatrix" was unfounded and his "bold comparison between the Virgin *Mary*, and Her Majesty" blasphemous, some Catholics were comfortable making this very comparison.[86] For instance, the author of *Maria Triumphans* dedicates the volume to Henrietta Maria, advising that if she would be patroness for his volume, Mary would repay her: "thus will *Mary* intercede for *Mary*; the *Queene of Heaven*, for the great *Queene* upon *earth.*"[87] Elizabeth Cary, dedicating her translation of Cardinal Jacques Du Perron's *Reply* to Henrietta Maria, praised the queen in language most often used to exalt the Virgin Mary: "you are a woeman, though farr above other wemen, therefore fittest to protect a womans worke."[88] To champion

85. Prynne, *Popish Royall Favourite*, sigs. G4v–H; I have removed confusing emphases. Veevers and Clark also quote this stunning passage (*Images of Love and Religion*, p. 108; "Iconography of the Blush," pp. 124–25). Hibbard argues that Prynne should be taken "seriously as a representative of moderate public opinion" rather than dismissed as an eccentric (Hibbard, *Charles I and the Popish Plot*, pp. 239–42, esp. 240).

86. *Vindiciae Caroli Regis*, sig. H2.

87. N. N., *Maria Triumphans*, sig. A3.

88. Elizabeth Cary, Lady Falkland, *The Reply of the Cardinal of Perron, to the Answeare of the Most Excellent King of Great Britaine* (Douai, 1630), sig. a2. Cary put Henrietta Maria in a very awkward position, enlisting the queen's support for her (belated) translation of a Catholic response to one of James I's defenses of sovereignty. James Du Perron, the cardinal's nephew, served as Henrietta Maria's almoner and blessed her new chapel at Somerset House in

the Virgin Mary or Henrietta Maria, Catholics needed either to downplay these figures' power or to justify it. The second strategy was both the more frequently chosen and the more challenging to assumptions about gender, since it thought outside of gender hierarchy and imagined a female power that was not usurped from men but rather separate, equal, and legitimate in its own right.

Henrietta Maria fueled the comparisons between herself and the Virgin Mary, flattering and unflattering, by openly devoting herself to the Virgin. Her elaborate new chapel at Somerset House was dedicated to the Virgin and became the center for the Arch-Confraternity of the Holy Rosary, which the queen led.[89] The Capuchins who arrived in the 1630s to staff that chapel and live adjacent to it adopted Mary as their patron. The queen's chapels contained many religious images, most representing the Virgin.[90] In thanks for the Virgin's intercessions on her behalf, the queen also gave expensive gifts to chapels in France honoring the Virgin.[91] The proliferation of female images in Henrietta Maria's chapels suggests how the queen's artistic patronage, penchant for performance, wifely influence, and Catholic piety all conjoined to elevate the image of woman in the Caroline court, creating what Sophie Tomlinson has called "a cult of woman, or focus on the feminine in Caroline culture."[92] Elizabeth I had sometimes drawn on imagery of the Virgin Mary, as well as Venus, to represent her own status as virgin queen. As Helen Hackett shows, Elizabeth's admirers stressed her resemblance to the Virgin more often than she did herself, and were especially likely to do so later in her life and after her death.[93]

1632 (see Havran, *Catholics in Caroline England*, p. 59; and Hibbard, *Charles I and the Popish Plot*, p. 52).

89. Cyprien of Gamache, "Memoirs," pp. 432–33; see also Veevers, *Images of Love and Religion*, pp. 92–109. Throughout his memoirs, Fr. Cyprien emphasizes the queen's devotion to Mary as well as the centrality of Mariolatry to the Capuchin mission under her auspices.

90. R. Malcolm Smuts, *Court Culture and the Origins of a Royalist Tradition in Early Stuart England* (Philadelphia: University of Pennsylvania Press, 1987), p. 228. Fr. Cyprien referred to the "beautiful image" of the virgin "which Queen Mary de Medicis had brought from Flanders" and given to Henrietta Maria for use in the devotions of the confraternity ("Memoirs," pp. 432–33).

91. Cyprien of Gamache, "Memoirs," pp. 350, 361–64.

92. Tomlinson, "She That Plays the King," p. 190.

93. Hackett, *Virgin Mother, Maiden Queen*. Frances Yates most vividly and influentially claims that Elizabeth was simply placed in a niche from which the Virgin Mary had been pushed: "The bejewelled and painted images of the Virgin Mary had been cast out of churches and monasteries, but another bejewelled and painted image was set up at court, and went on progress through the land for her worshippers to adore" (*Astraea: The Imperial Theme in the Sixteenth Century* [London: Routledge, 1975], p. 79). See also Carole Levin, *"The Heart and Stomach of a King": Elizabeth I and the Politics of Sex and Power* (Philadelphia: University of Pennsylvania Press, 1994), pp. 26–30; Leah S. Marcus, *Puzzling Shakespeare: Local Reading and Its Discontents* (Berkeley: University of California Press, 1988), pp. 67, 84–

James I had appropriated Catholic iconography to depict his role as the loving "nourish-father" of his people.[94] But this imagery took on different, and apparently more disturbing, meanings for a post-Reformation culture, when it was reconnected to Catholic theology in the service of a queen who was married, fertile, and openly Catholic.[95]

Iconography of the Virgin helped to idealize Elizabeth I's singularity, depicting her as an exception outside of usual human relations and therefore paradoxically able to participate in all of them; it enabled James to show how he absorbed into himself both female generativity and male authority. Henrietta Maria, however, was usually represented as wife and mother, as part of a family. Associations of her with the Virgin, whether positive or negative, stressed not her singularity but her influence over her husband and children, especially her oldest sons. Her husband's devotion to her and their intimate bond became central to Royalist idealizations of the couple and their rule, in which, as Roy Strong has argued, "the blissful royal marriage and her ever fruitful womb are exalted almost to the level of a state philosophy. Charles and Henrietta are the first English royal couple to be glorified as husband and wife in the domestic sense."[96] In this tradition, Charles worshiped his beloved. He was the knight, she the cherished lady. Idealizations of their courtship and marriage began with Royalist accounts of the couple's first meetings in the 1620s and were later promoted by the couple themselves.[97] Yet the attachment that Royalist masques, verse, portraiture, and polemic romanticize was one of the reasons that Parliamentarians and Puritans found Henrietta Maria so threatening; it was not the answer to their concerns but the cause of them.

The issue at the heart of debates about both Henrietta Maria's and the Virgin Mary's authority and influence was proximity to power and, more dangerous, intimacy. For it was indisputable that the queen lay, as Prynne charged, in the king's "own bed and bosome." Especially in the years of his

---

86; and Roy Strong, "The Popular Celebration of the Accession Day of Queen Elizabeth I," *Journal of the Warburg and Courtauld Institutes* 21 (1958): 86–103.

94. Jonathan Goldberg, *James I and the Politics of Literature: Jonson, Shakespeare, Donne, and Their Contemporaries* (Baltimore: Johns Hopkins University Press, 1983), pp. 90, 142; Debora Kuller Shuger, *Habits of Thought in the English Renaissance: Religion, Politics, and the Dominant Culture* (Berkeley: University of California Press, 1990), chap. 6, esp. p. 228. James refers to himself as a "nourish-father" in "Basilikon Doron," in *The Political Works of James I*, ed. Charles Howard McIlwain (Cambridge: Harvard University Press, 1918), p. 24.

95. Veevers also argues that iconography of the Virgin took on a different resonance in relation to an "overtly Catholic Queen" (*Images of Love and Religion*, pp. 11, 7).

96. Roy Strong, *Van Dyck: Charles I on Horseback* (New York: Viking, 1972), p. 70. See also Annabel Patterson, *Censorship and Interpretation: The Conditions of Writing and Reading in Early Modern England* (Madison: University of Wisconsin Press, 1984), chap. 4.

97. For a description of the couple's first meeting, see, for instance, *True Discourse of All the Royal Passages*, sigs. D3–4.

"personal rule" when Charles did not convene a parliament (1629–40), access to him was limited, interaction with him was informal, and even his own ministers strategized and worried about how to influence him. Kevin Sharpe argues that far fewer servants had intimate access to Charles I than to James I, and that "domestic proximity meant influence." As a result, the queen's proximity to the king was envied and disputed. Yet historians disagree as to whether the queen's access to the king translated into influence. Sharpe argues that Charles's relative inaccessibility made him more independent, even of his ministers, rather than more dependent on his wife: "it would seem that the queen exercised little influence or power."[98] Caroline Hibbard, however, claims not only that Henrietta Maria did indeed have influence but also that observers' perception of her influence was just as politically significant: "the king's policies from 1637 to 1642, if not actually shaped by the queen, could only too easily be identified with her point of view and that of her circle."[99] The queen's influence, and therefore her threat, were also perceived to increase over time. After 1640, Robin Clifton argues, there were no accusations of a Catholic plot against the king, since it was recognized that Catholics would only lose by his death. Instead, the threat was increasingly seen to emerge from inside England; indeed, from inside the king's bed curtains.[100] In the 1640s, hostility toward the queen was relatively widespread.[101] The "Declaration of Fears and Jealousies," for instance, composed by John Pym and debated in Parliament, focused on the queen as "a dangerous and ill-affected person [who] hath been admitted to intermeddle with the great affairs of state, with the disposing of places and preferments, even of highest concernment in the kingdom."[102]

98. Kevin Sharpe, "The Image of Virtue: The Court and Household of Charles I, 1625–1642," in *The English Court: From the War of the Roses to the Civil War,* ed. David Starkey (London: Longmans, 1987), pp. 248, 257.

99. Hibbard, *Charles I and the Popish Plot,* p. 228; Smuts, *Court Culture,* pp. 194–95.

100. Clifton, "Fear of Popery," p. 162. Attacking Henrietta Maria became so reliable a route for attacking Charles I that in "The Ready and Easy Way to Establish a Free Commonwealth," Milton argued that one problem with kings is that they come with queens: "There will be a queen of no less charge; in most likelihood outlandish and a papist; besides a queen-mother such already" (*Milton's Prose Writings,* ed. K. M. Burton, Everyman's Library [London: Dent, 1958], p. 225). Christopher Hill echoes this polemic, referring to "the disastrously popish and arbitrary Henrietta Maria" as "Charles' evil genius" (*The Century of Revolution, 1603–1714* [New York: Norton, 1961], pp. 74, 12).

101. See, for instance, *Some Observations upon Occasion of the Publishing Their Majesties Letters* (Oxford, 1645), sig. A4v; *Strange and Terrible Newes from the Queene in Holland Shewing Plainely the Intelligence of the King of His Intention to Raise Armes* (London, 1642), sig. A2v; and Edward Hyde, Earl of Clarendon, *The History of the Rebellion and Civil Wars in England* (Oxford: Oxford University Press, 1843), pp. 63, 67, 121.

102. As cited in Hibbard, "Queen as Consort," p. 414n63. Of twelve allegations made in the "Declaration of Fears and Jealousies," eight pertain to the queen. Both "A Remon-

Such charges attributed to the queen considerable, and detrimental, influence over the king, deflecting criticisms of Charles onto Henrietta Maria and locating her in the evil counselor tradition, in which political and sexual influence were often indistinguishable. This line of attack avoided the risks of directly criticizing a monarch by displacing blame onto his favorites and advisers, whom it would not be seditious to criticize.[103] After the "Spanish match," in Peter Lake's view, evil counsel became associated with popery.[104] For instance, as I mentioned earlier, criticism of James I's pursuit of the Spanish match was deflected onto Buckingham, and then from Buckingham onto his Catholic mother and wife.

The displacement of blame from sovereigns to their "evil counselors" often, as in Marlowe's *Edward II*, emphasizes the class inversions that result from empowering the baseborn and the disturbing redistributions of power that may attend the bodily intimacy between sovereign and favorite. This tradition sometimes, and complexly, associates homoeroticism and evil counsel.[105] Attacks on Charles and Henrietta Maria's relationship dwell instead on gender inversion, as do so many anti-Catholic discourses. In both cases, desire, affection, or dependency clouds the monarch's judgment, leading him to disparage his authority by relying on the advice or promoting the interests of an inferior, and thereby overturning the class, gender, and power hierarchies. One Royalist summarized the antiroyalist position as "The Queen governs the King, & doth something in his affaires that befits neither Her, nor Him"; *Mercurius Britanicus* reported that "some say she is the man, and *Raignes.*"[106] Decrying "evil counselors" in general, Lucy

strance of the State of the Kingdom" (Dec. 15, 1641) and the "Declaration" (Mar. 2, 1642) are reprinted in *An Exact Collection of All Remonstrances, Declarations, Votes . . . and Other Remarkable Passages betweene the Kings Most Excellent Majesty and His High Court of Parliament* (London, 1643), pp. 3–21, 97–102.

103. On "evil counsel," see Richard Cust and Ann Hughes, "Introduction: After Revisionism," in *Conflict in Early Stuart England: Studies in Religion and Politics, 1603–1642*, ed. Cust and Hughes (London: Longmans, 1989), pp. 1–46, esp. 20; Hibbard, *Charles I and the Popish Plot*, p. 233; Miller, *Popery and Politics*, p. 84; and Rachel Weil, "Sometimes a Scepter Is Only a Scepter: Pornography and Politics in Restoration England," in *The Invention of Pornography: Obscenity and the Origins of Modernity*, ed. Lynn Hunt (New York: Zone Books, 1993), pp. 125–53, esp. 139.

104. Peter Lake, "Anti-Popery: The Structure of a Prejudice," in Cust and Hughes, *Conflict in Early Stuart England*, p. 88.

105. Mario DiGangi, *The Homoerotics of Early Modern Drama* (Cambridge: Cambridge University Press, 1997), chap. 4.

106. *A Letter, in Which the Arguments of the Annotator, and Three Other Speeches upon Their Majestie's Letters Published at London, Are Examined and Answered* (Oxford, 1645), sig. A4; *Mercurius Britanicus: Communicating the Affaires of Great Britaine: For the Better Information of the People*, no. 44 (July 15–22, 1644), p. 347. This paper was a response to *Mercurius Aulicus*, which disseminated a court-centered perspective. See also *A Speech Delivered by Mr. Pym, at a Conference of Both Houses . . . Discovering the Dangers and Miseries the Three Kingdomes are Liable unto, by Reason of His Majesties Evill Counsellors* (London, 1642).

Hutchinson claimed that Henrietta Maria was worse than the rest because of "the power her haughty spirit kept over her husband, who was enslaved in his affection only to her, though she had no more passion for him than what served to promote her designs." Hutchinson warned that such inversion, "where the hands which were made only for distaffs affect the management of sceptres," inevitably doomed a kingdom: "Wherever male princes are so effeminate as to suffer women of foreign birth and different religions to intermeddle with the affairs of state, it is always found to produce sad desolations; and it hath been observed that a French queen never brought any happiness to England."[107]

Like Prynne's *Popish Royall Favourite*, *The Great Eclipse of the Sun, or Charles His Waine Over-Clouded, by the Evill Influences of the Moon* (1644) draws an explicit parallel between the inverse coverture Hutchinson identifies in the Caroline court and that in the Catholic cosmos, attributing the chaos in the kingdom to the fact that Charles prays to the Virgin Mary and allows himself to

> be rul'd by his little *Queen Mary*, for this was [not] Idolatry, but the way to increase his Royall Off-spring, and Progeny, whereupon the King being in full Conjunction with this *Popish Planet*, the Queen, hee was totally eclipsed by her Counsell, who under the Royall Curtaines, perswaded him to advance the Plots of the Catholikes, under the colour of maintaining the *Protestant Religion*. Ordinary women, can in the Night time perswade their husbands to give them new Gowns [and] Petticotes, and make them grant their desire; and could not Catholick Queen *Mary* (think ye) by her night discourses, encline the King to Popery?[108]

This diatribe assumes that wives often practice what Olympe de Gouges would later call "nocturnal administration," but in most cases the stakes were smaller, a clothing allowance rather than affairs of state.[109] Here, though, a "curtain lecture" instigates the disorder leading to civil war and regicide.

In the widely repeated analogy of husband and wife to sun and moon, the moon, or wife, borrows her light from the sun. The image of the royal

107. Hutchinson, *Memoirs*, p. 89. In Hutchinson's view, Queen Elizabeth was not an exception to this rule, since she submitted to the judgment of male advisers.

108. *The Great Eclipse of the Sun, or Charles His Waine Over-Clouded, by the Evill Influences of the Moon . . . Otherwise, Great Charles, Our Gracious King, Eclipsed by the Destructive Perswasions of His Queen, by the Pernicious Aspects of His Cabbinet Counsell, and by the Subtill Insinuations of the Popish Faction* (London, 1644), p. 3.

109. Olympe de Gouges, "A Declaration of the Rights of Woman," in *Women in Revolutionary Paris, 1789–1795*, ed. and trans. Darline Gay Levy, Harriet Branson Applewhite, and Mary Durham Johnson (Urbana: University of Illinois Press, 1979), pp. 87–96, esp. 93.

marriage as a "great eclipse" thus overturns a familiar figure for the happily married couple and borrows imagery from Royalist idealizations of Charles, which frequently associated him with the sun.[110] One defender of Charles's marriage to Henrietta Maria (in 1625) chided those who feared that the marriage would in any way affect Charles's commitment to reformed religion: surely the queen would not "offer to seeke to guide Him by whom She is to be directed, to be the sterne when She is but the vessell of which Hee is the Pilot; to be the Sun, when she is but the Moone, which must borrow light from his knowledge."[111] Yet almost twenty years later, that was exactly what was feared. The moon was eclipsing the sun, the Virgin Mary deflecting worship from her son, the *feme covert* subsuming her husband. *The Great Eclipse* concludes: "The King was eclipsed by the *Queen*, and she perswaded him that Darknesse was Light, and that it was better to be Papist, then a Protestant."[112]

Such suspicions were confirmed by the seizure of the "king's cabinet" of conjugal correspondence at Nazeby, which Parliamentarians read as evidence of inverse coverture in the royal household, and, as a consequence, in the kingdom. These letters and papers were published with annotations and glosses as *The King's Cabinet Opened* (1645). For the annotator, the secret the cabinet revealed was the already widely suspected one that "the King's counsels are wholly governed by the queen; though she be of the weaker sex, born an alien, bred up in a contrary religion, yet nothing, great or small, is transacted without her privity and consent"; "the queen's counsels are as powerful as commands."[113] Just as the secret hidden in a recusant woman's bed, a confessional, or James's privy chamber could turn out to be a heterosocial couple, so the scandal in Charles's "bed and bosom" was his wife. One Royalist reported that the publishers of the correspondence were "wondrous angry, 'cause the Queenes no Man."[114]

Where is the scandal in her being "no Man"? This Royalist writer assumes, despite considerable evidence to the contrary, that only a woman can have sexual intimacy with and influence over a king; were the queen a man, then presumably her influence would be less sexual, less seductive,

---

110. Smuts, *Court Culture and the Origins of a Royalist Tradition*, pp. 234–38.
111. George Marceline, *Epithalamium Gallo-Britannicum* (London, 1625), sigs. P3v–4.
112. *Great Eclipse*, p. 2.
113. From the "annotations" appended to *The King's Cabinet Opened; or, Certain Pacquets of Secret Letters and Papers* (London, 1645), in *The Harleian Miscellany*, 12 vols. (London, 1808–11), 5: 514–57, esp. 548. On the "King's Cabinet," see Lois Potter, *Secret Rites and Secret Writing: Royalist Literature, 1641–1660* (Cambridge: Cambridge University Press, 1989), pp. 57–64.
114. *A Satyr Occasioned by the Author's Survey of a Scandalous Pamphlet Intituled, The King's Cabanet Opened* (Oxford, 1645), sig. A3v.

less unseemly. Furthermore, were the queen a man, her exercise of political influence would not transgress the prohibition that women should stay out of politics. To make so extraordinary a statement, the writer must forget the history of hostility toward Buckingham's influence over first James, then Charles. A man in the king's privy chamber, let alone his bed and bosom, might indeed have been found objectionable. Yet this articulation of why Parliamentarians were "wondrous angry" contains an insight into contradictions inherent in the attacks on Henrietta Maria.

Outrage at Henrietta Maria's influence depended on several interconnected assumptions:

1. The private and the public are discrete arenas of action. Although they had not yet been fully disarticulated, they had to be construed as distinct before crossing from one to the other could provoke a scandal.
2. Women belong in the private sphere.
3. Kings should be able to distinguish between their personal pleasures and public obligations. Their wives serve only personal pleasure, except in producing an heir, which should be their only political contribution.
4. A queen consort who attempts to parlay sexual intimacy into political influence and a king who lets her do so break all these rules, promoting both gender disorder and political tyranny.

These assumptions contain the seeds of their own refutation. For instance, how can the queen consort be relegated to the private sphere if her principal function is to produce an heir? Does not this politically freighted act of reproduction make nonsense of a distinction between the domestic and the political, personal pleasure and public obligation? Mid-century political discourse is filled with attacks on women for "bringing the bedroom into matters of state," as Sharon Achinstein puts it, as well as attacks on men for allowing them to do so.[115] But sharper boundaries between spheres, the domestication of women, and a return to men on top cannot resolve the problems these discourses articulate. The vehemence of Henrietta Maria's attackers reveals that her offense is not simply crossing from an acceptable sphere of action (the private, the bedroom) to another deemed inappropriate to her (the public, the council chamber). In these texts, the private is a space too dangerous, inscrutable, and hard to regulate to leave to a woman. The queen's presence offends and disturbs anywhere.

115. Sharon Achinstein, "Women on Top in the Pamphlet Literature of the English Revolution," *Women's Studies* 24 (1994): 131–63, esp. 153.

Since coverture was so widely used as the model for right relations, Royalists found themselves looking for alternatives in an effort to justify a
more prominent role for the queen. Thus, while Royalists affirmed political hierarchy against the "leveling" impulse of Puritans and Parliamentarians, and sometimes used the traditionally hierarchical relation between
husband and wife as a model for the ideal relation between king and subject, they also, in defense of Charles and Henrietta Maria, argued *against*
gender hierarchy in marriage. Mobilizing sexual and social conventions to
question where the scandal lay in marriage, Royalists challenged the assumption that two spouses are inevitably unequal, and that the more powerful must either subsume the lesser or be eclipsed by it; Royalists articulated the possibility of partnership. In court drama, such as masques and
Sir William Davenant's works, according to Kevin Sharpe, "marriage was
the ultimate relationship of equals in love. Accordingly the queen might
counsel her husband to change his policies without arousing any suspicion
that she wished to compromise his authority. And their relationship too
might form the basis of that change of policy: towards a polity of community and mutual love."[116] In addition to such abstract idealizations of marital union and wifely counsel, Royalist polemicists who countered the direct attacks on the queen were forced to reassess and defend the status of
wife. How, they ask, can it be a criticism to say that a wife has intimate access to her husband? *Vindiciae Caroli Regis* declares that, as "for the Queen
who lyes in the Kings Bed and Bosome . . . She ought to do so, and the King
will have it so."[117] Other royalists go even further, defending the influence
the queen gains through proximity. One response to *The King's Cabinet
Opened* insists that "it is not onely not unfit for a wife to present advise to
her husband, but indeed extreamely proper, especially when she is not
only of great abilities, but of as great affection to her husbands affaires."[118]
In their guarded endorsement of wifely counsel such defenses of Henrietta
Maria closely resemble defenses of Marian devotion. In both cases, Catholic writers responded to their opponents' virulent misogyny by trying to
imagine an alternative to subordination or domination for women.

The positive spin Royalists placed on female influence and power is especially evident in discussions of Henrietta Maria's substantive interventions both on behalf of Catholics and especially in the Royalist war effort.

116. Kevin Sharpe, *Criticism and Compliment: The Politics of Literature in the England of
Charles I* (Cambridge: Cambridge University Press, 1987), p. 288; see also chap. 2, passim;
and Martin Butler, *Theatre and Crisis, 1632–1642* (Cambridge: Cambridge University Press,
1984), esp. chap. 3.
117. *Vindiciae Caroli Regis*, sig. H2.
118. *Letter . . . Arguments of the Annotator*, sig. A4v; see also *Key to the Kings Cabinet*, sig. G.

While commentators, at the time and subsequently, disagree about how much she accomplished and how big a difference it made, Henrietta Maria did considerably more than deliver curtain lectures to Charles. She collected money, raised troops, negotiated with the Irish in an attempt to recruit them to Charles's aid, and engaged in international diplomacy with her relatives.[119] Henrietta Maria seems to have played this role self-consciously. In letters to Charles, she refers to herself as "Your humble and faithfull Agent in accommodating and promoting your high affaires." Her detractors could parody this characterization, depicting her as a "generalissima" and a "*She-Tamberlaine.*"[120] But her apologists could also embroider on her self-representation. One Restoration biographer, John Dauncey, describes how, at York, "she uses her utmost diligence in promoting his Majesties affairs, and in a short time raises a pretty considerable force, which with an *Amazonian* courage she undertakes to command in person"; he urges the reader to envision "her Majesties self *Generalissima*, with an undaunted and more then Womanlike resolution in the head of her Army."[121] Royalists emphasize the queen's industriousness, presenting it as an extension of wifely care. She was not only "ready and willing to endure a part of her Husbands afflictions," as Dauncey claims, but eager to strive to alleviate or ameliorate them. "Nor need it be related what good offices shee did His Majesty during the time shee spent in those forraine parts, in furnishing him from time to time with *Money, Armes* and *Ammunition.* . . . It is enough to say, that never King had a better *Agent.*"[122]

Even Royalists could see the comic potential in this conjunction of the marital and martial in the queen's role as generalissima housewife. *A Satyr Occasioned by the Author's Survey of a Scandalous Pamphlet Intituled, The King's*

---

119. As a consequence of her negotiations with the Irish, which included promising them toleration if they helped Charles, the Irish Rebellion was also known as the Queen's Rebellion. "The Declaration of Fears and Jealousies" claims that Irish rebels "call themselves the Queens Army" and "the prey or booty which they take from the *English,* they marke with the Queenes Mark" (*Exact Collection of All Remonstrances,* p. 98). See also Hibbard, *Charles I and the Popish Plot,* p. 214.

120. *The Queens Majesties Message and Letter from the Hague in Holland, Directed to the Kings Most Excellent Majesty* (London, 1642), sig. A2. On the "generalissima," see Hutchinson, *Memoirs,* pp. 97, 227. For the term "She-Tamburlaine," see *Key to the Kings Cabinet,* sig. Dv. During these years, many other women also took active roles defending their property, spying, raising funds, etc. Each side ridiculed the activity of women on the other. See Anne Laurence, *Women in England, 1500–1760: A Social History* (London: Weidenfeld & Nicolson, 1994), pp. 244–45; and Achinstein, "Women on Top."

121. Dauncey, *History of the Thrice Illustrious Princess,* sigs. E12, F2.

122. Ibid., sig. D5; *Briefe Relation of the Remarkeable Occurences in the Northerne Parts* (London, 1642), sig. A2v.

Cabanet Opened praises *"She* that at once such *weightie* Acts can doe,/ That can be *Queene,* and yet *Negotiate* too"; "While this Hand holds *Instructions, that Receipts."*[123] This Royalist satire of critics' depictions of the queen is so subtle that it is almost indistinguishable from the criticism itself. One sarcastic Parliamentarian, for instance, describes the queen as a shopper for Catholic victory: "who went to the Broakers with the Jewells of the Crowne, and the Cupboard of Gold Plate? who bought *Pocket-pistolls,* barrells of Powder, and many such pretty toyes to destroy the Protestants? was it Queen *Mary?* The very same."[124] This passage simultaneously trivializes the queen's political interventions and deplores them as doing real damage to the Parliamentary cause. In the case of the queen's sale of crown jewels, suspected before and lamented after, critiques of wifely transgression (selling joint property without permission and spending extravagantly) and of political espionage intertwine.

Many historians dismiss Henrietta Maria as more interested in people than in politics; Samuel Gardiner argued, laying down the foundation for many subsequent characterizations of the queen, "Of politics the Queen was completely ignorant, and it was always difficult to interest her in them, unless some personal question was involved."[125] The queen is most often regarded as personally motivated, partisan, or "bigoted" in promoting Catholicism. Such judgments on Henrietta Maria participate in a more general habit of depicting Catholic women in seventeenth-century England as beneath politics. Foreign queens and papist mistresses, Catholic women in general distract men from political action rather than participating in it fully and legitimately themselves. Anti-Catholic and anti-Royalist polemic and the histories that reproduce their terms thus place Henrietta Maria in a double bind: consigning her to the private, they then censure her for taking everything too personally. Seventeenth-century Royalists try to break this bind by defending the queen consort's engagement in polit-

123. *Satyr Occasioned by the Author's Survey,* sigs. A4r–v.
124. *A Nest of Perfidious Vipers; or, The Second Part of the Parliaments Kalender of Black Saints* (London, 1644), p. 8.
125. Samuel R. Gardiner, *History of England from the Accession of James I to the Outbreak of the Civil War, 1603–1642,* 10 vols. (London: Longmans, 1884), 6: 367. According to Gardiner, Henrietta Maria could have used her influence to real political consequence, but "she was too happy in the immediate present, too little capable at any time of a sustained effort, except when some personal object was at stake" (7: 106). Following Gardiner's formative interpretation, Sharpe argues that in the queen's household, unlike the king's, "affection for persons and support for policies" were closely connected ("Image of Virtue," p. 256); Veevers argues that Henrietta Maria had an "interest in people rather than politics" (*Images of Love and Religion,* p. 1). In all her work, Hibbard questions the assumption that the queen was more motivated by the personal than any of the other players in Stuart court politics.

ical action as a form of wifely duty. They thereby question the standard of
an impersonal politics against which Henrietta Maria is found wanting.
Why wouldn't a wife work on her husband's behalf? Why wouldn't a sister
appeal to her brother for help?

Other advocates for the queen stress that she helped the Catholic cause
by acting independently of her husband, and even in opposition to him.
After Henrietta Maria's death, for instance, a member of her clerical staff
praised her as "the cause" of "great benefits" to English Catholics, and as
"the *primum mobile* that impelled the whole machine; nothing was done but
under her authority and protection."[126] Like defenses of Marian devotion,
then, defenses of Henrietta Maria both insist on the authority that women
can exercise legitimately through traditional roles, as wives and mothers,
and, erratically, press toward a positive conception of the inversion widely
feared not only in anti-Catholic texts but in early modern discourses generally. Some Catholic writers found it possible to describe a woman in the
terms used to describe a husband, a king, a god—as a *primum mobile*—and
to mean it as a compliment, as a justification for reverence rather than
abuse. While this positive interpretation of inversion is especially striking,
Catholic defenses of women as partners, as beside rather than on top,
make the more significant, if subtler, contribution to the history of gender. Misogyny was an invaluable tool for various political and rhetorical
projects. Yet, as Royalist and Catholic responses to writers such as Prynne
make clear, the very vigor and availability of misogyny reveals the instabil-
ity of heterosexuality. A social order that depends on both heterosexuality
and misogyny is a social order divided against itself. Attacks on the Virgin
Mary and Henrietta Maria teeter on the brink of wishing that Jesus had no
mother, that the queen were a man, that sovereigns of heaven and earth
could reproduce themselves without recourse to women. By pointing this
out, defenses of the Virgin Mary and Henrietta Maria undermined Protestant England—with all its purported investment in spiritual equality and
companionate marriage—more successfully than Guy Fawkes could do
with his barrels of powder.

The queen's role as mother was inseparable from her roles as wife and
queen. Her maternity was, quite literally, highly visible; she was often pregnant as she worked on her husband's behalf; she gave birth, for instance,
on January 29, 1639; July 8, 1640; and June 16, 1644.[127] While these pregnancies were central to Royalist praise of the queen, and, less directly, to

126. Cyprien of Gamache, "Memoirs," p. 453; see also p. 464.
127. From early 1642 on, Henrietta Maria and Charles were often apart. She presided
over troops at York and en route to Kineton, where she and Charles were reunited, in June
and July 1643.

Puritan and Parliamentarian suspicion of her, one must dig for the details of Henrietta Maria's fecundity in histories and biographies. Quentin Bone, who offers the most concrete information, subordinates it in a note: "Since the queen was frequently bearing children during these years, it would be monotonous to mention the birth of each child in the main body of this work."[128] Royalist discourses, however, emphasize the queen's fertility from the beginning. George Marceline's commemoration of the marriage, *Epithalamium Gallo-Britannicum*, expresses the wish that Henrietta Maria will be "the happie Mother of many children, and Hee [Charles] the fortunate Father and Progenitour of many Princes."[129] Such nuptial wishes relatively quickly turned to celebrations of the queen as a "fruitful vine."[130] Henrietta Maria had given birth to the two princes who would be kings by November 1633; she bore a total of eight children. As one late seventeenth-century biographer, John Verney, explains: "This was the service she did her King and his Government, to bring him each year a prop of Empire; and his people a security of Succession." The very "security of Succession" that heartened Royalists gave others pause. Verney also remarks that after the birth and death of her first child, the queen "endured . . . the muttering of others, who said, they could discern no cause of joy, in her being with Child, God having better provided for us, in the hopeful Progeny of [Charles's sister, Elizabeth,] the Queen of *Bohemia*," whose issue would presumably be Protestant.[131]

Attitudes toward Henrietta Maria's maternity did not divide neatly down party lines—Royalists in favor, Parliamentarians against; Catholics in favor, Protestants against. Nor were these attitudes focused solely on a secure succession and which party stood to gain by it. Let us return to the comparisons made between Henrietta Maria and the Virgin Mary. If the queen of England's role in the Caroline court resembles that of the queen of

128. Quentin Bone, *Henrietta Maria: Queen of the Cavaliers* (Urbana: University of Illinois Press, 1972), p. 86n58.

129. Marceline, *Epithalamium Gallo-Britannicum*, sig. H3.

130. *The True Effigies of Our Most Illustrious Soveraigne Lord, King Charles, Queene Mary, with the Rest of the Royall Progenie* (London, 1641). Henrietta Maria was only fifteen in 1625, when the marriage was solemnized; her pregnancies began when she was nineteen. It has been remarked that she did not become pregnant until after Buckingham's assassination. He was killed in August 1628; Henrietta Maria's first pregnancy was announced seven months later (Mar. 25, 1629) and ended in premature delivery and stillbirth in May 1629. This may not be as precise a passing of the torch, so to speak, as Derek Hirst suggests when he claims that "Henrietta Maria's first confinement came nine months after the duke's death," but the timing does seem significant (*Authority and Conflict: England, 1603–1658* [Cambridge: Harvard University Press, 1986], p. 156).

131. Verney, *Life and Death of That Matchless Mirrour of Magnanimity*, pp. 24, 19–20.

heaven, as Prynne contends, then her influence must emerge from her authority as mother rather than her intimacy as wife. Indeed, the couple at the center of Marian devotion is mother and son, not husband and wife, the mother, significantly, taking the lead position. Royalist idealizations of Henrietta Maria conjoin her roles as wife and mother in fascinating ways. *Epithalamium Gallo-Britannicum,* for instance, the same text that joyously anticipates Henrietta Maria's fertility, insists that Charles's new bride resembles his mother. He is, as a consequence, happy "in finding a kinde of mother in a wife, so like Her, who may serve Him for his mothers picture, at all times to looke on, with a respective, loving, joyfull remembrance, to see his mother living in Her."[132] The mother Charles sees in her is, of course, dead; she was also a mother with whom he spent little time, and who exercised little power over her husband or in his court. Marceline's remarkable conflation of wife and mother domesticates Henrietta Maria as a foreigner who has already been absorbed into the English royal family, and reduces her to a "picture" of a peaceful and safely completed past. Yet he also confers on her potential influence over her husband/son.

A later Royalist defense of the queen, against the charges made by the publisher of the "king's cabinet" of correspondence, does not so remarkably conflate wife and mother. But it does slide rapidly from one to the other, beginning in a defense of wives' right to give advice, moving on to a defense of queens (passing over the difference between a queen regnant and a queen consort), and building toward Henrietta Maria's status as mother:

> For among all sorts of men are Kings only bound their wives shall be no helpers to them? And what though the Queene be of the weaker sex, must she therefore have no share in Counsells? Sure he that will thus argue against Queen *Maries* advise, makes Libells against Queene *Elizabeth.* Nor are her abilities of the lesse use for being borne in *France.* For though a meere *Alien* may be suspected to incline too much to that Nation he was borne in, yet such suspicions vanish where greater reasons appeare; and sure none will deny me this, that to be a wife of *England* is a stronger tye,

132. Marceline, *Epithalamium Gallo-Britannicum,* sig. S3. Charles's grandmother Mary Stuart was also described by her staunch defender John Leslie as her husband's mother. Leslie insisted that she would never have conspired to kill Darnley because of the "verie motherlie care" she felt toward him: "for besids all other respects, thowghe they were not farre differente in yeares, she was to him not onlie a loyall Prince, a lovinge and deare wyfe, but a most carefull and tendre mother with all" (*A Defence of the Honour of the Right Highe, Mightye and Noble Princesse Marie Quene of Scotlande* [London, 1569], sig. a6v–7). Atkinson points out that medieval devotion to Mary often conflated the roles of consort and mother, placing Mary as both to Jesus (*Oldest Vocation,* p. 110).

then to be a Daughter of *France,* especially when she is become the Mother
of a Prince which she hopes may weare the English Crowne.[133]

Note how this defense of female authority resorts to the fiction of coverture to resolve the dilemmas of divided duty and dynastic alliance; through
the miraculous transformations enacted by marriage a daughter of France
becomes a wife of England. Her role as mother is not threatening here, but
redemptive, transcending conflicts of interest and erasing previous allegiances. Whereas Marceline attached Henrietta Maria to the past by casting
her as Charles's dead mother, this text insists that the queen's motherhood
attaches her to the future, reordering her priorities more significantly
even than matrimony. Read in retrospect, this text seems to anticipate the
ways in which Henrietta Maria's Restoration biographers turn to her role
as mother to justify her survival as widow, to give shape to her story after
her husband is dead.[134] Royalist discourses written across almost sixty years
(from the queen's marriage to the accession of her son James) defend the
queen as wife and mother, and by extension uphold women's authority
in both roles. Such discourses resolutely restrict women within traditional gender structures; yet Catholic female figures such as the Virgin
Mary and Henrietta Maria, however exceptional, provoked unease by operating within, rather than outside of, those structures.

After all, how "traditional" was motherhood for an English queen?
Henry VIII's wives were so numerous and so ill fated in large part because
of their collective inability to produce a hearty male heir; in their histories,
miscarriages, disappointing female births, and accusations of illegitimacy
precede and predict the sexual scandals and executions. Mary Tudor was
plagued by phantom pregnancies and never produced an heir. Elizabeth,
of course, never married; furthermore, while some contemporary writers
praised her as the mother of her people, Rose shows that she rarely presented herself this way.[135] Her reluctance to position herself as either the
Virgin Mary or a mother suggests her canny awareness that both positions
were too embattled to bolster her claims to legitimacy. James I owed his
throne to his two mothers, Elizabeth and Mary Stuart, and, with his wife,

133. *Letter, in Which the Arguments of the Annotator,* sig. A3v.
134. See Dauncey, *History of the Thrice Illustrious Princess;* and Verney, *Life and Death of that Matchless Mirrour of Magnanimity.* See also *An Elegie on the Death of the Most Serene Majesty of Henrietta-Maria* (London, 1669) and *An Elegy upon the Death of the Most Illustrious Princess Henrietta Maria* (London, 1670). Percy Herbert's Royalist roman à clef, *The Princess Cloria; or, The Royal Romance* (London, 1661), similarly dwells on the queen's role as mother.
135. Mary Beth Rose, "Gender and the Construction of Royal Authority in the Speeches of Elizabeth I," chap. 2 of "Gender and the Transformation of Heroism in English Renais-
sance Literature" (manuscript).

Anne, produced six children, of whom three lived past infancy: Henry, who died before he could succeed; the future Charles I; and Elizabeth of Bohemia, who had many children. Although James's (Catholic) wife, Anne, was crucial to his founding of a Stuart dynasty, James redressed his dependence on mothers, his own and his children's, by suppressing them in his account of a patriarchal genealogy proceeding directly from his own body. As Jonathan Goldberg has argued, in James's idealized genealogies, mothers are dead or absent or absorbed into fathers.[136] In addition to this symbolic appropriation of maternity into himself, James also attempted to limit his wife's control of their children, insisting that the queen not raise them herself.[137] For James, then, the symbolic power of motherhood was especially useful when it was separated from a pregnant, lactating body. In this history, the status of the queen regnant was distinct from and considerably higher than that of the queen pregnant.

Henrietta Maria's fertility, then, oft represented and far surpassing that of her recent predecessors, conjoined with her open Catholicism to make her a controversial figure. It is unclear how much influence Henrietta Maria actually had over her children. Despite her marriage articles, at least the two oldest boys had Anglican baptisms, which their mother may not have attended.[138] She made various efforts to urge the children toward Catholicism, including taking Prince Charles to mass with her in the 1630s, until the king intervened. In *Romes Master-peece; or, The Grand Conspiracy* (1644), William Prynne warns that the king's sons are "secretly instructed in the Popish Religion," and that the oldest prince, the future Charles II, was particularly "educated from his tender age, that hee might accustome himselfe to the Popish party."[139] Obviously, the queen was assumed to be a conduit, if not the source, of this influence on the royal children.

Conflicts over control of Prince Charles, more with Parliament than with her husband, contributed to Henrietta Maria's final flight from England.[140] According to Quentin Bone, "a prince under the religious influence of a strongly Catholic mother was for the Puritans an inadmissible danger to Protestantism in England."[141] After Charles I's execution, it is uncertain how much influence Henrietta Maria had on the prince;[142] but, as king,

136. Goldberg, *James I and the Politics of Literature*, chap. 2, esp. pp. 88, 99.
137. See Williams, *Anne of Denmark*, pp. 52–57.
138. Havran, *Catholics in Caroline England*, p. 57; Henrietta Haynes, *Henrietta Maria* (New York: Putnam, 1912), p. 117; Hibbard, *Charles I and the Popish Plot*, p. 39.
139. William Prynne, *Romes Master-peece; or, The Grand Conspiracy* (London, 1644), pp. 23, 18.
140. Hibbard, *Charles I and the Popish Plot*, pp. 221–23.
141. Bone, *Henrietta Maria*, p. 74.
142. Ibid., pp. 230–33; and Oman, *Henrietta Maria*, pp. 211–13.

Charles II was suspected of being "crypto-Catholic," a suspicion confirmed
when he converted on his deathbed; his brother James II was openly Catholic. As in disputes regarding Henrietta Maria's influence over her husband, the point is that contemporaries assumed that the queen had power,
and feared the power that they thought she had. In a period when Catholic mothers were thought to be dangerously influential and their contributions to children's education an insidious means of maintaining, even
disseminating, Catholicism, she came to stand as a symbolic figurehead for
Catholicism's generativity and motherhood's ascendancy.

CATHOLIC MOTHERS

Suspicion of Catholic mothers focused not only on the Virgin Mary's
heavenly court of appeals and on Henrietta Maria's London one. It extended beyond these extraordinary women to ordinary Catholic wives and
mothers, beyond polemical attacks to legislative attempts to intervene in
the daily practices of Catholic life. In Chapter 2 I argued that penal legislation focused on the wife, and on the dilemma of maximizing her accountability and accessibility without dismantling the legal fiction of coverture, which had become the model of right relations not only in the
household but in the nation and the cosmos. Penal laws were also concerned with women's authority as mothers.

Legal regulation sought to curtail Catholics' efforts to transmit their
faith to their children through education.[143] In early modern England,
both prescription and practice ascribed control over children's education
and marriages to parents, and defended this control as a basic prerogative.
Yet child-rearing practices at various social levels limited parents' direct,
daily influence on their children: families at the top of the social system
might first send infants off to a wetnurse, and later exchange children or
send them to serve at court or, in the case of Catholics, abroad to be educated; families lower down might send their children into service or ar-
range apprenticeships for them. The issue, then, was not proximity to
one's children but control over the decisions that determined who would
raise them and how. Aggressive attempts to abrogate Catholic fathers'
rights ultimately failed, in part because such legislation would have undermined paternal prerogative more generally. Still, a frank suspicion of

---

143. John Bossy, *The English Catholic Community, 1570–1850* (New York: Oxford University Press, 1976), p. 161; and A. C. F. Beales, *Education under Penalty: English Catholic Education from the Reformation to the Fall of James II, 1547–1689* (London: Athlone, 1963), chap. 6.

recusant mothers pervaded the enacted legislation, which sought less ambivalently to curtail mothers' power.

Polemical and legal assaults on Catholic mothers' influence assumed, as did attacks on the Virgin Mary and Henrietta Maria, that mothers were powerful and that they could determine their children's religion. In those households in which a husband and father conformed as a "church papist," leaving it to his wife to maintain the family's religious identity, she might do so not only by recusing herself from Anglican services but by catechizing her children. From the perspective of those who proposed and supported various bills to regulate the education of Catholic children, Catholic households were schools of disobedience and godlessness. Acknowledging the household as a crucial mechanism for propagating the faith, the staunchest Protestants wanted it to operate only according to their own interests. To protect Protestant families, Parliament proposed to invade and undermine Catholic ones, revealing thereby that they valued only certain families and promoted the authority of only some patriarchs, only conditionally. The father, like the husband, had to earn his privileges, and could always lose them.

Two different kinds of legislation were proposed regarding Catholic children. The first, which was frequently proposed and debated but never enacted, sought to wrest children away from recusant parents. The second, which was enacted but only erratically enforced, sought to limit parents' attempts to export their children to the Continent for a Catholic education there.

The first kind of legislation was largely a Jacobean and Caroline phenomenon. Parliament did not make an explicit proposal for "the taking of Papists' children from them" until 1605, although a sustained attempt had been made from 1593 to 1603. In almost every parliament under James, proposals to force Catholics to send their children to Protestant households or schools were renewed and debated. Parliament debated "seize the children" bills and motions in 1605, 1610, 1621, 1624, 1625, 1641, 1642, 1646, 1649 (when five educational laws were passed), and 1677. These parliamentary attempts to tamper with parents' otherwise sacrosanct control over their children's upbringing responded to what were viewed as the inadequate efforts of Stuart kings to suppress Catholicism; perhaps if Catholicism could be cut off at the root, the kings' temporizing would be less problematic. These bills and motions also struck at the paternal prerogative to which Stuart kings analogized their own sovereignty. It was a prerogative, however, that members of Parliament also enjoyed, and was inseparable from available notions of property and manhood. As a result, none of these bills was enacted into law. Yet the one stipulation of that first

explicit proposal in 1605 which did find its way into the penal code was
that "no man whose wife was a recusant could hold office unless he educated his children as Protestants and took them to church." "Thus," according to A. C. F. Beales, "was Parliament recognizing the key-position of
the mother in Catholic education."[144] This was a "key-position" that penal
laws recognized only in order to circumscribe.

Although these legislative initiatives failed, for the most part, a feudal
practice survived that sometimes enabled the crown to seize Catholic children—but only in the event of their fathers' death. Whatever authority fathers had and however reluctant the government was, finally, to set the
precedent of limiting that authority, fathers did not live forever. When a
father died, the wardship system intervened to ensure that his absence did
not necessarily empower the mother. A survival of feudal land tenures,
wardship dictated that if a landowning gentleman died while his heir was
still a minor, his estate temporarily reverted back to the "lord"—that is, the
sovereign—rather than pass directly to the heir or into his mother's governance. The sovereign therefore had the right to appoint a guardian at
his or her discretion. This guardian managed the ward's estate and over-
saw his or her education and marriage. The potential for corruption was
great. In practice, the wardship system operated as a kind of inheritance
tax; in choosing wardships, the crown could benefit those named guardians
and punish the ward's family.[145] Recusants were prevented from serving as
guardians, an indication that the position was considered one of power
and profit.

A Jacobean statute (3 and 4 Jac. I, cap. 5, sec. 21) dictated that "for the
better Education and Preservation" of recusants' children and their estates, custody of wards should go to the next of kin who conforms.[146] The
selection of guardians, however, was not so consistent in breaking up Catholic families as this legislation would suggest. First, the granting of wardships was a prerogative of the crown, and Stuart kings sought to eradicate
Catholicism only inconsistently and in conjunction with various other political aims. As a consequence, those instances in which Catholic children
were assigned to Protestant guardians cannot be taken "as evidence of any

144. Beales, *Education under Penalty*, pp. 91–92.
145. Joel Hurstfield, *The Queen's Wards: Wardship and Marriage under Elizabeth I* (London:
Longmans, Green, 1958); Lawrence Stone, *The Crisis of the Aristocracy, 1558–1641* (Oxford:
Clarendon, 1965), pp. 252, 440–41, 497–98, 600–605, 739–41.
146. William Cawley, *The Laws of Q. Elizabeth, K. James, and K. Charles the First. Concerning
Jesuites, Seminary Priests, Recusants, &c.* (London, 1680), sig. Hhv. See also *Statutes of the
Realm. Printed by Command of His Majesty King George the Third* (1819).

general policy of securing conformity by removing children from their parents," according to John Bossy. Royal discretion, especially as it operated regarding the property and interests of peers, could not substitute for the systematic disruption of Catholic parental power that Parliament repeatedly proposed. Not all Catholic wards were given to Protestant guardians. Bossy asserts that "by 1640 it was at least as common for the wardship of Catholic peers who succeeded as minors to be successfully acquired by their Catholic friends and relations. Outside the peerage, the prospects for successful intervention were very limited."[147] Interestingly, more Catholic children seem to have been made wards of Protestants during the Civil War and interregnum.[148]

Furthermore, wardship required the father's death. It was easier to intervene, practically and ideologically, when there was not "a Catholic father to contend with," Bossy avers. "Where there was, attempts went off at half-cock"; "the few cases where children of Catholics were brought up Protestants before the Civil War were all cases of wardship following a father's death." In Bossy's view, stepping into a father's absence "was about as much as the mainstream of opinion in the English governing class was prepared to tolerate."[149] That is, mainstream opinion could tolerate removing parental authority and control from mothers, but not from fathers. Since wardship could, at the crown's discretion, remove minors from their mothers' governance (and company) and limit mothers' control over estates and marriages, the parental prerogative the law and social custom respected did not necessarily belong to mothers. Even so, the death of fathers probably worked as often to increase mothers' authority as to strip them of their children. In practice, most wards probably remained with their mothers.[150] What the proposed legislation revealed, however, was that child rearing and education were too important to leave to women. Again, the problem was not that women strayed into the public sphere, but that the work they did in the private sphere had such important public implications. Yet, paradoxically, some penal laws worked, like mortality, to remove fathers rather than children from the household, and to leave mothers in charge. Furthermore, Parliament's most spectacular and unanticipated

147. Bossy, *English Catholic Community*, p. 162.
148. Beales, *Education under Penalty*, p. 107.
149. Bossy, *English Catholic Community*, pp. 163, 164, 162.
150. On the effect of fathers' deaths on mothers' power, see Amy Louise Erickson, *Women and Property in Early Modern England* (London: Routledge, 1993), p. 5; and Michael C. Questier, *Conversion, Politics, and Religion in England, 1580–1625* (Cambridge: Cambridge University Press, 1996), p. 106n28.

empowerment of a Catholic mother resulted from the execution of Charles I, which, ironically, left Henrietta Maria to rear England's next two kings alone.

Efforts to "seize the children" were obviously erratic. But a climate in which such action could be proposed and seriously debated was one in which Catholics had to seize their own children to ensure a Catholic education for them. It was difficult, but not impossible, to give children a Catholic education in England. One statute (1 Jac. I, cap. 4, sec. 9) dictated that schools must be kept publicly or in the houses of gentlemen who were not recusants. In other words, recusants could not have their own schools. Nor could they have their children privately tutored; to maintain a private schoolmaster could lead to a fine of 40 shillings per day. Despite these prohibitions, there were Catholic teachers in England: some taught in secret schools; some served in households under the cover of being stewards or music masters (or nurses?); some were mothers.[151] The hidden, often domestic locations of Catholic education in England were the same locations at which women were relatively powerful. Some evidence suggests that women played important roles in founding and running secret schools. In 1621, the "Great Committee" (i.e., Committee of the Whole House) expressed concern about the "Corrupt Education of their [recusants'] children either under Popish wives or Tutors."[152] Protestant polemicists often attributed early Catholic household instruction to mothers and nurses. *A Moderate Expedient for Preventing of Popery* advises that "if without great inconvenience the Children of Papists could be brought up out of their company, it were a happy turn: but I find it to be full of difficulty; there is provision made to avoid Popish School-masters, but there is no ward against Popish School-mistresses, that infect the silly Infants while they carry them in their Arms."[153] To view teaching as women's work is not to see it as unimportant, but rather to see it as pervasive and almost impossible to regulate.

Since schooling at home was, for the most part, in the hands of women, lay men, and the occasional closeted priest, it was inadequate to the needs of children intended for clerical vocations. Those who wanted to prepare their children to be nuns and priests sent them to the Continent to be

---

151. Caroline Hibbard, "Early Stuart Catholicism: Revisions and Re-Revisions," *Journal of Modern History* 52.1 (1980): 1–34, esp. 14.

152. Beales, *Education under Penalty*, pp. 208–15, 91–92, 93.

153. *A Moderate Expedient for Preventing of Popery, and the More Effectual Suppression of Jesuits and Priests, without Giving Them the Vain-glory of Pretending to Martyrdom* (London, 1680), sig. Cv.

trained in convents and seminaries.[154] Such a course was costly, entailing travel expenses as well as room, board, and tuition, and possibly fines. As a consequence, it was restricted to the relatively affluent or those with patrons.

When parliamentary rhetoric heated up, departures for the Continent increased. For instance, in anticipation and then in the wake of the educational statutes of 1649, which, according to Beales, "upheld the fundamental right of a parent's conscience to have his child brought up in his own faith" (unless "he" were Catholic), and ensured that every child would be raised Protestant, more than the usual numbers of children and adolescents went abroad. Beales relates that "the business of intercepting them was so brisk as to involve disputes among the port authorities themselves."[155] Under such circumstances, the Privy Council more closely scrutinized the granting of travel passes to recusants and watched the ports to monitor and restrict the traffic in children. Concern so focused on the transportation of Catholic children that in Cawley's late seventeenth-century guide to penal laws, the index entry for "Children" reads "see Seas."

Why not let these children leave? Why not encourage, or at least ignore, the export of Catholic children in the hope of decreasing the English recusant population? There were several concerns. One was the export of English resources, young people and cash. Another reason was surely an unwillingness to surrender children to Catholic influence and control, to let the children, and thereby the future, go. The most vehement objections to the transport of children warned that they would not stay away permanently, but would return strangers. Thomas Abernethie warns of the danger from "the education of your Nobilitie at schooles in forraine countries, who having drunke in the doctrine of iniquitie from their tender age, are both more perverse in themselves, and more dangerous, bringing in their friends and neighbours, by their Priests to perdition with them."[156] Privileging Catholicism over "Englishness," especially by seeking a Catholic education in a "foreign" country for their children, English recusants maintain international Catholic alliances to the detriment of English national security. Miles Prance explains

154. Hibbard, "Early Stuart Catholicism," pp. 18–19; Havran, *Catholics in Caroline England,* pp. 5–7; see also 117–18. On English Catholic convents, seminaries, and educational institutions on the Continent, see Peter Guilday, *The English Catholic Refugees on the Continent, 1558–1795,* vol. 1, *English Colleges and Convents in the Catholic Low Countries, 1558–1795* (London: Longmans, 1914).

155. Beales, *Education under Penalty,* p. 105.

156. Thomas Abernethie, *Abjuration of Poperie* (London, 1638), sig. F3v; cf. *A Worthy Speech, by Mr. Tho. Abernethie* (London, 1641), sig. A4.

the general practice of the Popish Gentry, to send over their Children thither, being made believe, that we have no good method of Learning in our English Schools or Universities; but that the onely grand Masters of Education in the world, are the Jesuits. By which means, not onely our Nation is scandaliz'd, and the Wealth thereof privately drain'd away, but also it comes to pass, that the Children of so many Noble and Considerable Families, being bred up from their tender years wholly under their Tuition, they have the better opportunities to instil Traiterous and Disloyal Principles into their minds, plant in them an endless hatred against the Protestant Religion, and in general, gain such an Ascendant over them, that as they were their Masters and Tutors in their Youth, so they behave themselves as their Governours all their lives afterwards: the Estates of many Popish Gentry being as absolutely at the Priests dispose, as at their own.[157]

The depiction of the "Popish Gentry" as priests' dupes impugned their manhood and their credibility; it might even serve as a warning to them. It also avoided the troubling question of Catholic gentlemen's consent.

In a similar vein, John Gee warns that, in the end, priests betray those who have sheltered them, "stealing away their children, and sending them beyond the seas, to their utter ruine and overthrowe. This is too common a practice."[158] Like Prance's, Gee's narrative of kidnapping masks the possibly more disturbing one of consent. Might not Catholic fathers *choose* to send their children to Catholic schools? If anyone or anything interferes with recusant fathers' paternal rights, it is not priests but penal laws. In her account of her own conversion to Protestantism, Helen Livingston similarly begs the question of Catholic fathers' responsibility. As an example of the disobedience and disorder fostered by the "Roman Kirk," Livingston cites "the disobedience of young infants towards their fathers and mothers, maintained & authorized by the Roman Kirk, when a young childe is entred into a closter contrare the will of his father."[159] The young child disobeys both parents, but "is entred into a closter" against the *father's* will. Unspoken, but just below the surface, is the mother's will, or perhaps the alliance of mother and priest. All of the writers I have quoted on this point—Abernethie, Prance, Gee, and Livingston—are apostates. Revealing the dirty little secret of how Catholicism corrupts youth, they insist that it countermands fathers rather than divides some fathers against others. By imagining all fathers as Protestants, these writers can argue that any in-

---

157. *A True Narrative and Discovery of Several Very Remarkable Passages Relating to the Horrid Popish Plot: as They Fell within the Knowledge of Mr. Miles Prance* (London, 1679), sigs. Bv–B2.
158. John Gee, *The Foot Out of the Snare* (London, 1624), sig. D2.
159. Livingston, *Confession and Conversion*, p. 16.

tervention in Catholic households promotes rather than undermines paternal power.

Operating on the assumption that all children transported across the
seas were being sent to seminaries, penal laws imposed increasingly harsh
penalties for sending children abroad "to prevent their good Education in
England, or for any cause." Elizabeth imposed a £100 fine for every offense. James added that children sent abroad would be disqualified from
inheriting unless they took the oath of allegiance and received the sacrament upon their return. Charles I's one contribution to the penal code
elaborated that any party involved in such a transaction—sending or
sent—"shall be disabled from thenceforth to sue or use any Action, Bill,
Plaint or Information, in course of Law, or to prosecute any Suit in any
Court of Equity, or to be Committee of any Ward, or Executor or Admin-
istrator to any person, or capable of any Legacy or Deed of Gift, or to bear
any Office within the Realm, and shall lose and forfeit all his Goods and
Chattels; and shall forfeit all his Lands, Tenements and Hereditaments,
Rents, Annuities, Offices and Estates of Freehold for and during his natural Life." This statute further emphasizes that children are not to be conveyed out of the king's dominions "to the intent and purpose to enter into,
or be resident or trained up in any Priory, Abbey, Nunnery, Popish University, Colledge, or School, or House of Jesuites, Priests, or in any private
Popish Family, and shall be there by any Jesuite, Seminary Priest, Friar,
Monk, or other Popish Person instructed, perswaded or strengthened in
the Popish Religion, in any sort to profess the same."[160] It was also illegal
to send financial support to children enrolled in schools abroad.

Penal laws increasingly, yet confusingly, associate children and women
and seek to prohibit the movements of both. Cawley summarizes the first
law prohibiting the export of children (27 Eliz., cap. 2 , sec. 6) as: "None
shall send *his* Child or other beyond the Seas without licence." Such li-
cense could be obtained only from the queen herself or from four Privy
Counsel members. This law later (by 1 Jac. 1, cap. 4, sec. 8) became: "*No
Woman*, nor any Child under the age of one and twenty years (except Sail-
ers or Ship-boys, or the Apprentice or Factor of some Merchant in Trade
of Merchandize) shall be permitted to pass over the Seas" without the
king's permission or that of six or more Privy Council members.[161] One of

160. Cawley, *Laws . . . Concerning . . . Recusants*, sigs. Ff4, Llv, Ll (on 3 Car. I, cap. 2). As
early as August 1625, Charles ordered English parents to bring back children sent abroad
to be educated in Catholic schools or seminaries (Bone, *Henrietta Maria*, p. 47).

161. Cawley, *Laws . . . Concerning . . . Recusants*, sigs. N3v (marginal gloss on 27 Eliz.,
cap. 2), X2. The emphasis is mine in both quotations.

the most stringent failed bills was the "Popish Recusants (Children's Education) Bill" of 1677, which proposed a £1,000 fine "for any boy under twenty-one years of age (or any woman at all) sent abroad in the care of any popish recusant."[162] In *Romes Master-peece,* Prynne, whose articulations of anxiety are always so telling, argues that the Earl of Arundel maintains at Greenwich "a feminine School" from which girls are "sent forth hither and thither into forraine Monasteries beyond the Seas."[163] In Prynne's intemperate tract, as in penal legislation, the suggestion is that English Catholics are mobilizing their resources to educate women as well as children. Here Catholicism, so often accused of promoting illiteracy and ignorance, is censured for promoting women's education. Why single out women in this way? Why target the mobility of adult women as more threatening than that of adult men? In part, both the legislation (enacted and proposed) and the polemic infantilize women, assuming that they, like children, are more vulnerable to seduction, more malleable. This assumed female vulnerability shapes many anti-Catholic discourses and underlies many eroticized constructions of that troublesome couple, the priest and the woman. Women are also allied with children through a lack of legal agency; neither the married woman nor the child is capable of choosing and consenting—or of being fined or punished. The dilemma in penal laws and in polemic about the traffic in children and women is exactly who is responsible. Who is to blame? Who is to be penalized?

On the one hand, fathers were most likely to have had the authority to make decisions about their children's education and vocations; they were also most likely to have been able to command the resources to support such a costly commitment. On the other hand, the laws avoid explicitly targeting fathers, in part because this would be too direct an assault on paternal prerogative. Thus paternal agency gradually disappears from the law. The phrasing moves from a direct prohibition of paternal action ("None shall send his child") to phrasing that bypasses the father to focus on his dependents ("No woman or child shall pass").

Many adult women "passed" over the seas to enter English convents; many also played some role in smuggling children abroad, sometimes with the consent of conforming or recusant husbands, sometimes in defiance of Protestant husbands, sons, or guardians. In this context, the now fairly well known story of Elizabeth Cary's audacity in kidnapping her youngest sons, Patrick and Henry, and smuggling them abroad seems less an idiosyncratic self-assertion than participation in a collective strategy to propa-

162. Beales, *Education under Penalty,* p. 113.
163. Prynne, *Romes Master-peece,* p. 23.

gate the faith. Indeed, according to Beales, Privy Council records suggest that in 1635–36, around the time this incident occurred, the traffic in children was greater, or the Privy Council was more interested in it, than "for any year before or since till the Catholic revival under James II"; Beales cites, for instance, heightened scrutiny of permits for foreign travel.[164]

The transfer of the Cary children occurred in 1636, three years after Cary's husband's death, while the two boys were living with Cary's oldest son, Lucius (a Protestant). According to the biography of Cary, apparently written by one of her four daughters (who became not only Catholics but nuns) as a somewhat ambivalent defense of her mother, Cary had warned Lucius that she would steal the boys away if he did not send them abroad. She chose her moment when two of her daughters, who would assist the plan from inside the house, were visiting Lucius. The daughters delivered the boys to two hired men, who then carried them on horseback to Abington, where they were handed over to a third man, who took them to London by water. There they awaited their carriage "beyond the seas," while their mother outfaced the Privy Council and marshaled needed funds and assistance.

The Lady Falkland, Her Life insists that Cary did not steal the boys against their will but responded to their own desires. In their mother's house they had "received great inclinations to the Catholic religion (though they were very young), which made her have some design from that time to steal them away." Even at Lucius's, they retained "the extraordinary desire . . . to see themselves Catholics." They cooperated with the scheme because their "desire to go was so great," even walking over a mile alone to meet the strange men waiting for them, "which plainly showed they were not brought away by force."[165] The *Calendar of State Papers, Domestic Series* also records Cary's insistence that her sons chose to leave, "both having been very desirous to be sent for away."[166]

After highlighting the young boys' "desire," the biographer then asserts Elizabeth Cary's right as widowed mother and the force of her "will." Before the Privy Council, by her daughter's account, Cary insisted that she could not steal something that was hers; decisions about the boys' residence and education were hers to make. "Though she had been forced to

164. Beales, *Education under Penalty*, p. 100.
165. Elizabeth Cary, *"The Tragedy of Mariam, Queen of Jewry," with "The Lady Falkland: Her Life,"* by one of her daughters, ed. Barry Weller and Margaret W. Ferguson (Berkeley: University of California Press, 1994), pp. 244, 249, 256, 259.
166. *Calendar of State Papers, Domestic Series,* ed. F. H. Blackburne Daniell (1921) (Nedeln, Liechtenstein: Kraus Reprints, 1968) (hereafter *CSPD*), 1635–36, pp. 431–32; on the "kidnapping," see also pp. 444, 451–52.

fetch them away from their brother's secretly, she had in that done nothing contrary to the law, since she could not be said to have stolen that which
was her own, her son having no pretense to right to keep his brothers from
her against her will and theirs, having never been committed to him neither by the state, nor their father."[167] Especially given that Lucius was not
the boys' legal guardian, the issue was not stealing them but transporting
them abroad.

When the Privy Council reminded her that "it was against the law to
send them to seminaries," Cary asked them to prove that she had done
so.[168] According to the *Calendar of State Papers,* Cary claimed not to know
where her sons were, and refused to say whether she had determined where
they would go; she did, however, insist "that she has not sent them to any
religious house or person, or to be instructed in any religion, but has left
them freely to that religion wherein they have been brought up."[169]

According to the *Life,* Cary pointed out that if it was possible to get
through the ports without a pass from the Privy Council, as required by
law, then officers of the port should be legally accountable, not she. De-
murring at the charge that she was trying to "teach [the Council] law," she
reminded the Council that she was a lawyer's daughter; this background
seems to have enabled her to zero in on the fuzziness of laws regarding the
traffic in children—they left accountability vague. If her children had
"passed" beyond the seas and it could not be proved that she knew where
they were, had determined their destination, or had participated in their
actual transport, whose criminality was under discussion? Because of such
"uncertain and illusory answers," she was committed to the Tower.[170]

Her sons in fact were still in London. As long as they remained there, no
crime had been committed, by any interpretation of the penal law. If Cary
had revealed their location, she would have been off the hook; yet she
would also have lost her chance to get them out of the country. By persist-
ing in equivocation, she outlasted the Council's interest and, with the help
of a priest, got the boys to Paris, where they settled in a Benedictine seminary, although both eventually abandoned their religious orders.[171]

However extraordinary Elizabeth Cary's "will" in opposing her eldest
son and the Privy Council, she could not have gotten the boys to that seminary by herself. Like other parents seeking a Catholic education and reli-

---

167. *Lady Falkland: Her Life,* ed. Weller and Ferguson, p. 258.
168. Ibid., p. 259.
169. *CSPD,* 1635–36, pp. 431–32. Cary stood before the Privy Council on May 16, 1636.
170. Ibid., pp. 451–52.
171. Patrick married; he also seems to have made excisions and annotations in the *Life*
of his mother.

gious vocations for their children, Cary needed powerful contacts and willing hirelings; she also needed money. In *An Antidote against Purgatory* (1634), Jane Owen tries to persuade Catholics of "the greater Ranke and best abilities" to finance the transportation and continental education of Catholic children. "For if neither any places of Residence beyond the Seas had beene provided, and furnished with sufficient maintenance for the bringing up of English Schollers; nor that there had beene any Catholikes, who would have opened their purses to this noble End, Catholike Religion had beene utterly extinct many yeares since, in England."[172] For even the most affluent families, sending one or more children abroad would require contacts inside England and abroad. The less affluent would also need financial help. Cary's situation was unique, then, not because she needed assistance but because she was in such a good position to command it. Her social position was high and her contacts were impressive: her husband had a title, Lord Viscount Falkland, and served as lord deputy of Ireland; one daughter served as maid of honor to Henrietta Maria, who recommended another daughter to the queen of Spain as a court attendant.[173] Powerful patrons helped Cary survive the indigence that resulted when her father and husband learned of her conversion to Catholicism and cut her off financially.

Much of the assistance Cary received came from other Catholic women. Many, including the Countess of Buckingham and Henrietta Maria, lent or gave her money; the queen also worked to reconcile the estranged spouses. While the king was censuring Cary's conversion and her refusal to produce the missing boys, his wife was working on Cary's behalf. Henrietta Maria's intercessions, financial and otherwise, worked in support of Elizabeth Cary's maternal "will"—Catholic education and religious vocations for the children. The biography suggests that Henrietta Maria financially supported Cary's children in their convents and seminaries, even after their mother's death: "For the maintenance of her sons where they were, she did allot something which she received from the charity of her most Excellent Majesty, who was graciously pleased to continue it to them after her death, till the extremity of these times." The queen commanded Lucius to allow one sister to become a nun; she spoke up for another to the king.[174] Hen-

---

172. Owen, *Antidote against Purgatory*, pp. 203, 204–5.
173. *CSPD*, 1635, p. 578.
174. *Lady Falkland: Her Life*, ed. Weller and Ferguson, pp. 263, 274. The daughter whose vocation Henrietta Maria defended was Mary, the daughter Cary had pledged to the Virgin (pp. 272–74). Henrietta Maria also helped Mary Ward, when she lived in London from 1639 to 1641. Pope Urban VIII suppressed Ward's unenclosed teaching order, the Institute of the Blessed Virgin Mary, in 1631; yet he provided Ward with a letter of introduction that she might present to the queen. See Henriette Peters, *Mary Ward: A World in Contemplation*,

rietta Maria's various interventions on behalf of other women reveal that, as anti-Catholic writers feared, Catholicism could unite women despite class and other differences. However exceptional her status, the queen was not just a symbolic figurehead for English Catholics but a material help to them. While Elizabeth Cary's husband, Henry, complained about his wife in terms very similar to those many used to describe the French queen— "How very unsafe it is for me to nourish that serpent longer in my bosom that deals so treasonably with me"—the alliance between his wife and the queen suggests that the problem was not individual traitorous wives, who might be expelled from one's "bed and bosom," but an insidious network of them.[175]

In the *Life* of Elizabeth Cary, written by a woman and from a pro-Catholic perspective, as in attacks on Henrietta Maria, the inspiration for this community of women is the Virgin Mary, who not only conjoins maternity with agency and authority but asserts that combination as "adorable." Unsurprisingly, the Virgin Mary appears in the *Life* at moments of maternal crisis. First, the author attests to Cary's proto-Catholic sympathies and beliefs even while she was "still a Protestant," by describing how she "bore a great and high reverence to our blessed Lady"; this devotion was particularly manifested during her pregnancy (in 1621/22) with her youngest daughter, Mary, whom she pledged *in utero* to the Virgin as a future nun. Next, after Cary's return from Ireland but before her conversion was made public, probably sometime in 1625, her eldest daughter, Catherine, died in her arms after the difficult delivery of a premature infant who died shortly thereafter. Cary apparently took comfort from evidence of Catherine's deathbed turn toward Catholicism, most vividly manifested in the vision she described of "a bright woman clothed in white, having a crown on he[r] head; which she then assuredly believed to be our Blessed Lady, and persuaded her daughter the same."[176] Similarly, a Catholic account of Henrietta Maria's Marian devotion links it to the perils of maternity. Since she "had always regarded the most Blessed Virgin as her good mistress and her dear mother," the queen prayed for her "powerful intercession" during a "bad lying-in." As a consequence, she "received immedi-

---

trans. Helen Butterworth (Leominster, Herts.: Gracewing, 1991); Margaret Mary Little-hales, I.B.V.M, *Mary Ward (1585–1645): A Woman for All Seasons* (London: Catholic Truth Society, 1974), p. 27; and Mary Ward, *Till God Will: Mary Ward through Her Writings*, ed. M. Emmanuel Orchard (London: Darton, Longman, & Todd, 1985), pp. 112–18.

175. Letter from Dublin Castle, dated Dec. 29, 1626, to "Right Honorable Sir," possibly Coke; see *The Lady Falkland: Her Life*, ed. Richard Simpson (London: Catholic Publishing, 1861), Appendix, p. 140.

176. *Lady Falkland: Her Life*, ed. Weller and Ferguson, pp. 196, 202.

ately an extraordinary ease, which was followed by a very happy delivery and perfect health."[177] Such intercessions would have been especially comforting to women who bore as many children as Henrietta Maria and Elizabeth Cary did, whose relatively privileged status could not protect them from the perils of pregnancy and childbirth. Appealing to Mary in the kinds of maternal crises she was herself spared—depressions, pain, death— these women challenged the assumption that the Virgin Mary made other mothers look and feel bad. For Henrietta Maria and Elizabeth Cary, she is presented as a source of comfort.

In the biography, Cary's emergence as a public Catholic and her movement into conflict with her father, husband, eldest son, and king occur under the auspices of two crowned women, the queens of heaven and England. While critics often depict Cary's conversion in terms of loss—of money and male support—it can also be viewed as a gain, especially in terms of female patronage. Cary's reluctant public conversion not only forced her into conflict with powerful men (her father, her husband, the king) but evoked the patronage of powerful women (the Virgin Mary, the queen, the Countess of Buckingham). It also became the occasion of her own assertion of authority, especially regarding her children. Her filial biographer emphasizes Cary's maternal will to convert: her vow to determine one daughter's destiny before she is even born; her eagerness to find evidence of Catholic leanings in another daughter's murmurings on her deathbed. Although criticism that emphasizes the parallels between Cary's life and work has tended to dwell on her role as wife, since her heroines, Mariam in *The Tragedy of Mariam* and Queen Isabel in *The History of . . . Edward II,* engage in fatal conflicts with their husbands, Cary was also a mother. Since her biographer was also her daughter, perhaps it is predictable that Cary's role as mother accrues increasing importance as the *Life* unfolds. Cary's promise to the Virgin and her daughter's vision of her occurred during years in which Cary was constantly pregnant: she gave birth in 1609 and 1610, then roughly once each year from 1614 to 1621, then again to her last two children in 1624 and 1625. As she sat by the bed in which her eldest child gave birth and died, her own youngest child was still unweaned; she contemplated nursing her granddaughter—"had it lived, the mother resolved to have nursed her daughter's child together with her own, not yet weaned"—but the infant died after a few hours.[178]

In the *Life,* as Cary moves from the phase of her life in which she bore and nursed her many children and secretly gestated her own Catholicism

177. Cyprien of Gamache, "Memoirs," pp. 316, 330–31.
178. *Lady Falkland: Her Life,* ed. Weller and Ferguson, p. 202.

into a phase in which she fights openly for control of her children's education and souls, women emerge as her allies and patrons. Supplanting the mother and mother-in-law with whom she has often been in conflict, these female allies and patrons are connected to her by Catholicism, not by familial relation.

If, as I have argued, much anti-Catholic polemic ridicules or denounces the possibility that women could have influence over men, commanding their love, devotion, and obedience, this polemic also downplays the possibility that a female figure could become the object of women's desire and reverence.[179] Certainly, anti-Catholic discourses insist that women are more susceptible to Catholicism, but this susceptibility is often associated with their vulnerability to seduction by men, not with their attraction to women. Yet the maligned, inverse couple at the center of so much anti-Catholic polemic (the Virgin Mary commanding her son, Henrietta Maria influencing her husband and son, Elizabeth Cary defying her oldest son and the king to control the fates of her youngest sons) obscures from view another kind of alliance—mothers in collaboration to wield power and influence. Responses to and representations of Catholic women's interrelations confirm Valerie Traub's claim that when early modern women's relationships with one another coexisted with rather than replaced heterosexual marriage, they were ignored, even tolerated. Yet they were also, through this neglect, eclipsed. Even the considerable scholarship on Cary focuses on her conflicts with male authorities rather than on her less fully articulated, less visible alliances with women.[180]

The *Life* reports that when Elizabeth Cary died in 1639, she was buried "by her Majesty's permission in her chapel, where the office was performed for her by the charity of the Capuchin Fathers."[181] At that time there were only two Catholic cemeteries, each attached to one of the royal chapels (at St. James's and at Somerset House). Although one of Henrietta Maria's Capuchins, Cyprien of Gamache, claimed that no one but the queen's "officers and servants, of both sexes, who die in the faith of the Church of Rome" could be buried in these cemeteries, the Queen occasionally granted this privilege to others as a special favor, as apparently she did to Cary.[182] The *Life* suggests that none of Cary's children attended the funeral, yet their absence does not mean that Cary died, as some scholars

179. Vanita, *Sappho and the Virgin Mary*, passim.
180. Valerie Traub, "The (In)Significance of 'Lesbian' Desire in Early Modern England," in *Queering the Renaissance*, ed. Jonathan Goldberg (Durham, N.C.: Duke University Press, 1994), pp. 62–83.
181. *Lady Falkland: Her Life*, ed. Weller and Ferguson, p. 275.
182. Cyprien of Gamache, "Memoirs," pp. 342, 447.

have insisted, "impoverished and alone."[183] Cary achieved a privilege available to only a very few English Catholics; this burial installed her at the physical center of Catholic life in England. Her children were not present, in large part, because of the triumph of her maternal will: most of them were where she had maneuvered to place them—"out of England and the occasion of danger of heresy," as the *Life* puts it.[184] They were in religious houses on the Continent pursuing vocations and praying for her. Because of her religious difference from her parents, her husband, and her eldest son, neither the family of her birth nor that of her marriage, each Protestant, could comfortably accommodate her in its tomb. The Tanfield family, which disowned her after her conversion, represents her in effigy on its tomb in Burford, Oxfordshire.[185] But her body does not seem to be there. Instead, it lies among the others, mostly women and priests, interred in London's Catholic cemeteries.

In focusing on the whereabouts of this corpse, I want to emphasize the possibilities both for a female community and for female command, as they were imagined both positively and negatively in association with Catholicism, and the historical elusiveness of that feared, perhaps briefly achieved command of Mary. Since neither Catholic cemetery in London survives, it is hard to be sure where Elizabeth Cary was buried. Although Barbara Lewalski interprets the passage in the *Life*, to which all conjecture about Cary's burial must return, as meaning that Cary was buried "in the burial ground of Henrietta Maria's private chapel at St. James's Palace—now covered by a road," it seems more likely to me that Cary would have been buried in the cemetery adjacent to the queen's relatively new chapel at Somerset House.[186] That chapel was closer to the queen's residence, and since its official opening in 1636 it had been the chapel of choice, since it was larger, more elaborate, and, unlike the chapel at St. James's, which Inigo Jones had originally planned for the Spanish infanta, had been designed specially for Henrietta Maria. The Capuchins lived next door to Somerset House and performed all of the services in its chapel. If Cary's funeral service took place in the Somerset House chapel, dedicated to the Virgin and decorated with her image, then that moment in that place brought together the three targets of Protestant anxiety about Catholic fe-

183. Germaine Greer, Susan Hastings, Jeslyn Medoff, and Melinda Sansone, eds., *Kissing the Rod: An Anthology of Seventeenth-Century Women's Verse* (New York: Farrar Straus Giroux, 1988), p. 54.

184. *Lady Falkland: Her Life*, ed. Weller and Ferguson, p. 274.

185. See Kenneth B. Murdock, *The Sun at Noon: Three Biographical Sketches* (New York: Macmillan, 1939), illustration facing p. 38.

186. Barbara Lewalski, *Writing Women in Jacobean England* (Cambridge: Harvard University Press, 1993), p. 388n53.

male power that I have been discussing—the Virgin Mary, the French queen, the commanding mother. In the 1630s "the command of Mary" was considerable, just as Prynne and others feared: the queen seems to have had the power to grant a prohibited Catholic burial and to break the law to support a Catholic mother's children. Yet the command of Mary was also moribund: at Cary's funeral in the Somerset House chapel, the figures for a feared Catholic maternity coalesce around a mother's now-unlocatable dead body, and on the brink of revolution.

The process by which this power moved from maligned to ignored to buried was not, of course, complete when Charles I lost his head. We can trace the process by looking at the fortunes of Somerset House and its chapel. In 1643, while Henrietta Maria was out of the country, Parliament ordered the Somerset House chapel broken open and defaced and the Capuchins imprisoned. The chapel was, then, "alas! sacrilegiously changed into an infamous meeting-house of Huguenots," as one Capuchin lamented. With the restoration of Charles II in 1660, however, his mother resumed residence in Somerset House and restored and enlarged her palace and its chapel.[187] In 1666, the Great Fire, which devastated so many Protestant churches, spared the chapel—miraculously, some said.[188]

After Henrietta Maria died in 1669, Charles II's wife, Catherine of Braganza, moved from St. James's to Somerset House. Catherine's story reveals, yet again, that Catholic queens could not win. If Henrietta Maria was suspect because of her fertility and her commanding presence as mother, Catherine of Braganza was held in contempt for her infertility, which contributed to anxieties about a Protestant succession. Dryden, for instance, mentions Catherine only briefly at the start of *Absalom and Achitophel*, not by name but as "a Soyl ungratefull to the Tiller's care." Her infertility excludes her from his story. Yet Catherine was an important figure of Catholic female power, even if, in her case, that power did not correspond to maternity. In 1670, Catherine employed twenty-eight priests; in 1680, two to three hundred people, mostly women, attended her chapel.[189] Like Henrietta Maria, Catherine was a survivor. In the perilous years of the

---

187. Bone, *Henrietta Maria,* pp. 160–61; Cyprien of Gamache claims that "at that time, you heard nothing talked of in London but the ruin and desolation of the Catholics. They had no longer any divine service; the Queen's chapel was shut up" ("Memoirs," pp. 344–45, 351–54; on the restoration of the chapel, see pp. 429–33). See also *Upon Her Majesties New Buildings at Somerset-House* (London, 1665) and *The Speech of Her Majesty the Queen Mother's Palace, upon the Reparation and Enlargement of It, by Her Majesty* (London, 1665), both presented in the voice of the reoccupied Somerset House.

188. Walter George Bell, *The Great Fire of London in 1666* (London: John Lane, 1920), p. 326.

189. Miller, *Popery and Politics,* p. 22.

Popish Plot and the exclusion crisis, she withstood charges that she conspired to murder her husband and a crisis organized around his illegitimate son and her own inability to produce a legitimate heir; she facilitated
Charles's deathbed conversion, then outlived him by about twenty years.

During the brief reign of James II (1685–88), the last of England's two
post-Reformation Catholic monarchs—or, as some said, "Queen Mary in
breeches"—his wife, Mary of Modena, used both the chapel at St. James's
and an elaborate new one designed for her at Whitehall by Christopher
Wren.[190] Following the precedent of his father and brother, James II never
converted an Anglican chapel to Catholic use, but rather built anew.[191]
This sprint of Catholic expansion was short-lived. Playing cards depicting
events during James II's reign depict Mary of Modena praying to Our Lady
of Loreto for a son (see figures 1 and 2). With his birth, viewed variously
as miraculous or as counterfeit, the problematic triumvirate of Catholic
queen consort, Virgin Mother, and maternity issues in triumph—a Catholic heir to the throne—and in ultimate defeat. There will not be another
Catholic queen consort in England; there will not be another Catholic heir
born.[192] Queens ceased to be active agents on behalf of Catholicism, or symbolic figureheads for it. When James II's daughter, Mary, took the throne
with her husband, William, in 1688, she declined to command. She em-
phatically subordinated herself to her husband, although they held the
throne jointly; she was also childless. With constitutional rule and a secured
Protestant succession, the command of Mary receded into a remembered
horror rather than looming as a feared prospect.

In 1688, after James II and Mary had both left Whitehall but before
William and Mary were in residence, rioters attacked the two chapels the

190. For the reference to James as "Queen Mary in breeches," see Richard L. Greaves,
Secrets of the Kingdom: British Radicals from the Popish Plot to the Revolution of 1688–89 (Stanford: Stanford University Press, 1992), p. 41; and Miller, *Popery and Politics*, p. 75. On
James's and Mary's chapels, see Martin Haile, *Queen Mary of Modena: Her Life and Letters*
(London: Dent, 1905), pp. 126; Mary Hopkirk, *Queen over the Water: Mary Beatrice of Modena, Queen of James II* (London: John Murray, 1953), pp. 106–7; and Little, *Catholic Churches
since 1623*, pp. 22–23. Catherine of Braganza at first refused to surrender the St. James's
chapel to Mary. See Carola Oman, *Mary of Modena* (London: Hodder & Stoughton, 1962),
pp. 36–37, 84.

191. Haile, *Queen Mary of Modena*, pp. 155–56.

192. On how propaganda surrounding the "warming-pan scandal" drew on a "long-
standing tradition of anti-Catholic bigotry" that associated Catholicism "with a kind of
monstrous motherhood that deprived men of their paternal rights," see Rachel Weil, "The
Politics of Legitimacy: Women and the Warming-Pan Scandal," in *The Revolution of 1688–
1689*, ed. Lois G. Schwoerer (Cambridge: Cambridge University Press, 1992), p. 76. Like
Elizabeth Cary's body—paved under somewhere—Mary of Modena's body is unlocatable.
During the French Revolution it disappeared from Chaillot monastery, where it was await-
ing future burial in Westminster Abbey (Oman, *Mary of Modena*, p. xvi).

The Duthes of Modena Presenting
an edge of Gold to the Lady of
Loreta that if Q: might Conceve a son

1. Mary of Modena presenting a gift to the Lady of Loreto, that she might conceive a son. Three of spades from playing cards depicting "The Reign of James II." (© Copyright the British Museum)

fleeing royals had used, at St. James's and at Whitehall, but did not molest that at Somerset House, perhaps because Catherine of Braganza was still in residence there—and remained so until she returned to Portugal in 1692. As a consequence, the Somerset House chapel continued in use a few years longer than the others: the chapel at St. James's was turned over

2. Clergy praying to the Lady of Loreto for a Prince of Wales to be born. Seven of spades from playing cards depicting "The Revolution." (© Copyright the British Museum)

to French and Dutch Protestants; that at Whitehall was dismantled.[193] William and Mary shifted their residences away from those associated with

193. Hopkirk, *Queen over the Water*, pp. 162, 202. One last priest remained in residence at Somerset House until his death in 1698 (p. 191). For a parallel narrative of "the end of dominion maternal," see Mikalachki, *Legacy of Boadicea*, chap. 4, esp. pp. 144–49.

court Catholicism—St. James's, Somerset House, and Whitehall, with their elaborate chapels—and toward Hampton Court, which Wren remodeled, and the newly purchased Kensington Palace. Somerset House was subsequently demolished in 1776 to make way for Sir William Chambers's new complex of administrative buildings.[194] While it is lamented as a lost Inigo Jones masterpiece, sacrificed to progress, it was also the temple of Catholic female power, symbolic and enacted, spiritual and temporal. That it is unlamented as such suggests how the terms of anti-Catholic polemic, particularly its hostility to female power, continue to shape approaches to Stuart history and assumptions about what constitutes loss, what constitutes progress, what defines an event as "glorious."

194. Christopher Hibbert, *London: The Biography of a City* (Harmondsworth: Penguin, 1969, 1983), p. 120; Harris et al., *King's Arcadia*, pp. 148, 153. There is some confusion in these sources regarding the date. The *DNB* suggests that Chambers was appointed the architect for the new Somerset House in 1775, and the demolition occurred in 1776.

CHAPTER FOUR

"The Wretched Subject
the Whole Town Talks of ":
Elizabeth Cellier, Popish Plots, and Print

The crisis known as the Popish Plot was about the power of stories—
testimony in court, rumors in the street, and narratives in print—
to persuade the English populace, and especially judges and juries,
that Catholics were conspiring to reclaim the kingdom by force and by
stealth. The power of stories to confirm, inflame, or create anti-Catholicism
was certainly not without precedent. In the case of the Popish Plot, an outrageous charge once again found confirmation not in physical evidence
but in its resonance with the cultural imaginary. The Popish Plot depended
almost completely on one witness, Titus Oates, and his claim that Catholics, particularly Jesuits, were conspiring to kill Charles II and his coun-
cilors, massacre Protestants, and set up a Catholic government under the
Duke of York (the future James II). The rumor of yet another popish plot
had legs because it served political needs. By discrediting Catholics, it fueled the exclusion crisis, a Whig attempt to bar James's succession.[1]

Oates's initial testimony anticipated rather than reported or explained
an "event." It then seemed to produce one: Sir Edmundbury Godfrey, the
justice who had received Oates's testimony, was found dead, supposedly
murdered. Had Catholics taken revenge against Godfrey, as well as si-

---

1. See Maurice Ashley, *James II* (London: Dent, 1977), chap. 9; J. P. Kenyon, *The Popish Plot* (London: Heinemann, 1972); John Miller, *Popery and Politics in England, 1660–1688* (Cambridge: Cambridge University Press, 1973); and Jonathan Scott, "England's Troubles: Exhuming the Popish Plot," in *The Politics of Religion in Restoration England,* ed. Tim Harris, Paul Seward, and Mark Goldie (Cambridge: Basil Blackwell, 1990), pp. 107–32, esp. 108–9, 111.

lenced him, as Protestants claimed? Or, as Catholics argued, was Godfrey's inopportune death simply interpreted in the context and the service of rising anti-Catholicism? Whatever the explanation, Godfrey's death worked, in many people's minds, to confirm Oates's charges; it also became a focus for the anti-Catholic feelings that had been stirred up.

Regarding the Popish Plot, then, it is impossible to distinguish between events and their narrative representations because those narratives—circulated as rumors, offered in court as testimony, published—were the event. Despite the Lord Chief Justice's claim that "Narratives are no Evidence at all," another commentator explains that "the whole Machine of this vast, and hideous Plott is built upon the bare testimony of the swearers."[2] Narratives were indeed evidence, if not of what real people actually did, then of what writers and readers feared and believed. As Rachel Weil has argued, witnesses' credibility was determined not so much by what they said, or even who they were, since many of the key witnesses in these trials were "infamous persons," but by how well their testimony served dominant political interests, confirmed long-standing prejudices, and conformed to familiar conventions.[3] On the "evidence" of those narratives found most convincing—that is, those describing a Catholic conspiracy—at least twenty-two persons were executed, none of whom ever confessed. In these deaths, the traditions for representing Catholicism issue in the most extreme of material consequences; the discursive reveals itself as the real.

Although the trials of the alleged conspirators were, according to Jonathan Scott, "not judicial events at all" but rather "acts of political theatre, to express, and to that extent assuage, a general public concern," they could not have functioned as such if they had not been widely represented in print.[4] Without the press, these trials would have had limited audiences and limited impact; the press did more to bring the Popish Plot into the public sphere than the courts or the scaffolds did. Coming at a crucial moment in the transition from a culture of spectacle to one of print, these trials formed a bridge between the two. Presses printed expanded versions of witnesses' testimony, rival accounts of the trials and executions, gossip

2. *The Tryall of Richard Langhorn Esq., Counsellor at Law* (London, 1679), sig. F; John Dormer, *The New Plot of the Papists: To Transform Traitors into Martyrs* (London, 1679), p. 14. According to Kenyon, "Not a jot of written evidence was given in, so everything hung on the oath of the witnesses" (*Popish Plot*, p. 203).

3. Rachel Weil, "'If I Did Say So, I Lyed': Elizabeth Cellier and the Construction of Credibility in the Popish Plot Crisis," in *Political Culture and Cultural Politics in Early Modern England: Essays Presented to David Underdown*, ed. Susan D. Amussen and Mark A. Kishlansky (Manchester: Manchester University Press, 1995), pp. 189–209.

4. Scott, "England's Troubles," p. 120.

about those suspected or accused, satires, "news." News also, obviously, circulated orally, at least in London. But this oral transmission, like the events in the courts, is accessible to us now only through the written record. In depending on this written record, reading between the lines and reading one text against another, I share the position of most English people who sought to learn about the plot and its discovery and punishment. John Evelyn, for instance, justifies to his diary his decision to attend the trial of Sir George Wakeman, the queen's physician, on July 18, 1679, at which Oates and William Bedloe, another important Popish Plot witness, testified. "Though it was not my custom or delight to be often present at any capital trials, we having them commonly so exactly published by those who take them in short-hand, yet I was inclined to be at this signal one, that by the ocular view of the carriages and other circumstances of the managers and parties concerned, I might inform myself, and regulate my opinion of a cause that had so alarmed the whole nation."[5] Even for Evelyn, who lived in London during the trials, checking what he read against his own ocular proofs was a rare and remarkable occurrence. Furthermore, whatever his eyes told him is both interested and accessible only through what he wrote down about it (nothing).

In the flurry of publications that not only represented but constituted the Popish Plot and justified fierce retaliations against Catholics, women and clerics once again assume prominence. Witnesses claimed that Godfrey had been murdered in Catherine of Braganza's palace, Somerset House. Many of those who were convicted for the murder were members of the Catholic queen's staff. Oates also accused the queen of conspiring to poison her husband; although the queen was never officially charged, her physician was tried (and acquitted). Given the controversy surrounding Henrietta Maria and her chapel at Somerset House, it is hardly surprising to find Catherine of Braganza and Somerset House the targets of renewed anti-Catholic feeling. Indeed, Oates's charges against the queen seem almost inevitable, given the ways that gender inflected and enabled representations of Catholicism throughout the century. Simultaneously suspected of high treason and petty treason, a foreigner and an English queen, Catherine of Braganza seems like the usual suspect. Yet she was never tried, nor was she as excessively represented as Henrietta Maria. Consequently, I would like to shift my focus here to a less obvious suspect, who was ultimately a more central figure in printed attacks on Catholicism around 1680. This less privileged woman who yet became a highly public

5. *The Diary of John Evelyn*, ed. William Bray, 2 vols. (Dent: London, 1966), 2: 137.

embodiment of Catholicism was Elizabeth Cellier, the so-called Popish
Midwife implicated in the Meal Tub Plot, a belated offshoot of the Popish
Plot. For Cellier, as for the other female figures for Catholicism I have discussed, representations owe as much to rhetorical and iconographic traditions as they do to any observation of actual persons or events. Yet I also
want to argue that the particulars of Cellier's persona and history exert
more pressure on the representations of her than was possible in representations of more socially and conceptually remote figures (even living
queens consort). However much she, too, was a figment of the culture's
imagination, she also had a specificity stemming from a particular cultural
moment. Representations of Cellier reveal the tension between as well as
the overlap of the real and the representational.

Charges of a Meal Tub Plot arose after the Popish Plot executions, when
the frenzy of prosecution and retribution had subsided but the exclusion
crisis was still on the boil. Purportedly a Catholic scheme to divert blame
for the Popish Plot onto Presbyterians, the Meal Tub Plot might also have
been a scheme by those who opposed James's succession to reanimate hostility toward Catholics.[6] Regardless, it was understood from the start as an
attempt to manipulate public opinion. Testing the power of a new charge
to reanimate a tired controversy, the Meal Tub Plot focused on the provenance and proof value of documents found hidden in Elizabeth Cellier's
"meal tub," or flour barrel. When one Thomas Dangerfield was arrested
for trying to frame the Whig politician Roger Mansel for treason, he cast
doubt away from himself by accusing Cellier (among others). Cellier was
available, so to speak, because she was using her mobility and her contacts
as a midwife with an aristocratic, even royal clientele to monitor and relieve Catholic prisoners in Newgate, to smuggle correspondence into and
out of the prison, and to support the defenses of Catholics on trial.[7] Funded
by contributions from powerful Catholic patrons such as Lady Powis and
Roger Palmer, Earl of Castlemaine, Cellier worked to relieve or provide
bail for the more than two thousand Catholics imprisoned in the London
area.[8] Cellier claimed that she had hired Dangerfield to provide informa-

---

6. Although Presbyterians and Catholics could be viewed as enemies and opposites, the
two groups were often lumped together as equally dangerous opponents of Anglicanism.
See, for instance, Joseph Glanvill, *The Zealous and Impartial Protestant, Shewing Some Great, But
Less Heeded Dangers of Popery* (London, 1681).

7. *Mr. Tho. Dangerfeilds Particular Narrative* (London, 1679), sig. Rv; Thomas Dangerfield, *The Grand Impostor Defeated* (London, 1682), sigs. B2v–C.

8. Anne Barbeau Gardiner, "Elizabeth Cellier in 1688 on Envious Doctors and Heroic
Midwives Ancient and Modern," *Eighteenth Century Life* 14.1 (1990): 24–34, esp. 25. See also
Gardiner, "Introduction," in Elizabeth Cellier, *"Malice Defeated"; and, "The Matchless Rogue"*
(Los Angeles: William Andrews Clark Memorial Library, UCLA, 1988).

tion on how Catholic prisoners were being treated in Newgate and to work as a servant, courier, and informant; he claimed that she had hired him to fabricate evidence of a Presbyterian plot to replace Charles II with his illegitimate son, the Duke of Monmouth, and to plant material incriminating the Earl of Shaftesbury in a plot against the king.[9] Dangerfield testified that his written reports on his "fact-finding" missions could be found concealed in a meal tub in Mrs. Cellier's house, as indeed they were. Whichever side concocted the Meal Tub Plot, it brought to the fore the central question at which the Popish Plot prosecutions had hinted: might one faction invent a plot to incriminate and discredit another? If evidence could be fabricated, how could it be trusted as "proof"?

Dangerfield's charges instigated a process that made Elizabeth Cellier notorious. She was indicted and tried for treason. Like everyone tried for treason before 1696, she had to act as her own defense attorney; unlike most, she did so successfully. Cellier was acquitted, in part because the fervor had passed and questions were already being asked about the legal procedures and witnesses used to convict the "traitors." Anger at the verdict, however, made it unlikely that she could proceed quietly with her life and work. Cellier compounded her notoriety when, in the three weeks after her acquittal, she wrote a self-justifying account of the trial, *Malice Defeated*, which she had printed for her, despite the Privy Council's attempts to seize sheets while they were in press, and which she sold from her house.[10] For this text Cellier was subsequently tried for and convicted of libel. Apparently, while the King's Bench was not willing to convict her of treason, the Whig-controlled Old Bailey could not allow so forthright an espousal of the Catholic cause in print to go unpunished, especially in view of Cellier's claim that Catholic prisoners were being tortured in Newgate. Although her treason trial was belated in regard to the Popish Plot, her libel trial reveals that much was still at stake.

The one thing about which Elizabeth Cellier and her detractors can agree is that paper and pens have become crucial weapons and the page a terrain of struggle as important as the courtroom or the scaffold. Both court cases against Cellier revolve around texts: correspondence smuggled into and out of Newgate, lists and schemes hidden in meal tubs, libelous publications, witnesses' examinations. Multiple accounts of both of Cellier's trials survive, including *Malice Defeated;* she is referred to in the *London*

9. Dangerfield claims that he was first hired by Cellier because he was "vers'd a little in the Law" and therefore could help her with her husband's debts; he also suggests that she wanted to employ him sexually (*Grand Impostor Defeated*, sig. C).

10. References to *Malice Defeated; or, A Brief Relation of the Accusation and Deliverance of Elizabeth Cellier* (London, 1680) appear parenthetically in the text as *MD*.

Gazette, a paper of record "published by authority," the only regular source of news being published during the months of her notoriety; in Henry Care's *Weekly Pacquet of Advice from Rome,* an opposition paper; and in multiple broadsides and ballads.[11] In accounts of her two trials, Cellier and her accusers fight over possession of papers, over authorship and accountability, over what papers can prove and how they can be manipulated, forged, altered, planted.[12] If we now understand these battles over texts only through texts, so, too, did the combatants. Asked how she knows something happened, Cellier replies: "I read it in a Pamphlet" (*MD,* sig. H2v). A witness at her trial testifies that he knows only "what he heard by Common Report, and read in the Prints" (*MD,* sig. K).

It was Cellier's punishment for libel that really made her a public figure, not just because she was literally exposed to public view (and assault) but because this public spectacle became such a popular topic for visual and verbal representation. The sentence was severe: she was fined the huge sum of £1,000 and on three occasions was placed on the pillory, where the crowd treated her brutally. On each occasion the hangman burned copies of her book. On her last two visits to the pillory, perhaps because she had complained in a petition to the king that "she might as well have been sentenced to be stoned to death," she was allowed to keep her head and hands out of the pillory and to protect herself by wielding a wooden shield "as a kind of battledore," as Lady Rachel Russell derisively reported.[13] Enthroned on the pillory, depicted in woodcuts, represented in effigy in a pope-burning procession, the target of at least twenty-five published at-

11. For notices of Cellier's trials and her sentencing, see *London Gazette,* nos. 1520 (June 10–14, 1680), 1546 (Sept. 9–13, 1680), and 1547 (Sept. 13–16, 1680). Neither of the rival papers that might well have discussed Cellier's case, Benjamin Harris's *Protestant (Domestic) Intelligence* and Nathaniel Thompson's *True Domestick Intelligence,* was published in the months when Cellier was notorious. Henry Care appended a brief commentary on the week's events, called variously the "Popish Courant" and "Popes Harbinger," to his *Weekly Pacquet of Advice from Rome.*

12. In *Malice Defeated,* Cellier claims that while she was in Newgate, the jailer's wife and sister copied her letters (sig. F); that when her letters were read into evidence, incriminating words and phrases were "thrust in" (sig. Gr); and finally that Sir William Waller ransacked her house after she had been arrested, "filling his own and his Footmans Pockets and Breeches with Papers of Private concern, which he never carry'd before the Councel, nor as yet restor'd, though some of them be of *Considerable value*" (sig. E2v). Even in prison, Cellier is accused of acting as textual midwife. The *Calendar of State Papers* claims that convicted priests in Newgate wrote texts arguing for a Presbyterian plot, which were then "midwived into the world by the assistance of their fellow prisoner, the infamous Mrs. Cellier and her printer, Thompson" (*Calendar of State Papers, Domestic Series,* ed. F. H. Blackburne Daniell [1921] [Nedeln, Liechtenstein: Kraus Reprints, 1968], vol. 22 [1680–81], p. 370 [July 23, 1681]) (hereafter cited as *CSPD,* followed by the years covered by the volume).

13. *CSPD,* 1680–81, p. 16 (Sept. 14, 1680); see also p. 30 (Sept. 20, 1680, Newmarket); Lady Rachel Russell to William, Lord Russell, Sept. 17, 1680, in *Some Account of the Life of Rachael* [sic] *Wriothesley, Lady Russell,* 3d ed. (London: Longmans, 1820), p. 228.

tacks, and a polemicist in her own right, Cellier was a highly public, visible, and audible figure in the London street cultures of both spectacle and print. She was, as Henry Care remarked, "a *wretched Subject*, that all the Town talks of."[14] Since her birth and death records have not survived, Cellier emerges as an object of study only by becoming the subject of town talk. It is almost as if she comes into being when Dangerfield accuses her; later, when polemic has passed her by and she has written and published her last text, she disappears. While being the wretched subject of London discourse is what inscribed Cellier into the historical record, it was, like many processes of subject formation, an extremely risky business. The image of Cellier on the pillory parrying rocks vividly sums up the dangers and humiliations of being the target of representation.

Yet Cellier was sentenced to the pillory for being a subject in the opposite sense—an author and a legally accountable agent. Thus, at least in her case, exercising some control over representation—acting as a producer as well as a topic—did not necessarily either set the record straight or protect her. Both Cellier's attackers and her defenders agree in censuring her movement into print as an act of aggression. *The Midwife Unmask'd* describes her as "a stout *Virago*, who having been Imprisoned for the *Cause*, and escaped the Law, now with bold and audacious Effronteries publishes her Adventures"; "she rants and scratches like another *Pucel d'Orleans*, or Joan of Arque; handling her *Pen* for the Papistical Cause, as the other did her *Lance*."[15] Even Cellier's one Catholic defender, John Warner, James II's Jesuit confessor, simultaneously praises Cellier for her skill and argues that she endangered herself (and her cause) by displaying it indiscreetly: "Mrs. Cellier had won her laurels in this rather small affair of her trial; with her remarkable powers of endurance and of skill, she had fought alone against many and had vanquished all opposition. In her eagerness to add to these laurels by publishing the history of her trials, she came near to ruining everything. For in her book she gave free rein to her skill, . . . thus she offered a handle to those who were looking for one, to charge her with libel."[16] For Warner, publication, not "remarkable powers of endurance and [legal] skill," makes Cellier a feme insufficiently covert. Warner's location of danger in Cellier's "publishing the history of her trials" and giving "free rein to her skill" deserves closer scrutiny. Why was it in this process,

14. O. W. Furley, "The Pope-Burning Processions of the Late Seventeenth Century," *History* 44 (1959): 21; Care, "Popes Harbinger," appended to *Weekly Pacquet of Advice from Rome* 3, no. 12 (Sept. 24, 1680): 95.

15. *The Midwife Unmask'd; or, The Popish Design of Mrs. Cellier's Mealtub Plainly Made Known* (London 1680), p. 1. For another comparison of Cellier to "La Pucelle," see Care, "Popes Harbinger," appended to *Weekly Pacquet of Advice from Rome* 3, no. 3 (Sept. 3, 1680): 71.

16. John Warner, *The History of English Persecution of Catholics and the Presbyterian Plot*, ed. T. A. Birrell, 2 vols., Catholic Record Society 47–48 (London, 1953), 2: 424.

rather than in any of her dangerous but more covert political activities, that Cellier "came near to ruining everything"?

Other early modern women made contested public appearances in the courts and in the press. Real consequences attended the skill of all who did so: all depended on how well they could represent themselves, how successfully they could manipulate the available terms. Gender set those terms, determining the conditions under which authorship and agency might be attributed to women. But gender did not act independently as a determinant; religious affiliation, for instance, combined with gender with uneven and unpredictable effects. For instance, Catholics, like other minority dissenters, such as Quakers, operated under legal restrictions and social prescriptions even more rigorous than those constraining all early modern women. If the limits were more clearly marked and stringently enforced for such women, and if their transgressions of those limits were more urgent and more harshly punished, then attention to such groups can reveal where those limits were set and what the possibilities for maneuvering within or pressing against them might have been. Since Elizabeth Cellier was often at risk but never decisively defeated—tried but not convicted, then convicted and pilloried but not executed, denounced in court and in the press but willing to venture into both arenas to defend herself, her books burned but not all of them—her case is especially revealing of how gender and religious affiliation conjoin and conflict in limiting the options for representing women as agents and authors. Shifting the focus away from what Cellier did or did not do, I will concentrate on the various ways she is represented and what contingencies (which court, what genre, what year or even month) shaped them.

"The Popish Romancer": Cellier as Author

Since writing for public circulation and consumption could be incriminating in itself, women's "apologies" or self-justifications were often self-defeating.[17] This was a particular problem for Catholic women.[18] Being

17. Margaret W. Ferguson, "A Room Not Their Own: Renaissance Women as Readers and Writers," in *The Comparative Perspective on Literature*, ed. Clayton Koelb and Susan Noakes (Ithaca: Cornell University Press, 1988), pp. 93–116; Susan Sage Heinzelman, "Guilty in Law, Implausible in Fiction: Jurisprudential and Literary Narratives in the Case of Mary Blandy, Parricide, 1752," in *Representing Women: Law, Literature, and Feminism*, ed. Heinzelman and Zipporah Batshaw Wiseman (Durham, N.C.: Duke University Press, 1994), pp. 309–36, esp. 329; Wendy Wall, *The Imprint of Gender: Authorship and Publication in the English Renaissance* (Ithaca: Cornell University Press, 1993); and Weil, "'If I Did Say So, I Lyed,'" pp. 203–6.

18. See also Ros Ballaster, "Fiction Feigning Femininity: False Counts and Pageant Kings in Aphra Behn's Popish Plot Writings," in *Aphra Behn Studies*, ed. Janet Todd (Cambridge: Cambridge University Press, 1996), pp. 50–65.

Catholic and female could doubly discredit an author attempting to compel belief, since both groups were assumed to be illiterate and deceitful. If Cellier had two strikes against her when she tried to raise an authoritative, persuasive public voice, the content of her message, quickly labeled libelous, provided her with an almost insurmountable challenge.

Given the climate, her topic, and her already well established public persona, Cellier's emergence into print was inevitably a highly political and therefore conspicuous and perilous act. Cellier picked up her pen / lance during one of several late seventeenth-century political crises that Rachel Weil claims "opened up the public airwaves to people outside the formal political nation, while at the same time making the credibility of those people an object of political struggle." She also tottered on the threshold of a period, the years from 1684 to 1740, that Ros Ballaster argues "provided significant and distinctive conditions of access for the woman writer into explicitly political discourse."[19]

Cellier's story might be approached either as a success narrative, in which a specifically female kind of authority becomes available in the public sphere, or as a failure narrative, in which Catholics steadily lose both authority and symbolic resonance in the public sphere and recede from engagement in the political process. That these two narratives work at cross-purposes—one step forward, two steps back—suggests their inadequacy to explain the phenomenon of Elizabeth Cellier. Cellier does not represent either group, Catholics or women; the history of either group, taken alone, does not prepare one to understand her. However demonized and criminalized, most Catholics did not wind up in court, even in those volatile years; conversely, those who did were rarely acquitted. Accounts of Cellier's two trials attribute to her the claim that she stood "singly and alone" before the court, that she lacked Catholic support; yet on both charges she was tried as "the Female Champion of the Cause."[20] Both might be true. A

19. Weil, "'If I Did Say So, I Lyed,'" p. 207; Ros Ballaster, *Seductive Forms: Women's Amatory Fiction from 1684 to 1740* (Oxford: Clarendon, 1992), p. 11.
20. In *Malice Defeated*, Cellier claims that in organizing her defense, she acted *"Singly and Alone,* without the Advice or Assistance of any Catholick breathing, Man or Woman. I was left to study, manage, and so support myself in all my troubles to my Expence and Loss *much above a thousand Pounds,* never receiving one penny towards it, directly or indirectly," except for £10 from a condemned priest (sig. Iv). An account of her libel trial presents her as using the same language to counter Baron Weston's assumption that she must suffer for her allegiance to Catholicism, even if she is not solely responsible for *Malice Defeated:* "Pray, my Lord, hear me one word; As to your saying, I do it to defend a Party, I profess I stand singly and alone; I have been so Barbarously used by those you call that Party, that the Protestants have been abundantly more kind to me then they. And I would not tell the least Lye to do them any good turn" (*The Tryal and Sentence of Elizabeth Cellier; For Writing, Printing, and Publishing a Scandalous Libel, Called Malice Defeated* [London, 1680], p. 27); *Midwife Unmask'd,* p. 1.

controversial figure, especially a woman, might bear the blame for Catholic affiliation without reaping any benefits.

Cellier also does not "represent" other women, even Catholic ones. Although most women were identified by their marital status, Cellier, who was married to a French merchant, is identified much more frequently as a midwife than as a wife. As an adult convert to Catholicism, Cellier, like Elizabeth Cary, contradicted the assumption that most women clung to Catholicism because they resisted change; for her, Catholicism was a choice and an innovation. As a midwife and a gentlewoman, Cellier also occupied a class position between the two groups of women who appeared most frequently in Popish Plot trials: working-class women (nurses, servants, and housekeepers) who were introduced as witnesses yet often ridiculed, and aristocratic and royal women who were suspected but, for the most part, protected. Even Cellier's hood served as a kind of habit, a distinguishing mark in woodcuts, linking her to matrons, who wore a scarf and hood (see figures 3 and 4, for instance). Finally, Cellier was a spatially as well as a

3. Elizabeth Cellier, in her hooded "habit," stands by as the incriminating documents are found in her meal tub. From *The Popish Damnable Plot against Our Religion and Liberties* (1681). (Beinecke Rare Book and Manuscript Library, Yale University)

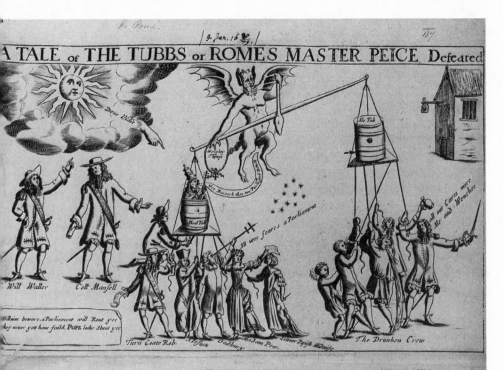

A TALE of THE TUBBS or ROMES MASTER PEICE Defeated

Will Waller   *Coll Mansell*

Villains beware, a Parliament will Rout yee, They never yet have foild. POPE looke About yee

Turn Coate Rob.   *Hun*   *Badburg.*   *Madam Pew*   *Scriver Popish Midwife*   *The Drunken Crew*

If Englands Prayers be heard, and Senate sit;   *Down goes proud Rome, French Arms, and Northern Wit.*

The Ale-Tub's Complaint.

Unkind Devil, thus at last deceive me!
Stay till the Ale was out, and then to leave me:
Hath not my service greater been by odds,
Than can be hop't from *Bread* and *wooden Gods?*
See how out off-spring altogether strive,
To keep the Ballance and the Ale alive,
Although at Bottom, while perfidious you
Tack to that *Tripple Dogs* and *Damned Crew*
Of *Loyala's*, till they Us all undo:
Sot that you are, to have a greater hope
From a few Priests, and an old doting Pope,
That their dry PLOTS, cau e're your int'rest farther
Than I have done, by Rapine, Whores, and Murder,
Who by the Liquor of my musty Cell
Hath sent you scores, nay hundreds, quick to Hell:
You are ungrateful, thus to leave old Friends,
And think *Rome's* Vassals e're can make amends;
Who when their work is done will Domineer;
And swear that hell was meally mouth'd for fear:
Then turn your hand, and on our side it give,
Or they will stave my Hogshead as I live,
And so grow sober, then shall both on's pass,
Ale for a *Witch*, thou *Devil* for an *Asse.*

The Devil (or *Jack* on both side's) Reply.

What Ails this Drunken Puppy to Complain,
Thinks he I know not where's my greatest gain:
That Pack of Bandogs, breed of Northern Tikes;
Shall Teize the fouls of all that us dislikes;
Must my Vicegerent with his *Tripple Crown?*
By Empty Ale-Tubs e're be weighed down?
No know I am wiser, Drunkards are but fools
Unto this MEAL-TUB and his Holinesses Tools.
'Tis true, the Ale-Tub, is our friend we know,
And oft from thence some Reeling to Hell go,
But these can Ruine Kingdoms at a Blow.
And where they Conquer, there the Herreticks feel,
Far greater Torments than our whips of Steel
We Exercise upon our Slaves below,
Who (but for them) did ne're such tortures know.
Flay men alive, then forth their Bowels tear,
Women rip up with Child, and on their Spear
Mount their young Infants, while in blood they sprawl,
The Catholicks may to quiet them that Bawl;
Cities Coasume with fire, Ravish Maid and Wife,
Destroy by Poyson, Pistol, Burnings, Knife,
With thousand other ways to End their hated Life.

But what is best of all: when they have done,
They call this holy work: most Christian——
Acted from pure zeal, and love so mild,
Makes them as guiltless as the Unborn Child;
Two *Anniversary*, and out *Pater-Nos*
Will make amends for all, and quit the Cost
They'r daring sinners, of the Popes first Rate,
With God himself they will Equivocate——
By Breaden Gods they can Absolve a Lye——
Nay by the Mass they dare do more than I,
Not Tremble at, but mock the Deity.
Then cease to murmur, they shall bear the Bell
For Damn'd Designs, and PLOTS that out-does Hell.

The Jesuits speak their merrits.

Most Holy Father, we do much admire
Your weighty Goodness, and your Reverend Sire,
Whose helping hand doth for us turn the Scale,
By him we have, and do, and shall prevail;
'Tis not Heavens Power that shall frustrate this
Most Brave design, which in the MEAL-TUB is;
Nor *Presbyterians* save their hated Throats,
Now at the last, by a Damn'd tell-tale Oats.
If Hell (for Heaven we matter not) Conceal
This Blest Intreague, by all our Gods the MEAL
Shall have high honour, on our Altars that
Made into Gods be worship't smoaking hot.
This matchless Treason, makes it holy all——
White as from Tower scrapt, or West-ward Hall;
This wonder-working Euch'rist shall do more
Tha a Jesuits Powder, Petitioner, or Whore,
Or all the Bassled Plots we e're Contriv'd before,
'Twill make the Herreticks all agast to see
Themselves the Plotters, murdered Legally.
And make us fat with Laughing, how they will
Divided fall and one another Kill——
'Tis holy sport to see their blood run down
In every Channel of the Borned Town,
While Changeling *Robin*, Bugbear in the City,
Dye the *Green Ribbans* Red; by Hell that's pretty:
Then shall that Mote, in Northern eye be sped,
After Exile call'd back to lose his head.
But these are scraps of what our TUB contains,
And do these Coxcombs, with their addled Brains,
Think e're to weigh us down with Ale and Grains?
No Punies know, your Reeling throng's out-done,
Wee'l make all England stagger e'er't be long:
But taking's idle, let's t'oaction come,
And strike the stroak, may Ruine Christendom.

Sir *William Waller* to Col. Mansell.

See *Mansell* where that Damned hellish Crew,
Are plotting Murders, and begin with you;
See heaven discovers unto thee and I.
Their horrid Treasons, hellbred Villany,
Coucht in that pacquet brought by *Willoughby.*
Oh Blessed God! whose mercies infinite
Do yet preserve us from Eternal Night;
It's thou alone whose heavenly goodness still
Defends our Lives (almost) against our will,
From these vile Plotters, Miscreants of *Rome,*
Blood-thirsty Villains, *Pests* of Christendom.
Direct me Heaven to take them in their toyl,
And all their Treasons, and their plottings spoil.
Let's in amongst them, *Mansel,* heres my hand,
I'le lose my life to save my native Land.
'Tis done, says *Mansel* brave Sir *William;* I
In such a cause with you am proud to dye.
We'll make those Vermin know, we scorn their rage,
Our noblest Souls dares *Rome* and Hell ingage.
And if such manhood Reigneth in us two,
What can't the Courage of our *English* do?
But Ruine all its Foes, when once provoke thereto.
Let's search that Pesthouse, where the Midwife's broad
Who brings *Rome's* Bastards and their Plots to bed,
Methinks it looks, as if the *Tower* Beasts
Had there some Prey on which they often feast.
'Tis there my Lady meets her trusty Steer;
Some *Newgate*-Birds and Sir Examiner.
There's Stars amongst them whence young *Tycho* drew
The Plots good fortune, but his own not knew;
See how the V Whores of either Sexes Tugg,
While the *Grand Bawde* sits Brooding on the TUB,
We'll turn the Bottom upwards ere we go,
I'le lay my Life there's a Treason at his Toe.
So oft they fetch him, with his Tripple Crown,
And threw the Crosses, and the MEAL-TUB down;
Whence came such stuff the Devil frighted, swore,
He never saw such Pricklesofp stuff before.
The VVest must yield the Belt unto the Nore.
Thus *England* once more is delivered from
Rome's Rogues abroad, and Plotters here at home:
Stand on your Guard, now hold your selves awake,
Lest their next Plot (you careless) Napping take.
Respice & Cave.

F I N I S.

Printed for the Loyal Protestant, at the Sign of the True Englishman in *Great Britain,* Nov. 13. 1679.

---

4. Cellier and other supposed conspirators. Cellier appears to be holding a knife, partially concealed behind her back. This detail may refer to the accusation that she was involved in a conspiracy on behalf of the Duke of York to have the king killed. From "A Tale of the Tubbs; or, Romes Master Peice Defeated" (broadside, 1679). (By permission of the British Library, Wing T128)

socially mobile figure, circulating through London's prisons and aristocratic households, gathering and disseminating intelligence. Even when at
home she seems to have run her household as a base of political operations—she lodged, and perhaps coached, the thirty Catholic boys from
St. Omer's seminary who came over to be witnesses on behalf of six men
accused by Titus Oates and tried in 1679; she sold her texts; she employed
scribes and secretaries; according to her accusers, she plotted treason and
hid incriminating documents in her flour tub. In sum, despite her motto,
"I never change," Elizabeth Cellier can be difficult to locate in relation to
the categories that often organize historical study.

Although the fiction of the "Meal Tub Plot" depended on a notion of
Cellier as an "author" who invented a sham plot and blamed it on Presbyterians, the extent of Cellier's responsibility for *Malice Defeated* was a point
of contention in her libel trial and in the various polemics written around
and in response to it. Cellier was tried for the "virulency and Malice" of her
pen, yet most of the legal personnel at the trial and the polemicists who
wrote about Cellier as author assumed that she could not have written the
text alone; she must have been guided, for instance, by Jesuits, those "Scrib-
ling Fathers"; or "a priest got into her Belly, and so speaking through her,
as the Devil through the Heathen Oracles," simultaneously impregnated
and possessed her with the book (see figure 5, in which Cellier is depicted
taking dictation from Jesuits).[21] Priests were often suspected as the ghost
writers, as well as ghostly fathers, behind those Catholics who found themselves in court, on the scaffold, and in print.[22] For Cellier, too, eloquence
could be heard as evidence not of authenticity and integrity but of con-
federacy and design. Her gender and her profession made skeptical observers and readers even more inclined to question her ability to create
without assistance, and to view her as the midwife to a text of which she was
not the parent.

In this context, any attempt on Cellier's part to own *Malice Defeated* can
be viewed as self-defeating presumption. One account of the libel trial, for
instance, ridicules Cellier for affirming her authorship: "she loudly answered,—*My Lord, I wrote it every Line my self.* So Ambitious she was of being *Gossip* to the Spurious Libel, though 'tis well known to be *The whole
Troops Child.*"[23] Cellier obviously had reasons for renouncing this bastard

---

21. *Tryal and Sentence of Elizabeth Cellier*, p. 14; *The Complaint of Mrs. Celliers, and the Jesuits
in Newgate* (London, 1680); *The Scarlet Beast Stripped Naked* (London, 1680), sig. A2v.

22. See, for instance, Capt. William Bedloe, *A Narrative and Impartial Discovery of the Horrid Popish Plot* (London, 1679), sig. A2.

23. *The Tryal of Elizabeth Cellier, the Popish Midwife, at the Old Baily, Septemb. 11 1680. For
Printing and Publishing the Late Notorious Libel, Intituled, Malice Defeated* (London, 1680), p. 2.

5. Cellier as author. She appears to be taking dictation from the Jesuits behind her. Queen of spades from playing cards depicting "The Meal Tub Plot." (Beinecke Rare Book and Manuscript Library, Yale University)

text, such as averting conviction; indeed, in another account of the trial she engages in some slippery maneuvering about what it means for the book to be "hers": "I said it was my Book, and so it was, because it was in my possession, but not that I writ it. This is my Fan, but it does not follow that I made it."[24]

Taken together, the various accounts of the libel trial suggest that, at least at the discursive level, Cellier is held accountable for the book—and

24. *Tryal and Sentence of Elizabeth Cellier*, p. 17.

held in contempt for trying to avoid that accountability—while she is yet
dismissed as an author—and held in contempt for claiming to be one. Insisting that the identity of "the worthy Author (whether *Lord,* or *Priest,* or
Monk, or *Bawd,* or *all* together)" of *Malice Defeated* is irrelevant to the prosecution, the legal and polemical cases against Cellier manage to convict
her of libel without ever conceding her competence as a writer or political
analyst.[25] As Sir Richard Weston explains in one account, "I think it is not
severe that you, who stand at the stake for all, must bear the blame of
all."[26] In short, a government outraged at the accusation that it tortured
prisoners and a legal system that needed someone to "stand at the stake
for all" required an author; that author was Elizabeth Cellier.[27] Although
various accounts of the libel trial evince interest in the processes of collaborative authorship—taking dictation and hiring copyists, for instance—
they make clear that in Cellier's case, authorship is not a process but a position. That position is at the stake or, more literally, on the pillory. By
whatever process *Malice Defeated* was composed, Cellier's name was on the
title page, and she sat on the pillory and did the time. Thus, from the perspective of Cellier's accusers and attackers, authorship becomes a kind of
martyrdom; she is a "Joan of Arque handling her *Pen* for the Papistical
Cause."

Yet, as this same writer goes on to lament, Cellier did not share the
"glory" of Joan of Arc's martyrdom; that is, she did not die.[28] As an autobi-
ographical account of a treason trial, *Malice Defeated* is highly unusual because so few persons tried for treason survived to write; certainly, no other
woman or Catholic wrote such a text. Cellier is thus unlike those women
for whom the prospect of death, whether in childbed or on the scaffold,
became the enabling condition of authorship or public speech;[29] she
writes *rather than* dies (instead of writing because she is about to die). Thus
the existence of *Malice Defeated* is more important than its accuracy, which
is, in any case, difficult to determine.

25. *Mr. Prance's Answer to Mrs. Cellier's Libel* (London, 1680), sig. Bv.
26. *Tryal and Sentence of Elizabeth Cellier,* p. 30.
27. I call Cellier an "author" on very different grounds than does Elaine Hobby, for
whom the author of *Malice Defeated* displays "the typically feminine need to clear Cellier
from charges of dishonesty and immodesty" (*Virtue of Necessity: English Women's Writing,
1649–88* [Ann Arbor: University of Michigan Press, 1988], p. 22).
28. *Midwife Unmask'd,* p. 1.
29. Catherine Belsey, *The Subject of Tragedy: Identity and Difference in Renaissance Drama*
(London: Methuen, 1985), pp. 190–91; Frances E. Dolan, "'Gentlemen, I have one thing
more to say': Women on Scaffolds in England, 1563–1680," *Modern Philology* 92.2 (1994):
157–78; Mary Beth Rose, "Where Are the Mothers in Shakespeare? Options for Gender
Representation in the English Renaissance," *Shakespeare Quarterly* 42.3 (Fall 1991): 290–
314, esp. 310–13; and Wall, *Imprint of Gender,* pp. 283–96.

In *Malice Defeated,* Cellier takes the inaccuracy of the charges and testimony against her as a gauge of the fictionality of the purported Meal Tub Plot: "If there be no more Truth in the whole Story, than there is in what relates to me, every Play that is Acted has more Truth in it" (sig. H2v). Yet *Malice Defeated* is itself another of the rival fictions that constitute this plot, rather than the truth against which they can be checked. Like any of the other texts, it uses conventions and form to interest and persuade. However, in struggling to contradict the "whole Story" with another, equally interested story, Cellier in *Malice Defeated* faced a particularly difficult choice when it came to form, a choice complicated by both her gender and her religious affiliation. Of the available forms, none of the more obvious options quite fitted the project, all exacted costs, and all could be turned against Cellier by her detractors.

Neither confession nor spiritual autobiography would work for Cellier because her story lacks an appropriate beginning. As Cellier tells it, it begins in adulthood and after marriage; it begins with conversion, a conversion more incriminating than justifying, rather than building toward it. Cellier presents her conversion not as a retreat into inwardness but as motivated by her reflections on political struggle: her horror at the treatment of Charles I and Royalists "for their being Papists and Idolaters." The conversion, in turn, motivates political resistance: her suspicion that the Popish Plot was merely "pretended" and her determination "to relieve the poor imprison'd Catholicks" (*MD,* sig. A2r–v). Her conversion initiates a story characterized by action, not by reflection or private devotions; justifying herself more by works than by faith, Cellier presents herself as an agent, not as a vessel through whom the spirit works.

Criminal (auto)biography is the last form Cellier would want, because she does not concede guilt, therefore does not repent, and, at the time she writes, has miraculously "delivered" herself from punishment. Similarly, Cellier does not present her text as a scandalous memoir, another genre available to notorious women. Instead, she insists that her sexual conduct or choices are not at issue, despite efforts in court and in print to shift the focus to them. Furthermore, the tendency of both scandalous memoir and criminal biography to criminalize self-determination runs counter to the positive depiction in *Malice Defeated* of Cellier's ability to deliver herself. Although the saint's life, the opposite of the criminal's biography, would appear to be an obvious choice for a Catholic woman's self-justification, there are no miracles in Cellier's story; she insists that she herself deserves the credit. Finally, Cellier's "Brief Relation" is more suspenseful and provisional than any of these forms would allow because it does not lead to the foregone conclusion of almost all of them—death. Even within Protestantism, as J. Paul Hunter points out, "the person whose life was published was nearly always someone already dead."[30] Just as Cellier's story does not begin with birth, in *Malice Defeated* or in the historical record, it does not end with death. She appears full-blown in scandal, then never subsides into repentance. Vital and vocal, Cellier evades this conventional closure, yet in her evasion she also misses out on the authorization that dying well confers on a life.

Querulously in this world rather than safely in the next, her narrative voice offers no assurances to readers. In refusing to wrap up the ends, Cellier insists that the future is uncertain not only for her but for England: "But how long either my self, or any other Loyal Subjects, shall be secure from the like Conspiracy, God only knows," Cellier concludes (*MD,* sig. L2v). This uncertainty, attended by a sense that she might alter a course not already determined, motivates action and speech.

Identified with a cause and with a community, Cellier also spills over the contours of the highly individualized narrator or protagonist: the speaking subject of autobiography, the lawbreaking subject of criminal biography, the suffering subject of hagiography and martyrology. While Cellier keeps her focus squarely on herself, she cycles through a variety of roles, which Weil catalogs as the royal jester, the martyr, the tragic heroine, and the clever legal tactician, discarding each as she reaches the limit of its usefulness.[31] This sequence of postures and voices suggests both self-consciousness about the options available for self-representation and an awareness of the shortcomings of any one. As a vehicle for depicting this discontinuous subjectivity, *Malice Defeated* is not as much shapeless as it is multiform, compounded of many voices, texts, and genres. In the frequent passages of dialogue set both inside and outside of court, *Malice Defeated* most resembles a play. At other moments it resembles a published archive of Cellier's case; at the risk of obscuring a coherent narrative of events, Cellier provides the reader with most of the documents through which she built her case, and with the evidence that condemns as well as supports her. As a consequence, *Malice Defeated* is noisy and visually chaotic.

Viewed as a whole, however, *Malice Defeated* is more than the sum of its parts; for Cellier does not simply move through forms and personae, revealing their inadequacy to the story she wants to tell and the self she wants to represent. Ultimately, she combines aspects of various forms and the subject-positions they confer on their protagonists to invent a new hybrid

30. J. Paul Hunter, *Before Novels: The Cultural Contexts of Eighteenth-Century English Fiction* (New York: Norton, 1990), p. 314.
31. Weil, "'If I Did Say So, I Lyed,'" p. 201.

form—the trial account written from the defendant's perspective, the legal romance, the criminalized-politicized-spiritual autobiography—and a new position and voice—the midwife who delivers herself, the "lady errant" who relieves her own distress. Cellier does not achieve the authority to set new terms or to invent new forms. Nor is experimentation unique to her. The climate of formal restlessness in the late seventeenth and early eighteenth centuries opened up the category of "writer" to many persons it had excluded previously and promoted many uncategorizable texts. In 1680, every publication was politically inflected and necessarily partisan. But Cellier's double jeopardy as female and Catholic forces her to expose the very inadequacy of the available forms and pushes her to the limits of the available options.

Even for those who wished to criminalize or dismiss Cellier, genre posed a dilemma, forcing them to combine old forms in new ways to tell her story. Cellier's many detractors invariably respond to her own self-presentations, picking up the terms she uses, trying on the forms she rejects, attempting to fit her into roles she spurns. Their many such attempts reveal the insufficiency of those forms as much as her own text does.

Although Cellier occasionally proclaims her willingness to die in defense of the truth, she focuses on the strategies by which she avoids conviction, suffering, and death. Many attacks on Cellier condemn just this strategic avoidance of suffering, distinguishing her from martyrs and interpreting her survival as a defeat. The pillory, a roughly cruciform "wooden engine," served as the focal point in parodic accounts of Cellier's "martyrdom." Intended to display and humiliate more than to injure, the pillory was supposedly a site of shame rather than an instrument of torture. On the pillory, the offender's head and hands were thrust through openings between two adjustable boards placed atop a pillar. Thereby exposed, the offender could not move to dodge the objects and abuse that might be hurled at him or her. According to Tim Harris, "the use of the pillory as a form of punishment effectively left execution of the sentence to the crowd," which might be lenient—even protecting the offender—or brutal, as it was to Cellier on her first appearance.[32] While the king's concession that Cellier could wield a racket to shield herself on subsequent occasions protected life and limb (see figures 6 and 7), it also provided even

---

32. Tim Harris, *London Crowds in the Reign of Charles II: Propaganda and Politics from the Restoration until the Exclusion Crisis* (Cambridge: Cambridge University Press, 1987), pp. 20, 130, 187. *The Life and Death of Mrs. Mary Frith* (London, 1662) describes "that Terrible Tempest of *Turnip Tops, Garbage, Dirt,* and *Brick-bracks*" prostitutes endure on the pillory as a "Martyrdome" (sigs. G4v–5).

6. Cellier on the pillory. From *The Popish Damnable Plot against Our Religion and Liberties*
(1681). (Beinecke Rare Book and Manuscript Library, Yale University)

more fodder for those who wished to mock her. Shielded physically, she
was more exposed in print. Freed from viewing her as a victim, her detractors, who were far more numerous and vociferous than her defenders, ridicule her misplaced sense of importance, her grandeur amidst *"rotten Eggs*
and *Turnip-tops,"* her sense that she was somehow above taking her lumps.[33]

33. Care, "Popes Harbinger," appended to *Weekly Pacquet of Advice from Rome* 3, no. 11
(Sept. 17, 1680): 87. Peter Lake and Michael Questier argue that Protestant accounts of
Catholic martyrdoms usually downplayed pain ("Agency, Appropriation, and Rhetoric under the Gallows: Puritans, Romanists, and the State in Early Modern England," *Past & Present* 153 [November 1996]: 64–107, esp. 79).

7. Cellier "disgracing" the pillory. Note that she seems to be wearing breeches here. Queen of diamonds from playing cards depicting "The Meal Tub Plot." (Beinecke Rare Book and Manuscript Library, Yale University)

Representations of Cellier on the pillory appropriated and parodied the rich Catholic iconography for representing the suffering female body. Some downplay her suffering; *Mr. Prance's Answer to Mrs. Cellier's Libel,* for instance, assures readers that "really she receiv'd no hurt from the Multitude, yet she pretended herself *half-Martyr'd.*"[34] Others emphasize how

34. *Mr. Prance's Answer to Mrs. Cellier's Libel,* sig. E2v.

hard she struggled to stay off the pillory. The construction of Cellier as martyr or "she-Saint" is invoked only in satires of her punishment. No Catholic texts constructing Cellier as a martyr survive, although the production and consumption of saints' and martyrs' lives, in print and in manuscript, were thriving, if clandestine, in post-Reformation England.

Catholic martyrologies contested Foxe's aggressively Protestant version of the history of Christian martyrdom. Whereas Foxe's *Actes and Monuments* led up to the Marian martyrs, Catholic martyrologies culminated in the Elizabethan and Jacobean executions of Jesuits, such as Edmund Campion and Henry Garnet, and in the Popish Plot casualties.[35] Like legal prosecutions, Catholic martyrologies focused on priests, and therefore tended to exclude women. Those few female martyrs who were executed for harboring priests were revered, but accounts of their martyrdoms circulated orally and in manuscript rather than in print. For example, Fr. John Mush's "Life" of Margaret Clitherow, who was pressed to death in York in 1587 because she refused to plead to the charge of harboring priests, survives in multiple manuscript versions, but was not published in its entirety until the nineteenth century.[36]

Women figured more prominently among saints' lives, which were more widely circulated in both manuscript and print. For post-Reformation Catholics, the saint's life became a feminized genre. According to J. A. Rhodes, in the late sixteenth and early seventeenth centuries, "nearly half the printed lives were about women saints and the majority of dedications were addressed to women."[37] Women also played important roles as translators (making texts written on the Continent more accessible to English readers, especially other women with more limited language skills), copyists (aiding the manuscript transmission of saints' lives), and consumers, especially in convents abroad. Yet the role of martyr or saint is one Cellier's detractors mockingly thrust upon her rather than one she assumed herself.[38]

35. A. G. Petti, "Richard Verstegan and Catholic Martyrologies of the Later Elizabethan Period," *Recusant History* 5.1 (1959): 64–90; Elizabeth Hanson, "Torture and Truth in Renaissance England," *Representations* 34 (1991): 53–84; and John R. Knott, *Discourses of Martyrdom in English Literature, 1563–1694* (Cambridge: Cambridge University Press, 1993), esp. chap. 2.

36. Fr. John Mush, "Life of Margaret Clitherow," in *The Troubles of Our Catholic Forefathers Related by Themselves*, ed. John Morris, 3 vols. (London: Burns & Oates, 1877), vol. 3. On Clitherow, see Megan Matchinske, *Writing, Gender, and State in Early Modern England: Identity Formation and the Female Subject* (Cambridge: Cambridge University Press, 1998), chap. 2.

37. J. T. Rhodes, "English Books of Martyrs and Saints of the Late Sixteenth and Early Seventeenth Centuries," *Recusant History* 22.1 (1994): 7–25, esp. 18. See also Helen White, *Tudor Books of Saints and Martyrs* (Madison: University of Wisconsin Press, 1963).

38. Visual representations of Cellier similarly parody Catholic iconography. In fig. 6, Cellier's shield resembles a *tavoletta*, a panel painted with images of the crucifixion and of

A look at one prototype of the genre suggests why Cellier would eschew it, as well as how it served the turn of her detractors. The most popular collection of saints' lives, John Heigham's translation of Alfonso Villegas's *Lives of Saints,* which went through many editions, offers some sense of the conventions that Cellier's detractors parodied. In Villegas's chronicle, the majority of female saints are martyred; these saints are usually nobly born, beautiful virgins; they lose copious amounts of blood and even body parts without dying; they can withstand extraordinary torments; they transcend all efforts to shame or humiliate them; they long for death but are extremely difficult to kill. According to Heigham, saints are "steadfast and unapalled in daungers; never ama[z]ed nor changed with the force of fortune: never moved with hatred, nor pricked forth with anger, nor wonne by fondnesse of affection." Although Heigham also claims that saints are "spiritual warriers" who must depend on "counsailes, advises, strange plottes and admirable stratagems" to "vanquish their enemies," most of the female saints whose lives he tells are more longsuffering than strategic.[39]

Various satires, which reveal an intimate familiarity with these conventions, depict Cellier as the opposite of a virgin martyr. The most sustained instance of the parodic antimartyrology, the *Adventure of "The Bloody Bladder": A Tragi-Comical Farce, Acted with Much Applause at Newgate by . . . Madam Cellier,* appended to Miles Prance's *Answer to Mrs. Cellier's Libel,* demonstrates how deftly satirists inverted the conventions of hagiography and martyrology. Although Antonia Fraser accepts Prance's scurrilous attack as an accurate description, I read it as evidence not necessarily of Cellier's conduct but of how her gender and religion combined to make her a particularly vulnerable target of satire.[40]

While the stories of martyred saints focus on the gory details of the ingenious torments they can survive without abjuring their faith, Prance's "tragi-comical farce" focuses on the shams Cellier supposedly employed to avoid standing in the pillory. First she takes a purge, but a day too soon; as a result, as a satire presented as *Maddam Celliers Answer to the Popes Letter* has her say, she "feigned to be monstrous sick and discharged my whole Artillery at both ends, with such fury, that what for fume and noise, none

---

martyrdoms held before the eyes of a condemned person in Catholic countries to console and distract him or her on the way to the place of execution and during the execution itself. On the *tavoletta,* see Samuel Y. Edgerton Jr., *Pictures and Punishment: Art and Criminal Prosecution during the Florentine Renaissance* (Ithaca: Cornell University Press, 1985), chap. 5; and David Freeberg, *The Power of Images: Studies in the History and Theory of Response* (Chicago: University of Chicago Press, 1989), pp. 5–9. I am grateful to James Grantham Turner for pointing out the resemblance between Cellier's shield and a *tavoletta.*

39. John Heigham, "Preface to the Reader," in Alfonso Villegas, *The Lives of Saints,* trans. Heigham (London, 1621), pp. *2v, *3.

40. See Antonia Fraser, *The Weaker Vessel* (New York: Knopf, 1984), p. 459.

durst approach me."[41] Then she declares herself with child, which "appear'd very improbable in a person of her *reverend years* [described later as "50-odd"], and one Midwife being sent to her retorn'd a *Non Inventus* on her Belly."[42] But the ruse does not end with this confrontation between a popish midwife and a credible one. When Cellier is about to be transported to the pillory, she claims to be in labor. Cellier's vociferous and seasoned performance of labor creates such a disturbance that it convinces those who are, according to Prance, already disposed to believe. "By this time some of her female popish Gang were got about her, and all agreed, that she was *just on point of delivery*. . . . She bellow'd out so hideously that one of the Popish Priests was over-heard to say *she over-acts it,* and some of the spectators thought her possest" (sig. E2). When at last "an able Physician and several discreet Women" search Cellier, they discover a blood-filled bladder. She "had used her skill in creating the necessary *Symptomes,* and preparing certain *Clotts* of it, and put them into her Body, (some of which sort design'd for a fresh supply, were also found elsewhere about her)" (sig. E2v). In Prance's view, if midwifery has taught Cellier anything, it is only how to deceive. Cellier has the skill to ape the symptoms of labor, but not so much skill that she cannot be found out and exposed by an "able Physician" and "discreet women." In Prance's text, she is finally undone by the very association with the female body that she tries to use to escape the pillory.

Thus Prance's *Adventure of "The Bloody Bladder"* and other antimartyr-ologies of Cellier depict her as the exact opposite of a virgin martyr. She is common, old, homely, and promiscuous; she is undesirable, but she makes claims to her own lust and her ability to provoke lust in others; the blood she loses is not even her own, only part of a ruse to avoid suffering; she complains bitterly about minor discomfort and scrambles to avoid her just punishment; she brings shame on herself through her disgusting and undignified attempts to avoid the pillory. She is cowardly, inconstant, and emotional. Her lack of bodily integrity—bleeding, bellowing, claiming to be pregnant—manifests her lack of spiritual integrity, just as the impenetrable virgin martyrs, whose bodies miraculously heal from attempts to rend them asunder, embody spiritual integrity. Far from resolutely silent,

41. *Maddam Celliers Answer to the Popes Letter* (London, 1680), p. 3.

42. *Mr. Prance's Answer to Mrs. Cellier's Libel,* sig. E2. Subsequent references in this paragraph are to this pamphlet. This incident is also mentioned in the broadside "Commentation on the Late Wonderful Discovery of the New Popish Plot" (London, 1680): "She who midwifes Trade well understood / Miscarried with her bladders Cram'd with blood." This broadside describes those who would defend Cellier as willing to "stoop to wipe clean madam Celliers Tail."

Cellier farts, belches, and bellows.[43] While her books are burned, her body is not. The various satires of Cellier's conduct on the pillory criticize her for making too much of her own suffering, for trying to avoid it, for not wanting to die, and for not dying. Deflating her pretensions to either heroic endurance or heroic action, to use Mary Beth Rose's helpful terms, such attacks cast Cellier into a narrative she does not choose for herself, only to insist indignantly that she does not belong there.[44]

If martyrology, "an intensely corporeal genre," as Elizabeth Hanson has called it, depicts spiritual agency that operates against or in spite of the suffering body, Prance's text suggests that Cellier's agency is wholly and degradingly corporeal.[45] Cellier's shameful performance of lack of bodily control—vomiting, shitting, and bleeding—associates her with the feminized body Gail Paster describes, whose emissions and porous boundaries are not under voluntary control.[46] This is the body that virgin martyrs transcend and whose meanings Catholic images—the sacred heart, the lactating virgin, the bleeding Christ—transform into positive icons of patient suffering and submission to forces beyond one's control. Yet Cellier's detractors censure her as much for her acts of will—taking the purge, devising the bloody bladder scheme—as for the resulting disorder and mess. It is her attempt to vomit, shit, and bleed on cue that is so objectionable. She may be an immodest schemer, but she is a failed one, her disorderly body defeating her pretensions to skill. Her body—obviously past pregnancy, too quick to respond to the ill-timed purge—outwits her attempts at counterfeiting, confirming that women's bodily disorders are involuntary and that some fluids and some orifices are more redemptive or sacralizable than others. In thus marking her body as carnivalesque rather than saintly or heroic, Cellier's lack of bodily control diminishes the threat she poses.

Consider Cellier in the context of the available traditions for depicting the Catholic female body. Anti-Catholic polemic dwells on women's lack of bodily closure and control in order to discredit them. Both Pope Joan and Joan of Arc, for example, are exposed by their pregnancies; like Cellier,

43. One pamphlet claims that the groans Cellier attributed to tortured prisoners in Newgate were actually the belches and farts of her female drinking buddies (*Modesty Triumphing over Impudence* [London, 1680], sig. B).

44. Mary Beth Rose, *The Expense of Spirit: Love and Sexuality in English Renaissance Drama* (Ithaca: Cornell University Press, 1989), chap. 3; and "'Vigorous Most / When Most Unactive Deem'd': Gender and the Heroics of Endurance in Milton's *Samson Agonistes*, Aphra Behn's *Oroonoko*, and Mary Astell's *Some Reflections upon Marriage*," *Milton Studies* 33 (1997): 83–109.

45. Hanson, "Torture and Truth," p. 68.

46. Gail Kern Paster, *The Body Embarrassed: Drama and the Disciplines of Shame in Early Modern England* (Ithaca: Cornell University Press, 1993).

"La Pucelle" is compromised by her attempt to use pregnancy to avoid martyrdom. Against this tradition, Counter-Reformation hagiography and martyrology emphasize holy women's extraordinary control over their bodies and fervent desire for death. Although saints' lives describe in gruesome detail the horrible mutilations and tortures inflicted on virgin saints, they observe a bodily decorum. The virgin martyrs' bodies are fountains of blood, yet they are not sexually penetrable and, apparently, excrete only from their wounds, not from the usual orifices. In many ways, Margaret Clitherow seems more like Cellier than like the virgin martyrs; she was a married mother who suffered imprisonment and execution in York within recent memory. However, by repeatedly telling readers that Clitherow refused to avoid or defer martyrdom by pleading her belly, *The Life of Margaret Clitherow* places her in the virgin martyr tradition and preserves her from the implication that she belongs with the fecund Joans. By Fr. Mush's account, Clitherow would have a good case: she is thirty, lending such a claim credibility; four women who search her pronounce her with child, and she herself confesses that she is inclined to believe that she is pregnant, although she cannot be sure, "having been deceived heretofore in this."[47] Since she is married, such a plea should not incriminate her. Her friends and family, even her judges, beseech her. Yet she refuses. Martyrs, of course, always prefer death to the alternatives. But the gendered theological and narratological traditions that shape depictions of Pope Joan, Joan of Arc, virgin martyrs, and Margaret Clitherow help to explain why Prance focuses his abusive satire on Cellier's attempt to avoid the pillory by pleading her belly. Seeking to avoid suffering and death, demonstrating lack of control over her body, and confessing sexual activity (even if the confession is not believed) all exclude Cellier from that elite group of holy—and dead—Catholic women. These alleged activities thereby ally her with the discredited women who hold center stage in anti-Catholic discourses: the two Joans. Lack of bodily control, then, does not really make Cellier a disorderly figure; instead, it puts her in her place.

The stones cast at Cellier in the pillory become crucial both to the purported attempts to construct her as a "she-Saint"—attempts registered, as I have said, only as they are countered by her detractors—and to polemical efforts to discredit Cellier as a candidate for sainthood or martyrdom.[48] According to some witnesses, Cellier pocketed stones pitched at her on the pillory.[49] She is later accused of storing them up as potential

47. Mush, "Life of Margaret Clitherow," p. 421.
48. *Scarlet Beast Stripped Naked*, p. 2.
49. Lady Russell reports this story, for instance, in a letter to her husband dated Sept. 17, 1680 (*Some Account of the Life of Rachael Wriothesley, Lady Russell*, p. 228).

relics. *The Popes Letter to Maddam Cellier* has her explain that "these hard Stones I carry home, / . . . / Which shallest soon be sent to *Rome*, / There to be Sanctify'd"; *The Devil Pursued* mocks that "these Stones and Dirt ought to be Relicks high."[50] In one satire presented as Cellier's own "Lamentation," she describes her "hopes of Saint *Celier* at last: Ile now begin to be in Love with a Pillory, and strive to merrit it as oft as I can, and every Stone they throw I'le labour to preserve as Monuments of my Sufferings, and secure them for Rellicks to Posterity."[51] The disdain both for the Catholic reverence for relics and for Cellier's claims to sanctity is also served by a crude sexual joke, since "stones" is a slang term for testicles. Cellier cannot resist collecting these stones because she has always had a weakness for them. The Cellier of *The Popes Letter* reminisces: "for stones I veneration had / . . . / Those given by many a Lusty Lad."[52] Whether as relics of her own martyrdom or as souvenirs of her promiscuity, the stones are viewed as embarrassingly literal and corporeal. Miring Cellier in her body and anchoring her to the earth, the stones she puts in her pockets contradict any claims she may make for her faith or purity.

Satires of the supposed sanctification of Cellier drew on a constellation of objections to Catholicism more generally, in which the theological cannot be disentangled from the political. First, the Catholic reverence for relics—otherwise ordinary, even distasteful objects (such as body parts), through which once-living persons continued to perform good works in the world—was widely disdained as a particularly superstitious, idolatrous practice.[53] Up to death, Catholic and Protestant martyrs were much alike. After death, Catholic saints distinguished themselves from the merely holy or venerable through their ability to effect miracles and intercede in the world of the living, an ability focused in the concrete yet wonder-working relic. As Protestantism labored to achieve what Lyndal Roper has called a "desomatization of the spiritual," its difference from Catholicism was often described in terms of the latter's inability to distinguish the material from the spiritual, the mortal from the divine. Just as the deft inversion of martyrology in attacks on Cellier reveals how complexly intertwined were the Catholic and Protestant imaginaries in this period, so, in a culture in which

50. *The Popes Letter to Maddam Cellier in Relation to Her Great Sufferings for the Catholick Cause, and Likewise Maddam Celliers Lamentation Standing on the Pillory* (London, 1680), p. 4; *The Devil Pursued; or, The Right Saddle Laid upon the Right Mare: A Satyr upon Maddam Celliers Standing in the Pillory* (London, 1680).

51. *Mistress Celiers Lamentation for the Loss of Her Liberty* (London 1681), sig. Av.

52. *Popes Letter to Maddam Cellier*, p. 4.

53. Patrick Geary, "Sacred Commodities: The Circulation of Medieval Relics," in *The Social Life of Things: Commodities in Cultural Perspective*, ed. Arjun Appadurai (Cambridge: Cambridge University Press, 1986), pp. 169–91.

corpses' wounds opened to accuse murderers, making a wax image was illegal, and iconoclasts found images so powerful that they had to destroy
them, Protestants strenuously repudiated belief in the efficacy of objects
because it still shaped many of their own practices. For instance, the attribution of magical properties to dead bodies, especially the bodies of executed criminals, was not restricted to Catholics. Because the criminal and
the saintly were never clearly distinguished in Christian tradition, many
people viewed a criminal's body as "a collection of magical talismans, the
pieces invested with supernatural power akin to the healing potential
which relics contained," as Roper puts it.[54] Protestantism could distance itself from its own reverence for the material by suggesting that Catholics
were indiscriminate in their approach to objects, turning anything re-
motely associated with the Catholic cause into a relic. In the almost complete absence of material evidence of Catholic conspiracy at this time, polemicists had a hard time naming the evidence of crime and punishment
that Catholics could transubstantiate into relics. The Meal Tub Plot was a
more fruitful field than the Popish Plot: one satire claims that the pope has
ordered the Franciscans to "preserve the *Meal-Tub*, in which lay hid the
Design of the holy Cause, among their chiefest Reliques."[55] And, of course,
there were those stones.

The antimartyrologies of Cellier also drew on widespread contempt for
what John Dormer describes as Catholics' "whole design of Canonizing
those men for Saints, whom the Justice of the Nation hath Condemned for
Traytors."[56] In this process of transforming criminals into saints, Catholics
published the last speeches of those condemned in relation to the Popish
Plot, all of whom protested their innocence, and revalued objects associated with them.[57] Polemicists castigated this process as an affront to the
English nation and to English law, as well as laughable proof that Catho-

---

54. Lyndal Roper, *Oedipus and the Devil: Witchcraft, Sexuality, and Religion in Early Modern
Europe* (London and New York: Routledge, 1994), pp. 177, 189. On the magical attributes
of criminal bodies, see also Peter Linebaugh, *The London Hanged: Crime and Civil Society in
the Eighteenth Century* (Cambridge: Cambridge University Press, 1992); and Katharine Park,
"The Criminal and the Saintly Body: Autopsy and Dissection in Renaissance Italy," *Renaissance Quarterly* 47.1 (1994): 1–33.

55. *Popes Letter to Maddam Cellier*, pp. 2–3.

56. Dormer, *New Plot of the Papists*, p. 5. This complaint was also made about attempts to
sanctify the "traitors" executed for their involvement in the Gunpowder Plot. See Robert
Picket, *The Jesuits Miracles; or, New Popish Wonders* (London, 1607).

57. Kenyon, *Popish Plot*, pp. 181–82. In an appendix Kenyon summarizes the slow process by which many of those executed for involvement in the Popish Plot were granted
the status "venerable" by Pope Leo XIII in 1886, then beatified by Pope Pius XI in 1929.
A lucky few (six) were finally canonized by Pope Paul VI in 1970.

lics could not tell a saint from a traitor. Catholics were not, in fact, indiscriminate in electing saints or collecting relics; they revered as martyrs those very persons whom the state had marked and eliminated as traitors. They viewed a place of punishment as a site for pilgrimage (as Henrietta Maria's supposed march to Tyburn suggested). Reducing this complex cultural struggle to some nail parings, polemicists could minimize what they feared as dangerous. Similarly, in the case of Elizabeth Cellier—female, lay, alive—polemicists found a particularly opportune occasion for ridiculing the whole project of transforming criminals into saints.

If the parodies of "saint Cellier" drew their terms from Catholic traditions, forcing Cellier into forms that ill suited her and simultaneously parodying both those narrative conventions and her failure to conform to them, then parodies of Cellier as a "heroina" drew their terms from *Malice Defeated* itself. These attacks actually build on more observant readings of *Malice Defeated*, if on equally great hostility and misogyny. For, while Cellier never depicts herself as a saint, she does borrow some elements from chivalric romance in telling her story. Unlike either the martyrology or the criminal biography, the romance does not necessarily require that the protagonist die (although many women in romances do) or admit guilt.

The basic outlines of the romance, as found in the oft-told stories of English knights errant such as St. George and Guy of Warwick, are simple: a knight slays dragons, conquers giants, and frees "tender Ladies from their harmes." As Guy of Warwick explains in Samuel Rowlands's version of the story, first published in 1609 and reprinted at least nine times by 1680, "Men easily may revenge the deeds men doe,/But poore weak women have no strength thereto." In a dedication "To the Honourable Ladies of England," Rowlands suggests that this is one of the ways romances are rooted in the past: "Ladies in elder times your sex did need/Knight-hoods true valour to defend your rights."[58] Through this association with a safely remote, fairytale past, the romance enables Cellier, like those women writers of romance whom Ballaster discusses, to justify her presence in the public sphere by "dehistoricizing and mythologizing" it.[59]

Defending her refusal to pay the jury that acquits her of treason the customary guinea per man, Cellier expresses her confidence that they "will

---

58. Samuel Rowlands, *The Famous History of Guy Earle of Warwick* (London, 1649), sigs. A3, N, A4. For the print history of this and other romances, see Tessa Watt, *Cheap Print and Popular Piety, 1550–1640* (Cambridge: Cambridge University Press, 1991), esp. chap. 7. Along with endless versions of popular stories of "knight-hoods true valour," however anachronistic, some stories of female warriors, usually dressed as men, also circulated in the seventeenth century.

59. Ballaster, *Seductive Forms*, p. 35.

not forfeit your Spurs by oppressing the Distressed She, Your selves and the Laws have preserv'd from a raging Dragon." While Cellier never explains exactly who plays the dragon in this scenario, she does insist that to pay the jurors would be to disqualify them from knighthood. Furthermore, if Cellier could pay them, she would not be as "distressed" as she has claimed to be throughout the trial. But, conversely, she would also have to defer more to her champions than she seems to want to do in *Malice Defeated*. Given her innocence and her skill in demonstrating it, how could they have done otherwise than acquit her? Why should she pay them, when she did the work? As she concludes her text, she expresses her hope that "the judicious Reader will pardon what is either forgot, or not well express'd, in consideration that I was forc'd to defend my life, both against the Knights and the Dragon, for in this unequal Combate there was no St. *George* to defend me against him" but rather an array of titled gentlemen in cahoots with the dragon. The "knights" before whom she stood accused should "blush at the weakness of their Combatant" (sig. L2v). Cellier does not depict herself as a fierce female warrior, but neither does she depict herself as a martyr. She emphasizes her economic distress, dependency, and gratitude to explain why she will not sacrifice her fragile finances to a custom; she simpers about her weakness as a combatant just after she has pointed out that she has acted as her own St. George, stepping in for England's absentee patron saint to save herself. At various points in *Malice Defeated*, Cellier appeals to the jury, the law, and her readers to "deliver" her, but she also emphasizes that in the end, the midwife has had to deliver herself. Cellier does not just regender the knight errant as feminine, creating the "lady errant," as her detractors claim; she combines in one the "Distressed Damosel" and the rescuer (sig. H). Only by placing its female protagonist in two distinct narrative roles at once can *Malice Defeated* tell the story of a woman who cannot defend her life "like a man" yet "will not part with it in complement to your Lordships" (sig. H2v). By intermarrying the chivalric romance with the trial account, Cellier creates a hybrid role—the heroine/defendant/attorney—which enables the female protagonist to be simultaneously active and innocent, heroic and alive. This was as great a challenge in secular fictions as it was in sacred ones.

The suffering female protagonist had a long tradition; as I have just shown, in representations of virgin saints, virtue equals suffering, and the more one suffers, the more, paradoxically, one triumphs. Surprisingly, this narrative pattern in pre- and Counter-Reformation texts was not doomed by its association with Catholicism, but rather became increasingly prominent and pervasive. According to Laura Brown, for instance, defenseless, victimized, masochistic figures in the drama and the novel are "discursively passive" but also "structurally threatening."[60] Mary Beth Rose has demonstrated that texts as diverse as conduct books, sermons, epics, novels, and plays in seventeenth-century England explore the "heroics of endurance."[61] While the value placed on this heroism made it possible to include women and a much broader range of men in the category "hero," it did not open up a place for someone like Elizabeth Cellier. Describing how she ends her suffering, and building toward escape and survival rather than defeat and death, Elizabeth Cellier's *Malice Defeated* departs from those genres in which, according to John Richetti, "utter helplessness" is "required for heroic status," especially for women.[62] To depict her competent, energetic, and successful strategies for avoiding the pyre, Cellier adapts the vocabulary and roles of chivalric romance to depict female agency positively.

Romance carried some hazards, however, in that it was easy for Cellier's detractors to turn the form against her. By the mid–seventeenth century, in the wake of Cervantes's *Don Quixote*, it was hard to distinguish earnest representatives of the romance from parodies.[63] Before she was threatened with standing at the pillory herself, Cellier ridiculed Dangerfield for his stint "mounted upon the Wooden Engine": he "peep'd through it like *Don Quicksot* through his Helmet, when he was mounted upon *Rosinant,* and going to encounter with the *Windmil*" (*MD,* sig. D2). After she makes her own visits to the pillory, satires turn Cellier's wit against her, mounting her, like Dangerfield, on a stationary and humiliating steed. Much is made of the fact that Cellier was allowed to face her final two encounters with the rowdy crowd wearing armor of sorts, described as a "wooden Buckler and Fence of trusty Bull-hide" in *Maddam Celliers Answer to the Popes Letter.* As *A Letter from the Lady Cresswell* elaborates, "This *She-Donna Quixot* . . . encounters with many *Wind-mills,* and is armed *Cap-a-Pe* with *Impudence* and *Lying . . .* she is armed with a *Jesuits Launce* and a *Sword for the Cause,* which she furiously brandishes," especially at Dangerfield. *Maddam Celliers Answer to the Popes Letter* simultaneously heroizes and ridicules Cellier, exaggerating her torments (she is battered with thousand-pound millstones and hundred-pound iron globes) and her panache in resistance (she catches

---

60. Laura Brown, *Ends of Empire: Women and Ideology in Early Eighteenth-Century English Literature* (Ithaca: Cornell University Press, 1993), pp. 67, 74.

61. Mary Beth Rose, "Gender and the Heroics of Endurance."

62. John Richetti, *Popular Fiction before Richardson: Narrative Patterns, 1700–1739* (Oxford: Clarendon, 1969), p. 208.

63. *Don Quixote* was translated into English in 1612 and 1620. By that time, romance and antiromance were intermingled in England. See Paul Salzman, *English Prose Fiction, 1558–1700* (Oxford: Clarendon, 1985), chap. 15; and Michael McKeon, *Origins of the English Novel* (Baltimore: Johns Hopkins University Press, 1987), pp. 52–64.

cannonballs "like Sugar-plums . . . between my Teeth"). Rather than dwell on her stratagems for avoiding the pillory, this satire depicts Cellier as a fierce virago whose skills are entertainingly gladiatorial: "Strenuously (as *Romes* Championess) Like *Jezabel* I marched along to the War Charriot that they had prepared to transport me to the Theater wherein I was to Act my part, in view of all the gaping Heriticks."[64] She is still "standing at the stake for all" against her will, but now she is chained to it like a bear, raging against those who amuse themselves by baiting her. Like the *Adventure of "The Bloody Bladder,"* this text confers power, skill, and agency on Cellier, yet depicts a woman's defense of herself as inevitably grotesque. An active rather than passive female heroism can easily be caricatured; the slide from "heroina" to Gargantua is a short one.

Romance was also a risky choice for Cellier's self-justifying narrative because the form, "perceived as catering to a growing and commercially important female audience," was "denigrated as a 'women's genre.'" According to Helen Hackett, "women were fed with romance as consumers, while being simultaneously castigated for accepting it, and categorically excluded from its manufacture."[65] For the most part, men wrote romances, and they reserved all the juiciest parts for themselves. As Anthony Fletcher points out, works such as *Guy of Warwick* offered guidelines for becoming a man and espoused a masculine form of heroism; "there was no comparable literature for girls who were learning to become women."[66] Yet women did read romances, as frequent attacks on their doing so reveal. These attacks articulate the fear that female readers may learn a great deal about becoming women from *Guy of Warwick* and other romances, and that much of what they learn may work against their industriousness, chastity, and contentment at home. Furthermore, women may not identify with the "poor weak woman" the hero rescues, avenges, marries, abandons. They may identify instead with the wandering and adventurous hero; or they may resist, supplement, or adapt the narrative.[67] Certainly, *Malice Defeated* suggests that a female subject may insert herself into a romance narrative in highly creative and unpredictable ways.

64. *Maddam Celliers Answer to the Popes Letter,* pp. 3–4; *A Letter from the Lady Cresswell to Madam C. the Midwife* (London, 1680), p. 4.

65. Helen Hackett, "'Yet Tell Me Some Such Fiction': Lady Mary Wroth's *Urania* and the 'Femininity' of Romance," in *Women, Texts, and Histories, 1575–1760,* ed. Clare Brant and Diane Purkiss (London and New York: Routledge, 1992), pp. 39–68, esp. 40, 46. See also Ballaster, *Seductive Forms,* chaps. 1 and 2.

66. Anthony Fletcher, *Gender, Sex, and Subordination in England, 1500–1800* (New Haven: Yale University Press, 1995), p. 89.

67. Caroline Lucas, *Writing for Women: The Example of Woman as Reader in Elizabethan Romance* (Milton Keynes, Pa.: Open University Press, 1989).

Objections to women's relation to romance can be charted through dismissive or censorious references to the "lady errant," a term that, as Hero Chalmers says, was often used "for the parody of improper feminine pretensions."[68] While romances were sometimes depicted as compensations for women's exclusion from public life, harmless if indolent distractions, these compensatory fantasies could also be depicted as encouraging women to leave their closets for a life of adventure, thereby making themselves even more ridiculous. In a widely quoted character sketch of a chambermaid, for instance, Thomas Overbury describes her as reading *"Greenes* workes over and over, but is so carried away with the *Myrrour of Knighthood,* she is many times resolv'd to run out of her selfe, and become a Ladie Errant."[69] To identify with the lady errant is to long to "run out of" one's self and one's life toward social mobility, sexual fulfillment, and adventure.

Cellier's detractors invariably disparage her by claiming that she is motivated only by an unseemly and laughable sexual desire, despite the fact that Cellier's quest as described in *Malice Defeated* is not in the least amatory or erotic.[70] The most sustained send-up of Cellier as lady errant is *Modesty Triumphing over Impudence; or, Some Notes upon a Late Romance Published by Elizabeth Cellier, Midwife and Lady Errant* (1680). The author claims that since "our *Lady Errant* is resolved to keep up the Antick Mode of *Romances,*" he will also, and proceeds to depict an encounter between "our *Dido* and *Aeneas*" (that is, Cellier and Dangerfield) in which "she huffs with many rants and resolutions, stollen out of Romances and Playes."[71] In this "romance," Cellier resembles Lady Wishfort, an older woman made ridiculous by desire.

Thus the lady errant was another manifestation of the unruly woman, distinguished by her engagement in public life. Like Cellier, women peti-

---

68. Hero Chalmers, "'The Person I Am, or What They Made Me to Be': The Construction of the Feminine Subject in the Autobiographies of Mary Carleton," in Brant and Purkiss, *Women, Texts, and Histories,* pp. 164–94, esp. 186. Henry Care compared Cellier to Mary Carleton (1634–73), also known as the "German Princess": "The *German Princess* her *Townswoman,* though great in the *Rolls of Fame,* is yet quite obscured by the Exploits of this more *Illustrious Heroina*" ("Popes Harbinger," appended to *Weekly Pacquet of Advice from Rome* 3, no. 16 [Oct. 22, 1680], p. 136). Carleton was tried twice for bigamy (1660 and 1663) and ultimately hanged for theft in 1673.

69. Thomas Overbury, *New and Choise Characters* (London, 1615), sigs. J4v–5.

70. See Weil on the aggressive eroticization of Cellier in the various attacks on her ("'If I Did Say So, I Lyed,'" pp. 202–6). Contemporaries routinely assumed Cellier to be guilty of sexual misconduct. Gilbert Burnet, for instance, describes her as "a popish midwife, who had a great share of wit, and was abandoned to lewdness" (*Burnet's History of My Own Time,* pt. 1, *The Reign of Charles the Second,* ed. Osmund Airy, 2 vols. [Oxford: Clarendon, 1900], 2: 244–45).

71. *Modesty Triumphing over Impudence,* sigs. Bv, C2v.

tioners during the Civil War were called "brave Virago's" and "Ladyes-errants" largely because they refused to stay home and out of the political process.[72] Satires on Cellier censure her for trying to "run out of" the self that is held accountable for libel, and depict female self-assertion as silly and ribald. They also often suggest that a lady errant is not only one who wanders or travels but one who strays, errs, makes mistakes, in part because, for a woman, to move out of acceptable roles and relationships, to leave home, is itself to transgress.[73]

Yet another danger in Cellier's borrowing from romance to tell a story she insists is true is that "romance," like "fiction," was commonly used to mean a lie or an exaggeration. Cellier herself uses the word this way when she explains in *Malice Defeated:* "I durst not trust my self with such a Doughty Knight as Sir William [Waller] was, lest he shuld make Romances of me, as he had done of others" (sig. G). In its association with lying, the romance stands in the same double jeopardy that plagues Cellier, thus intensifying its riskiness for her. Fictionality and artful duplicity were often equated with femininity. In addition, Catholics were widely presumed to be adroit and shameless liars. *Mr. Prance's Answer to Mrs. Cellier's Libel* warns readers: "The more Groundless and *Improbable* such their Lies are, with so much the greater *Assurance* do they Print, and Brazen them out to the World, to make them Credited. . . . *Cellier* and her *Inspirers,* wanted not *Presidents* for their Fiction, their Party having so long *inur'd* themselves to Forging Untruths, that now they think they may lawfully *Lie* by *Prescription.*"[74] In the week of Cellier's sentencing, Henry Care claimed that "'That's a Cellier Sir'" was "a modern and most proper Phrase to signifie *any Egregious Lye.*"[75] Because of the association of Catholicism and femininity with lying, a female "popish" narrator would have had a hard time asserting herself as reliable, even in the novel, the "new," more capacious form that supposedly emerged from the generic dissatisfaction and experimentation in which texts such as *Malice Defeated* participated.[76]

72. The phrases are quoted from Patricia Higgins, "The Reactions of Women, with Special Reference to Petitioners," in *Politics, Religion, and the English Civil War,* ed. Brian Manning (London: Edward Arnold, 1973), p. 205. See also Sharon Achinstein, "Women on Top in the Pamphlet Literature of the English Revolution," *Women's Studies* 24 (1994): 131–63; and Phyllis Mack, *Visionary Women: Ecstatic Prophecy in Seventeenth-Century England* (Berkeley: University of California Press, 1992).

73. According to the *OED*, the meanings of two originally distinct words—one meaning to journey or to travel, the other meaning to stray or to wander—became confused. As a consequence, to be a knight or lady errant might mean either to be itinerant or to be wayward (that is, to stray from the proper course or place), or both.

74. *Mr. Prance's Answer to Mrs. Cellier's Libel,* sigs. Cr–v.

75. Care, "Popes Harbinger," appended to *Weekly Pacquet of Advice from Rome* 3, no. 10 (Sept. 10, 1680), p. 79.

76. Ballaster, "Fiction Feigning Femininity."

Thus, used in reference to Catholics, the word "romance" took on all the resonances of "Rome." Owing their first allegiance to Rome, Catholics would "make romances" rather than face the truth of Protestantism or of their own treason. In Defoe's *New Family Instructor* (1720), the Father provides what Michael McKeon calls "a false but suggestive" etymology for "romance." In the absence of real miracles, priests had to fabricate stories; ultimately, any lie came to be known as a "Roman Legend." "Hence, I derive the Word Romance, (*viz.*) from the Practice of the *Romanists*, in imposing Lyes and Fables upon the World; and I believe . . . that Popery is a *Romantick Religion.*"[77] Strengthening the connection between romances and Romanists, most chapbook romances were set in a pre-Reformation world, and are difficult to distinguish from saints' lives.[78] Like Catholics, often accused of "backwardness in religion," the romance nostalgically imagined a lost world, even if it did not try to restore it. When Cellier, the "Popish Romancer,"[79] combines the pretensions to fact of the trial account with the presumed fantasy of the romance, when she tells the story of "now" in the form and conventions of "once upon a time," she compromises her already wounded credibility.

Yet, if the Meal Tub Plot is a fantasy, whose fantasy is it? Since by 1680 it had become clear that both Whigs and Tories could and did engage in suborning witnesses, the Meal Tub Plot provided particularly shaky ground for contesting Catholics' willingness to believe "Roman Legends" and to tell lies, since it was itself dependent on improbable narratives and witnessings from the grave. What proof was there that Whigs could tell the difference between representation and reality? That there was such a difference? Many scholars have argued that the seventeenth century was a period in which the division between fact and fiction was uncertain, yet distinctions were starting to be made, especially in legal and narrative terms.[80] By combining the trial narrative, the romance, and autobiography

---

77. McKeon, *Origins of the English Novel*, p. 89, quoting Defoe. Romance was also associated with Royalists, who used the form to represent their experience of the Civil War and to explore the ideal relationship not only between men and women but between sovereigns and subjects. See Victoria Kahn, "Margaret Cavendish and the Romance of Contract," *Renaissance Quarterly* 50 (1997): 526–66; Annabel Patterson, *Censorship and Interpretation: The Conditions of Writing and Reading in Early Modern England* (Madison: University of Wisconsin Press, 1984), chap. 4; Salzman, *English Prose Fiction*, chap. 11; and Susan Staves, *Players' Scepters: Fictions of Authority in the Restoration* (Lincoln: University of Nebraska Press, 1979), pp. 51–73.

78. Hunter, *Before Novels*, p. 87; and Margaret Spufford, *Small Books and Pleasant Histories: Popular Fiction and Its Readership in Seventeenth-Century England* (Athens: University of Georgia Press, 1981), pp. 219–20.

79. *Scarlet Beast Stripped Naked*, p. 3.

80. See Lorraine Daston, "Marvelous Facts and Miraculous Evidence in Early Modern Europe," *Critical Inquiry* 18.1 (1991): 93–124; Lennard J. Davis, *Factual Fictions: The Ori-*

in the remarkable way that it does, *Malice Defeated* participates in the inter-
rogation of standards of evidence that emerged from the Popish Plot trials.
While Cellier's references to romance made it even easier to dismiss her
and the veracity of her text, they also seem to have provoked anger and
anxiety by forcing attention to the crucial roles of narratives as evidence
and to the interconnection of politics and "romance" at this moment.

As a result, many responses to *Malice Defeated* and to Cellier's public appearances more generally attempted to redraw a line between fact and
fiction and to fix Cellier in place. In various satires, Newgate prison becomes an "inchanted castle." According to *The Tryal of Elizabeth Cellier*, for
instance, "the *distressed Damosel* was forced to take up her Lodging for that
Night in the *Inchanted Castle* of *Newgate*."[81] Since Cellier insists that Captain
Richardson, the keeper of Newgate, tortures Catholic prisoners, *A Letter
from the Lady Cresswell to Madam C. the Midwife* satirically warns her not to
venture "within his *Inchanted Castle* again, lest you want an *Knight Errant* to
release you, for he is a *Fell Gyant* as you have made him."[82] Extending the
vocabulary of romance from the personnel of Cellier's trials to the site of
her punishment, these satirists depend on readers to recognize that crime
and romance are incommensurate. Newgate is not an enchanted castle
from which a knight can spring Cellier, but a prison into which she is committed. Captain Richardson is not a "Fell Gyant," despite her outrageous
and incredible charges; he is a responsible government official, and one to
whom she may appropriately be subject. These writers concede that Cellier is "distressed," but even if she needs a knight errant, she will neither
find one nor be able to become one. Written after Cellier's conviction for
libel, in response to her now criminalized text and qualified legal victory,
such vituperations expose the intransigence of the "real," which is understood in terms of punishment and suffering. However imaginative she may
be, she cannot turn Newgate into an enchanted castle, attract a knight's
protection, or effect her own escape. If she wants to imagine herself in a
romance, they will humor her. But her skills as a litigant and a storyteller
cannot really transport her from the criminal biography in which her detractors think she belongs, with its grim and intractable conclusions, into
a romance. She may think of herself as a lady errant, but the law will keep
her in her place—at the pillory, in prison.

The many attacks on Cellier suggest that forms such as hagiography and
romance cannot accommodate the aging female body, with its "fume and

---

gins of the English Novel (New York: Columbia University Press, 1983); and Barbara Shapiro,
Probability and Certainty in Seventeenth-Century England (Princeton: Princeton University
Press, 1983).

81. *Tryal of Elizabeth Cellier*, p. 2.
82. *Letter from the Lady Cresswell*, p. 4.

noise," without collapsing into satire. They also express such obsessive interest in her body that they almost seem to lose track of their political project; misogyny so facilitates the attack that it almost pushes it out of control. Tory and Whig propaganda in this period were equally scurrilous, scatalogical, even pornographic; men's bodies and their sexual conduct might also become targets.[83] But the long-standing alliance between Catholicism and depictions of the female body and between misogyny and anti-Catholicism made a woman such as Cellier an especially easy target, and one almost impossible to defend. The apparent hostility of the crowd that threw things at her suggests how difficult a figure Cellier was to champion. Catholic iconographic traditions provided her attackers with precedents for displaying the suffering female body in vivid terms, thereby turning her "own" traditions against her. As a result, it was difficult for English Catholics to reclaim the depiction of the female body in this political context. Perhaps this is why virtually no defenses of Cellier were published after her visits to the pillory, and why she apparently insisted in both her trials that she stood "singly and alone." As I have argued, this sense that she can depend only on herself infuses Cellier's depiction of herself as a romantic figure; through romance, Cellier can recast abandonment as independence. Cellier's claim that she stands "singly and alone" can also be read as an admission that she is indefensible, that she has become, by the time of the libel trial, impossible to represent in positive terms. She was even less defensible after her visits to the pillory and attacks such as Prance's *Adventure of "The Bloody Bladder."* She was too female, too staunchly Catholic, too sloppily embodied. To engage in representing her was to wade into a mess, both literally (the bloody bladder, the stones, etc.) and generically. What middle ground might Catholic apologists have found between the hagiographic idealization of suffering and death and the ridicule that attends nonlethal punishments for women, such as the pillory, cucking, and bridling? Between the "holy joy" martyrs experienced in the divine comedy of their executions and the ribald "tragi-comic farce" of the bloody bladder?[84]

---

83. Harris, *London Crowds*, pp. 146–48; James Grantham Turner, "Pepys and the Private Parts of Monarchy," in *Culture and Society in the Stuart Restoration: Literature, Drama, History*, ed. Gerald Maclean (Cambridge: Cambridge University Press, 1995), pp. 95–110; Rachel Weil, "Sometimes a Scepter Is Only a Scepter: Pornography and Politics in Restoration England," in *The Invention of Pornography: Obscenity and the Origins of Modernity*, ed. Lynn Hunt (New York: Zone Books, 1993), pp. 125–53; and Steven N. Zwicker, *Lines of Authority: Politics and English Literary Culture, 1648–1689* (Ithaca: Cornell University Press, 1993), chap. 4.

84. On "holy joy," see John R. Knott, *Discourses of Martyrdom in English Literature, 1563–1694* (Cambridge: Cambridge University Press, 1993), pp. 78–83. On how the cucking stool and bridle encouraged the ridicule of afflicted women, see Lynda E. Boose, "Scolding Brides and Bridling Scolds: Taming the Woman's Unruly Member," *Shakespeare Quarterly* 42.2 (1991): 179–213.

Even if there had been forms available for defending someone like Cellier, it is not clear that there was a Catholic propaganda machine that could counter the Whig one at that moment. By that time, even Tory propagandists had tried to distance themselves from, and even to define their position against, Catholicism. Few and narrowly distributed, Catholic pamphlets had little chance of convincing the unconverted.[85] As a result, the surviving defenses of Cellier are either retrospective or unpublished; there was not a positive counterdiscourse in defense of Cellier as there was in defense of the Virgin Mary and Henrietta Maria. John Warner argues that Cellier "deserved a happier fate, whether we consider her mental abilities, or her blameless morals, or the courage of mind with which she rose above every danger, or her zeal in defending the Royal Authority, which was the sole cause of her coming into danger and stirring up the hornets' nest, or finally her constancy in the Faith which she embraced as an adult."[86] Henry Foley discusses a manuscript headed "A true relation of some judgments of God against those who accused the priests and other Catholics after the pretended plot in England," which reported that

> nearly all those who had a hand in her accusation and unjust sentence were manifestly chastised by God. Two of them afterwards went mad. Many of those who cast stones at her in the pillory were wounded by their own companions. Another youth who was very active at this work, instantly fell sick, and, retiring to a stable close by, remained there for some days unknown, and then being carried to his parents' house, died there within three days, unable to pronounce any other words than *"Sellier, Sellier."*[87]

Belief in such divine retribution, even if it did circulate among Catholics as a cheering rumor, has barely made it into the historical record. At one point in the treason trial as Cellier relates it, she says to the Lord Chancellor: "I know I am the talk of the Town; but what do the Judicious say of me, for it is that I value, and not the prate of the Rabble" (*MD,* sig. Gv). Unfortunately, those whom Cellier might have regarded as judicious do not seem to have published. Against the many attacks on Cellier, little was said in print in her defense. Nor does *Malice Defeated* set the record straight. In the case of a notorious woman with a missing past, what constitutes truth? Yet some copies of *Malice Defeated* escaped burning. As a consequence, Cellier's detractors did not get the last word. Furthermore, *Malice*

85. Harris, *London Crowds,* p. 169; cf. chap. 6, passim; Miller, *Popery and Politics,* p. 177.

86. Warner, *History of English Persecution of Catholics,* 2: 425.

87. Henry Foley, *Records of the English Province of the Society of Jesus,* vol. 5 (London: Burns & Oates, 1879), p. 74.

Defeated suggests that the town talk was more contentious than a Protestant-biased print record would lead us to believe.

" 'TWAS TRIAL NOT OF LIFE AND DEATH, BUT SKILL": CELLIER AS DEFENDANT

My organization misleadingly suggests that Cellier's positions as author and as defendant are separable. They are not. The fullest account of her operations as a defendant is attributed to her authorship; this attribution led, in turn, to her second stint as defendant. Indeed, Cellier claims to have intended it that way. According to a postscript to *Malice Defeated*, dated three weeks before her libel trial, which describes attempts to stop the printing, Cellier claims: "I publish'd it because I would come again before their Lordships" (sig. M). Why would she wish to do so? To turn the tables by accusing Sir William Waller, Dangerfield, and others of high treason. By this account, *Malice Defeated* was intended not to put closure on Cellier's treason trial but rather to instigate a new trial in which Cellier would play the roles of accuser and prosecutor. Despite the fact that the libel trial again cast Cellier as the defendant, this second trial confirmed that her roles as author and defendant were intertwined.

Like the representations of Elizabeth Cellier as author and protagonist, the diverse representations of her encounters with the law center on the roles that her legal prosecutions and punishment thrust upon her: the accused, the convicted, the target of stones and abuse. For it was, after all, through accusation, prosecution, self-justification, conviction, and punishment that Elizabeth Cellier entered into public discourse. Cellier was not unique in having agency (and authorship) conferred on her only so that she might be held accountable for her actions; the accused was one of the roles most readily available to women outside of the home. Representations of Cellier often depict her criminalized agency as an inappropriate incursion into public life and political affairs. Detractors routinely describe her as "busie" and officious;[88] they ridicule her "impudent" claim that she is, as *The Scarlet Beast Stripped Naked* sneers, "the only woman-Living, by her own Talk, that minded the future State and welfare of the Government."[89]

---

88. For instance, she is referred to as "that busie, Lustful *Cellier*" (*Reflections upon the Murder of S. Edmund-Bury Godfrey* [London, 1682], sig. Ev) and as "so notable a *Busie-body*" (*Mr. Prance's Answer to Mrs. Cellier's Libel*, sigs. Bv, Ev). The *OED* lists the following negative connotations for "busy": active in what does not concern one; prying, inquisitive, meddlesome, officious; restless, fussy, importunate; overdecorated. "Busy" could also be a euphemism for sexually active.

89. *Scarlet Beast Stripped Naked*, sig. Bv.

If she had minded her own business and known her place, they suggest, she might never have gotten into trouble. Yet if the criminalization of Cellier's agency is predictable, the outcome is less so. Convictions were much more likely to be described in print than acquittals; and prosecutions of the most infamous and therefore best documented and now most studied felonies, such as treason, rarely ended in acquittal. Furthermore, when acquittals did occur, they hardly seemed newsworthy. *Malice Defeated,* however, offers a lengthy narrative of a trial ending in acquittal. While the construction of female agency as criminality had material consequences and could even be fatal, it was not inevitably so; even in court, constructions of women's agency were flexible, conditional, and unpredictable.

In turning to representations of Cellier as defendant, I do not understand myself as shifting from the representational to the real. Her trials cannot serve as a standard or benchmark against which to check less reliable representations, since they themselves are available for study only through these representations, which create and perpetuate the conflicts adjudicated in court. For this reason, I have refused a chronological approach, which would suggest that representation is subsequent or secondary; that the trials were the event and that the representation followed after. Many competing accounts survive, each partisan and partial. Taken together, they convey a rich impression, not perhaps of what actually happened in a given courtroom on a given day but of how the event was perceived, imagined, invented. In representations of Cellier as defendant, gender continues to be as crucial as it is in representations of Cellier as author and protagonist. Yet in narratives of the trials, gender operates even less predictably; its meanings are even more conditional.

While all early modern trials depended on the storytelling ability of witnesses, the standard practice in treason trials of denying defense counsel placed even more emphasis on the defendant's ability to tell his or her own story without guidance or mediation. When, in her trial for treason at King's Bench on Friday, June 11, 1680, Cellier was responsible for defending herself, she shared the dilemma everyone tried for a felony faced; she was denied the assistance of counsel, except when a dispute over a point of law arose. Since most people without legal training might not recognize a "point of law," and counsel was not assigned until one had been identified, defendants with limited legal knowledge were the least likely to receive professional advice. This practice was justified on the grounds that the trial judge would serve as the accused's counsel; the case for the prosecution should be incontrovertible; and all the defendant needed to do was to tell the truth. The practice also reduced the length of trials: Cellier's treason trial took one day; her libel trial took two, but would have been one of many cases heard on those days. Although defendants in state trials complained for centuries about the injustice when the prosecution was represented by counsel but the defendant was not, only in 1696 (7 and 8 Wil. III, cap. 3) was right to counsel fully extended to them.[90] This legal reform seems to have been prompted in part by the recognition that those convicted in the Popish Plot trials had been innocent, and that judges had not performed adequately as their counsel.

Before the Treason Act of 1696, the accused was limited to a reactive role in conducting his or her defense: interrupting and contesting proceedings whose course and terms she could not direct. Rather than mount a defense, she could only try to undermine the prosecution. In treason trials, defendants could challenge up to thirty-five jurors for no reason, more for cause. They could also bring in witnesses, although these were not sworn (as witnesses for the prosecution were) and could not be bound over to attend; with no legal pressures to attend, defense witnesses often failed to appear.[91] Cellier herself apparently backed out of testifying on behalf of Richard Langhorne, fearing the unruly crowd outside the courtroom.[92]

Tracking down witnesses and persuading them to appear in court were especially difficult for the defendant to do from jail. Because defendants depended on friends and relatives to inform and help them, women may often have organized defenses behind the scenes. *The Tryals of Robert Green, Henry Berry, and Lawrence Hill, for the Murder of Sr. Edmond-Bury Godfrey Knt.* (1679), for instance, suggests that the defendants' wives sought out legal advice and rounded up witnesses. The court acknowledged their efforts—the lord chief justice called in *"Greene's* wife, and all her Witnesses"—but would not allow the women to address it directly. Nor did the court take the wives very seriously. Mrs. Hill concludes: "Well, I am dissatisfied; my

---

90. My discussion here is informed by J. H. Baker, "Criminal Courts and Procedure at Common Law, 1550–1800," in *Crime in England, 1550–1800,* ed. J. S. Cockburn (Princeton: Princeton University Press, 1977), pp. 15–48, esp. 36–37; J. H. Baker, *An Introduction to English Legal History,* 3d ed. (London: Butterworths, 1990), pp. 581–83; J. M. Beattie, *Crime and the Courts in England, 1660–1800* (Princeton: Princeton University Press, 1986), chap. 7; Thomas Andrew Green, *Verdict According to Conscience: Perspectives on the English Criminal Trial Jury, 1200–1800* (Chicago: University of Chicago Press, 1985), chap. 6; and John H. Langbein, "The Criminal Trial before the Lawyers," *University of Chicago Law Review* 45.2 (1978): 263–316.

91. Baker, *Introduction to English Legal History,* pp. 581–82.

92. Cellier apparently appeared in court but said that "she dirst not speak, unless the Court would promise her protection against the Rabble." The court offered only to punish those "that offered to meddle with her" after the fact (*Tryall of Richard Langhorn Esq.,* sig. N2v).

Witnesses were not rightly examined, they were modest, and the Court laught at them."[93]

Thus the practice of denying counsel to those accused of a felony forced women as well as men to learn about the law and to act as advocates in court. Yet it did not authorize or legitimate their appearances there. Assumed to be guilty, ignorant, and interested (to say the least), all defendants would have struggled to gain the court's attention and respect. Women representing themselves or their husbands faced the additional obstacle of the court's assumption that they were disorganized and uninformed; Catholics faced the special problem of the assumption that they were all inveterate liars. Caught in this double bind, Catholic women would seem to have faced insurmountable obstacles as defendants and advocates. Yet, while *Malice Defeated* suggests that Cellier received many slights as both a woman and a Catholic, she was one of the very few tried in connection with the Popish Plot who were acquitted. Her gender and religious affiliation disadvantaged her only to the extent that they made it difficult for her to speak credibly.

If Catholic women's legal rights were doubly constrained, they could counter one set of legal disabilities with another. Elizabeth Cellier adopts a version of this strategy of playing the status of married woman, or "feme covert," against that of recusant in a discussion with Sir William Waller regarding whether she will take the oaths of supremacy and allegiance. For Waller, the issue is how far Cellier is willing to go in support of her claim that she is a loyalist rather than a traitor. Cellier, by her own account, reminds Waller of her position as "a Forreign Merchants Wife" as well as an English subject. As a feme covert whose husband is a subject of the French king, she cannot be required to swear these oaths because she cannot swear an allegiance independent of and contradictory to her husband's allegiance (*MD*, sig. E2). This would be a risky strategy in a treason trial, in which allegiance to the crown is as much at issue as acts committed. But in this conversation, which occurs in Cellier's home before her arrest, she points out from the start the slippery nature of trying a married woman, especially the wife of a foreign subject. Married women could certainly be tried for a felony; in fact, this is the one area in which legal status as independent and accountable agents was unambiguously conferred on them. Cellier reminds the court, however, that marriage subsumes her status as subject into her husband's, thus eclipsing her loyalty; it is still there, she insists, but it cannot be hauled out and exposed to scrutiny. Cellier compli-

93. *The Tryals of Robert Green, Henry Berry, and Lawrence Hill, for the Murder of Sr. Edmond-Bury Godfrey Knt.* (London, 1679), pp. 61–62, 71.

cates the usual choice presented to Catholics, between the king and the pope, by adding her husband into the mix. She does not confess to a divided duty; rather, she suggests that the complexities of her attachments cannot be registered through the swearing of oaths. Although some of those tried in relation to the Popish Plot questioned whether they, as subjects of other countries, were subject to English penal laws or to the jurisdiction of English courts, Cellier does not; nor does she remind the court of her legal status as a feme covert to demur from accountability. Rather, she shifts the burden of proof from oath-swearing to her self-representations. When it comes to her claims that she is a Catholic and a defender of the crown, rather than a traitor, the court will just have to take her word for it.

In *Malice Defeated*, Cellier most tellingly deploys her legal knowledge in her treatment of witnesses. First, she attempts to convince the court that her own witnesses should be sworn, contrary to the usual practice. When the lord chief justice (Sir William Scroggs) reminds her that witnesses cannot be sworn against the king, that is for the defense, she objects to this construction, ably citing precedent and authority in support of her claim:

> And by the Statute of the Fourth of King James, it is ordered that persons accus'd shall have Witnesses produc'd upon Oath, for his better Clearing and Justification. And the Lord Cook [Sir Edward Coke?] says, That he never read in any Act of Parliament, Author, Book, Case, nor ancient Record, that in criminal Cases, the Party accus'd should not have sworn Witnesses: And therefore there is not a spark of Law against it. And the Lord Cook dyed but lately; and if there was no Law against it then, I desire to know by what Law it is now denyed me; for the common Law cannot be altered. (*MD*, sig. K2; I have eliminated confusing emphases)

Cellier reveals here that the process by which she learned about the law was neither diabolical nor mysterious; she was not even coached by Jesuits, who were assumed to be behind most inconvenient displays of knowledge or bold-faced defiance. Rather, she, like "Lord Cook," reads books. The lord chief justice, however, does not concur with Cellier's claim that she has identified a point of law, or that she needs counsel. His easy dismissal of her claim suggests the limited influence of even the most assertive and learned defendant.

Although Cellier does not persuade the court to swear in her witnesses, she does succeed in blocking the testimony of Thomas Dangerfield, once her employee and now the chief witness against her; she does so by proving that he is not qualified to be a witness in a treason trial. She produces "Witnesses and Records" to show that Dangerfield, who had been convicted of twenty-eight crimes by the age of twenty-five, has been "Burnt in the Hand, Whip'd, Transported, Pillorie'd, Out-law'd for Felony, Fin'd for Cheating, and suffer'd publick Infamy for many other notorious Crimes" (*MD*, sig. K2). The issue is not just that Dangerfield is an infamous person, and therefore not a credible witness, but that he cannot be sworn because he is a convicted felon. Although Dangerfield was pardoned so that he could testify against her, Cellier argues that he was not pardoned of all his offenses.

Arguing that "the King cannot give an Act of Grace to one Subject, to the prejudice of another" (*MD*, sig. K2v), Cellier challenges the practice by which a member of a conspiracy can secure a pardon by agreeing to give evidence against his accomplices; that is, by turning "King's Evidence." By the mid–eighteenth century, such evidence was not accepted without corroboration; but the Popish Plot trials depended on it. Cellier refuses to acknowledge the message of the penal laws and of coverture: that she is not fully a subject, and that the crown must be protected from her, not she by it. She also challenges the assumption that a witness for the defense is a witness against the king. Asserting her own belief in and knowledge of English common law, Cellier warns that extraordinary measures to protect king and country might, instead, undermine basic liberties: "If such Witnesses be allowed, Liberty and Property are destroyed" (*MD*, sig. L2). A Law that can so thoroughly strip Catholic subjects of their rights offers little protection to anyone.

Cellier's objection to Dangerfield touches off a debate among the legal personnel at the trial, which participates in a larger controversy. In the absence of material evidence of a popish plot, the "King's Evidence" and the credibility of the witnesses in the Popish Plot trials were widely debated, not only in courtrooms but in scores of pamphlets. The informers and witnesses who gave evidence regarding the Popish Plot and the Presbyterian or sham plot were, as Rachel Weil sums up, "sometimes criminal, often lower-class, and occasionally female."[94] Many were themselves implicated in the conspiracies they alleged, and testified on the condition that they would be pardoned. Opinion regarding their credibility divided largely along partisan lines. Those who felt that charges of a popish plot were groundless and that the case against Catholics was being fabricated argued that even the king's pardon was not sufficient to make a criminal a credible witness. They also argued that prosecutions depended heavily on professional witnesses who, as Cellier complains in a later text, "would swear

94. Weil, "'If I Did Say So, I Lyed,'" p. 190. On credibility, see also Shapiro, *Probability and Certainty*, esp. pp. 185, 188.

anything for Money."[95] Those who believed the accusations and defended the prosecutions argued that Catholics were the least qualified to discredit others. *Reflections upon the Murder of S. Edmund-Bury Godfrey* remarks, "Of how little value Oaths and Perjury are among the *Papists* is well known"; *The Kings Evidence Vindicated* proclaims, "I scruple more the Evidence of a Real Papist, than I do of a Perjur'd Protestant."[96] Catholics were unreliable because of their tendency to equivocate, and also because they could so readily achieve absolution from their priests for any outright lies they might tell. *Reflections upon the Murder* warns that "there is little credit to be given to the Popish *Witnesses,* who may perjure themselves to day, and be Absolv'd to morrow."[97] This belief that priestly absolution convinced Catholics that they were innocent helped to explain how those executed for their involvement in the Popish Plot could so passionately proclaim their innocence on the scaffold. It also made it an outrage that they should question the redemptive power of the king's pardon. *Reflections upon the Murder* explains:

> For the *Papists* are to understand, that the King of *England's* Pardon is of greater efficacy to cleanse a man from his offences, than if he should bath in a Tub of Holy Water every day i'the Year, and then receive Absolution from ten thousand Lubberly *Priests.* Being then made *good men* by the high Prerogative of the Kings Mercy, tho Fools and Knaves still take the boldness to defame them, they are Witnesses legal, every way justifiable, and not to be disputed against by any good or loyal Subject of the King. (Sig. E2)

Apologists for the prosecution also argued that if the witnesses against the plotters were disreputable, the reason was that only such persons would participate in conspiracy. The blameless would not know anything about Catholic schemes. Miles Prance, whom Cellier claimed had been tortured in Newgate, distanced himself from her by claiming that it was Catholics who were responsible for torture, if not of living bodies, then of life stories: "Must the *Lives* of *Witnesses* be not onely *fairly examined,* but also *set* upon the *Rack,* and so made to *speak,* not what *They* would Themselves, but what Their *Tormentors* please?"[98]

Cellier's successful legal strategies had ramifications beyond her own acquittal: Dangerfield was an important anti-Catholic witness who needed to

---

95. Elizabeth Cellier, *To Dr. — — An Answer to His Queries, Concerning the Colledg of Midwives* (London, 1688), sig. A2v.

96. *Reflections upon the Murder,* sig. Hv; *The Kings Evidence Vindicated, as to the Imputation of Perjury* (London, 1680), p. 3.

97. *Reflections upon the Murder,* sig. Hv.

98. *The Additional Narrative of Mr. Miles Prance* (London, 1679), sig. E.

be rehabilitated; prosecutions depended on the king's evidence and this resource could not be lost; finally, Cellier herself was slated to testify on behalf of the "lords in the Tower," and therefore her subsequent libel trial may have aimed, in part, to discredit her and prevent her or her "party" from capitalizing on her success in her treason trial.[99] Thus, although Cellier had to learn the law in order to defend herself, those who tried her, even Lord Chief Justice Scroggs and Judge William Dolben, both of whom she presents as concurring with her claim that admitting Dangerfield's evidence would set a dangerous precedent, did not necessarily view the mastery she achieved as admirable and exonerating.

Other evidence suggests that Scroggs and Dolben were already beginning to have legal and political reservations about infamous witnesses such as Dangerfield and Oates, and about the credibility of the "King's Evidence." By Cellier's account, however, she teaches them to raise these questions; she instills doubts; she articulates the principles that are at stake. From the start of *Malice Defeated,* Cellier challenges the assumption that the court represents the crown's interests, let alone hers, and that her interests and the king's are opposed. Since James, the Duke of York, was already being openly accused of involvement in the plot, Cellier opens up to question just what the relationship between the crown and Catholicism, the king and the King's Bench, Charles II and his brother James might be.[100] Is evidence of a popish plot, which is taken as evidence against James's succession, really the "King's Evidence"? In suggesting that the "King's Evidence" might be the Whigs' evidence, Cellier may have marked herself as more sinister rather than less so, a formidably incisive observer of the exclusionist, Protestant juggernaut gathering steam in the Popish Plot trials, as well as an unjustly suspected ally of the crown.

In *Malice Defeated,* Cellier demonstrates simultaneously that she relies on her legal knowledge to defend herself and that her knowledge irks her judges. Early in her account of her trial, she describes an exchange with the lord chief justice that occurred between her arraignment (April 30) and her actual trial (June 11). By that time, she had been in prison for twenty-two weeks.[101] Coming before the bar expecting to be tried, she

99. The lords in the Tower, Arundel, Powis, Bellasis, Petre, and Stafford, stood accused of treason and awaited trial. Only Stafford was ultimately tried (November 1680) and executed.

100. According to Miller, by the late 1670s "a transition had taken place from a situation where Popery was seen as the enemy of crown and nation to one where Popery and the crown were seen as dangers to the Protestant nation" (*Popery and Politics,* p. 84). As a result, Charles II was forced to sacrifice English Catholics to his brother's chance for succession, enforcing penal laws and crediting witnesses so as not to seem pro-papist.

101. In prison, Cellier was kept apart from other prisoners; a maid attended her. Her husband was not allowed access to her.

finds that the trial is being postponed indefinitely and objects that her lengthy imprisonment is costing her money. When told that she will have to wait "but a little while" more, she responds that her "Husband will think it a great while; at which the Court laugh'd." This laughter seems to suggest that it is trivial, ridiculous, even unseemly for Cellier to mention that her husband misses her; Cellier, who the lord chief justice has claimed is "fit for anything," must be "speak[ing] Bawdy" again (*MD*, sigs. I2v, Hv). The laughter may also express the court's incredulity that any Catholic would want to be tried promptly, given the usual outcome. Cellier then explains: her husband has "great cause to think it long" because he needs her legal advice. In her absence, her husband is conducting "a suit in Chancery to a considerable value," but since he cannot consult with her, he, "not knowing how to defend the Cause," is losing the suit.

Cellier's claim that she acts as her husband's legal counsel provokes the court's indignation. The lord chief justice accuses Cellier of "arraign[ing] the Councel," that is, putting them on trial. Sergeant John Maynard,[102] representing the crown, asks: "Why could not your Husband follow his Law-Suit without you?" Cellier replies, "Because he is a Stranger, and does not understand the Law." Maynard then says, "Then you do, Gentlewoman[?]" Cellier hastily replies, "No Sir, but I have got enough to make a Country Justice, and I pray that I may be tryed" (sig. I2v).

On the one hand, Cellier backs away from too confident an assertion of her knowledge; on the other hand, she claims that her knowledge is equal to that of many an assize court judge, and that she is not afraid to be "tryed." Cellier both requests that the court get on with it and throws down a gauntlet. If they want to find out how much she knows, they should try (or test) her. After she has secured the court's assurance that she will be discharged if she is not tried by the first day of the next term, she concludes by reasserting her confidence in the law and in her judges: "The Laws I am to be Tryed by have sufficiently compensated their denying me other Councel, by allowing me you my Lords that are my Judges, for Councellors, and I will depend on your Faithful advice with confidence, and humbly pray fair play for my life" (*MD*, sig. I2v). Here Cellier reminds the court that she is at a considerable disadvantage—she has been denied counsel—at the same time that she discounts her handicap in order to express gratitude toward and dependency on the judges. If the king's counsel has viewed her assertion of her legal competence as antagonistic, she

102. Cellier faced off against a formidable group of jurists. Maynard, the king's sergeant, was about seventy-eight at the time of this trial; widely respected for his legal learning and a political survivor, he participated in prosecuting most of those charged in connection with the Popish Plot (*DNB*).

insists that they are not her adversaries but her allies (which was, in fact, the case in the eyes of the law). While she may know more about English law than a French merchant, she relies entirely on the superior knowledge of her judges.

Cellier's strategy here suggests that she could try to deflect anger by appearing less competent. It also points to the double bind in which the law placed her; denied counsel, she needed legal knowledge to defend herself, but if she asserted that knowledge too confidently, she risked seeming presumptuous and provoking her judges' wrath. It was one thing for a lord chief justice to tolerate the inadequate efforts of Mrs. Berry, Mrs. Hill, and Mrs. Green behind the scenes; it was quite another to be confronted by a woman who actually knew the law and, what was more, challenged his own grasp of it.

Cellier's legal competence is not an issue only in *Malice Defeated.* Those who write defamatory responses to her text ridicule her claims to legal knowledge, joining in the anger and contempt Cellier attributes to her judges, but also confirming that Cellier's assertion of competence is as outrageous as her supposed treason. Unable, in the face of her acquittal, to accuse her of treason, Cellier's detractors resort to complaining that she is a know-it-all. *Modesty Triumphing over Impudence* complains: "Our *Lady Errant* runs on, quotes Statutes, dictates Law to the Judges." This pamphlet engages Cellier on the terrain of legal expertise, arguing that she is not as smart as she thinks, and, by implication, that the judges missed an important chance to trip her up. The author points out that Cellier's conversion to Catholicism, described at the start of *Malice Defeated,* could itself be viewed as illegal: "You are too well skilled in the Statutes to be Ignorant that this first Page of your Pamphlet, upon prosecution, without a *Dangerfield,* may truss you up."[103] A broadside, "To the Praise of Mrs. Cellier, the Popish Midwife, on Her Incomparable Book," pretends to exalt Cellier's knowledge: "You taught the *Judges* to interpret Laws,/Shewd Sergeant *Maynard* how to plead a Cause." But it stresses that this superior knowledge led to a travesty of justice: "You turn'd, and wound, and Rogu'd 'em at your will,/'Twas Trial not of Life and Death, but Skill."[104] Whereas, as Weil argues, it is unclear in *Malice Defeated* whether Cellier celebrates "the justness of the law" or her own "capacity to manipulate it,"[105] for Cellier's detractors the two are inversely related. If a Catholic woman can manipulate the law, then it must be unjust.

103. *Modesty Triumphing over Impudence,* sigs. D2v, A2.
104. "To the Praise of Mrs. Cellier, the Popish Midwife, on Her Incomparable Book" (London, 1680).
105. Weil, "'If I Did Say So, I Lyed,'" p. 196.

In *Malice Defeated,* Cellier's judges often seem to dismiss or belittle her because of her gender; in both *Malice Defeated* and the many attacks on Cellier, Catholicism and gender combine to undermine credibility. Yet Cellier's acquittal, especially at a time when it took little evidence to secure a conviction, suggests that not being taken seriously could occasionally have benefits. Being a woman was not only or not simply a liability. Furthermore, gender was not the only variable that mattered, nor was its meaning or effect consistent. Examining an account of another treason trial will reveal some of the other variables in play and how they could shape legal outcomes and representations.

The trial of Richard Langhorne, a lawyer who had provided counsel to the Society of Jesus, and who, like Cellier, was a Catholic implicated in the Popish Plot, took place before the same court one year before Cellier's treason trial. Because he was a "Counsellor at Law," Langhorne's claims to legal knowledge cannot be considered unlikely or presumptuous, as Cellier's can. Like Cellier, Langhorne reminds the lord chief justice and the court that he looks upon them "as my Counsel, to advise me in matters of Law."[106] But where Cellier can plead ignorance, Langhorne is chided for not knowing better. In a lengthy pamphlet account of the trial, the court repeatedly enlists his agreement when it rejects his various attempts at a defense: "You understand that being a Lawyer" (sig. N2); "You are a man of the Law, and therefore you know it is not fair to ask any Person a Question about a Criminal matter that may bring himself in danger" (sig. F). The court's treatment of Langhorne is genial, even respectful. At one point, the court both admires and rejects Langhorne's attempt to discredit a witness for the prosecution: "'Tis very fine, but the Court over-rules it" (sig. I). Perhaps because of his knowledge and experience as a lawyer, Langhorne is especially exasperated by the disadvantages under which he must labor and by the hopelessness of getting the court to accept what defense he can cobble together: "You take off the Defence that I have, and make it as if I had never any" (sig. M2). The court assumes Langhorne's knowledge, anticipating and countering his every move. In part because the court is never taken off guard, Langhorne is convicted.

Of course, the outcome of the two trials did not depend only on the evidence presented or the defendant's skill. The provenance of the accounts of these two trials sharpens the distinction between them: the account of Langhorne's trial, "published by authority," justifies that verdict and the

---

106. *Tryall of Richard Langhorn,* sig. H2; subsequent references in this paragraph are to this pamphlet. On Langhorne, who served as lawyer to the Society of Jesus and may have revealed many of the society's investments in an attempt to save himself, see Thomas M. McCoog, "Richard Langhorne and the Popish Plot," *Recusant History* 19.4 (1989): 499–508.

probity of the court, whereas Cellier's *Malice Defeated* promulgates her own
perspective. Furthermore, in the year between the two trials—from
June 1679 to June 1680—the political climate had shifted. There were
doubts about the plot and suspicions of false accusations and perjury; between July 1679 and December 1680, no one was convicted in London for
association with the Popish Plot.[107] In July 1679, Lord Chief Justice Scroggs
had acquitted Sir George Wakeman, the queen's physician, of the charge
of conspiring to poison the king, in large part because he questioned the
veracity of Bedloe and Oates. Since Scroggs had accepted their evidence
in thirteen earlier trials, many observers suspected that he acquitted Wakeman to please the king or in response to bribery or coercion. The uproar
attending this acquittal contributed to an attempt by parliamentary Whig
leaders to impeach Scroggs for treason, a process that began in November 1680, on charges that included "favouring Papists and Persons Popishly
affected" and "'defaming' and 'disparaging' the evidence of witnesses," as
Lois Schwoerer explains.[108] Thus, when Cellier raised doubts about witnesses and evidence, she addressed a court willing to listen and a lord chief
justice who had already taken enormous political risks to question the veracity of the "King's Evidence," and who was, as a consequence, soon to
face treason charges himself. Contrasting these two texts, and the two trials as those texts represent them, suggests that a female defendant did not
inevitably fare worse than a male one. The difference gender made depended on how it intersected with a host of other variables.

Interestingly enough, when Cellier did have counsel, in her trial for libel (in the Old Bailey [Newgate Sessions] on Saturday, September 11, and
Monday, September 13, 1680), her defense did not succeed. Cellier had
counsel in this trial because the charge was a misdemeanor rather than a
felony; this advantage actually seems to have curtailed her authority and
limited her options in the trial. The venue was also different; the Old Bailey
courts were controlled by Whig sheriffs, particularly unsympathetic to Catholic Tory polemicists.[109] Furthermore, Cellier did not write an account of
this trial, impeded, perhaps, by imprisonment, a heightened awareness of
risk, and the grim project of narrating "malice triumphant." Accounts writ-

107. Kenyon, *Popish Plot*, pp. 191, 201; Miller, *Popery and Politics*, chap. 8, esp. p. 176.
108. See Lois G. Schwoerer, "The Attempted Impeachment of Sir William Scroggs, Lord
Chief Justice of the Court of King's Bench, November 1680–March 1681," *Historical Journal* 38.4 (1995): 843–73, esp. 867, 859.
109. Cellier was also tried during those years (1679–85) in which the Licensing Act had
lapsed and the press could be controlled only after the fact, through charges of seditious
libel. Although attempts were made to seize sheets of *Malice Defeated* in press, there were no
legal grounds for doing so. See Harris, *London Crowds*, pp. 28, 130, 154; and Schwoerer,
"Attempted Impeachment of Sir William Scroggs," pp. 860–64.

ten by anonymous others cast Cellier in the role of the discomfited and outmatched, the role usually played by those accused in relation to the Popish Plot. In *The Tryal and Sentence of Elizabeth Cellier; for Writing, Printing, and Publishing a Scandalous Libel* (1680), the fullest account of the libel trial, Cellier complains that she was not given time to prepare her defense; she did not receive the indictment until the morning of her trial "and my Counsel could not Inspect it, nor speak a word with me about it," and as a result, "I am surprized and have no witnesses."[110] In a petition to the king, Cellier similarly complains that the court tried her "without giving her time for her defence, and they would not hear her witnesses."[111] Attempting to reproduce her former triumph, Cellier tries to challenge the members of the jury, only to be informed that she may not do so without cause (as she had been able to do at the King's Bench). She also challenges the witnesses brought against her (they have not been sworn, they are lying). Despite John Langbein's claim that in Old Bailey trials a defendant never even alludes to a "privilege against self-incrimination," Cellier insists that the burden of proving her authorship of *Malice Defeated* is on the court: "I bee'nt bound to accuse my self."[112]

Yet her objections are dismissed, and her counsel, Mr. Collins, offers her little assistance and scolds her own initiatives. When she calls for a witness who will corroborate her claim that Catholic prisoners were tortured in Newgate, Mr. Collins warns her, "You cannot do your self greater wrong than by such talk as this" (p. 28). When she asks whether her counsel may speak on her behalf and be heard, Collins interjects, "I have nothing to say for her," and sternly reprimands her for her own defense efforts: "If you had said less for your self it had been better" (p. 29). In control neither of the defense nor of the representation of it, Cellier is depicted as succumbing to defeat: "I have done then my Lord; for not having time to get my Witnesses, I cannot make my Defence so fully, as else I should have done: only I desire you to consider I am a poor ignorant Woman, and have erred out of ignorance: I thought nothing, but that I might publish what others had said and told me, and so I have offended in Ignorance, if I have offended" (p. 29). While Cellier makes some claims to feminine weakness when it suits her in *Malice Defeated,* she never presents herself as a "poor ignorant Woman"; indeed, as I have shown, she robustly asserts her legal knowledge. But the author of *The Tryal and Sentence of Elizabeth Cellier* coun-

---

110. *Tryal and Sentence of Elizabeth Cellier,* pp. 28, 16; subsequent references to this pamphlet are given parenthetically in the text.
111. *CSPD,* 1680–81, p. 16 (Sept. 14, 1680).
112. Langbein, "Criminal Trial before the Lawyers," p. 283; *Tryal and Sentence of Elizabeth Cellier,* p. 27.

ters that self-representation by emphasizing that Cellier's legal knowledge is limited, that her assertions of it are misguided and self-defeating, and that, in the end, her best recourse is to admit her ignorance.

If representations of Elizabeth Cellier's two legal engagements, culminating in her conviction for libel, are a limit case for the options for representing women as legal agents, what limits do they suggest? Like other evidence to which scholars are increasingly turning, such as probate accounts and church court records, accounts of Cellier's trials hint at the gap between the legal fiction of the feme covert and what married women's engagements with the law may have been.[113] The obviously exceptional cases of women who were charged with crimes, in Cellier's case both a felony and a misdemeanor, force into visibility the competence and industry that the fiction of coverture strove to eclipse. Cellier operated as her own defense counsel, secured an acquittal, and even, by her own account, lectured the court on the law. Far from being inhibited by a notion of herself as a feme covert, she introduced that legal fiction when it could help her. Cellier argued that if the court viewed her, as a woman and as a Catholic, as so exceptional that precedents and legal authorities did not apply to her case, then her conviction would undermine the very English law and English state it sought to protect. She assumed that her case had something to teach her judges: that it could establish precedents, uncover contradictions in recent practice, challenge assumptions, reveal partisanship. The courtroom was not an arena of self-realization and unfettered agency for Cellier, especially since one of her trials did end in a conviction. Yet all accounts of her court appearances, whether celebratory or vituperative, represent her as an agent.

While women were most likely to appear in court as defendants and to be construed as legal subjects when they were accused of felonies, that dubious recognition did not inevitably end in their conviction. Most of the considerable work on treason has focused on trials that ended in conviction and execution, in part because these were the most well documented and sensational cases; it has also focused largely on male offenders. With the notable exception of work on property and defamation, most work on women's relation to the law has focused on those women who were convicted of crimes (especially "feminized" crimes, such as infanticide and witchcraft) and, usually, executed, again because such cases are most likely to be well documented and to include some record of women's testimony.

113. On the complexities of women's relation to the law, see Amy Louise Erickson, *Women and Property in Early Modern England* (London and New York: Routledge, 1993); and Laura Gowing, *Domestic Dangers: Women, Words, and Sex in Early Modern London* (Oxford: Clarendon, 1996).

Cellier's case complicates the picture painted by these two overlapping bodies of scholarship because she was a woman charged with treason, because she wrote her own account of her trial, and because her case ended in acquittal. She survived—practicing her trade, continuing to be the producer and the topic of polemic—long after the spectacles of courtroom and pillory were over.[114] Although Cellier was hardly unscathed by her brushes with notoriety, any closure less decisive than death complicates the map of early modern options for representing criminalized women and our understanding of the conditions under which these representations were recorded, published, and read.

Cellier wisely feared the tyranny and intractability of literary forms and the unacceptable endings they might impose on her story and her life: "for Tragedies whether real or fictious [*sic*], seldom end before the Women die" (*MD*, sig. H2v). But her life, as it can be pieced together from surviving records, does not seem to have conformed to any of the genres thrust upon her, in large part through accidents of history and dogged longevity. Unable to pay the huge fine that was levied against her, Cellier spent about two years in prison; Charles II may then have remitted her fine in response to her petition.[115] With the accession of James II in 1685, Catholics briefly found political favor; the key witnesses against the supposed Popish Plot conspirators were convicted of perjury and publicly punished. Like the infamous Titus Oates, Dangerfield, Cellier's nemesis, was tried and convicted of perjury, lashed, and set on the pillory. In a broadside published later, Dangerfield confesses to Cellier that the Meal Tub Plot was his invention, and that she suffered unjustly for it. When he asks in amazement: "Hast thou outliv'd my Fury? Withstood all the Volleys of Turnips and rotten Eggs, and lives yet to be my Tormenter?" she confirms: "I have outlived the Pillory, to see thee recant at the gallows." The broadside ends with Dangerfield led off to Newgate.[116] Thus the changed political climate conferred innocence on Cellier, just as it had previously conferred guilt, and granted dignity to the very endurance that had once been ridiculed. The king's corroboration transformed Cellier's version of events into the official story, "published by authority."

114. After James's accession, for instance, Cellier proposed a scheme for educating and professionalizing midwives. See *A Scheme for the Foundation of a Royal Hospital, and . . . for the Maintenance of a Corporation of Skilful Midwives*, in *The Harleian Miscellany*, 10 vols. (1809) (New York: AMS Press, 1965), 4: 142–47; and Cellier, *To Dr. —— An Answer to His Queries*.
115. For the petition, see *CSPD*, 1682, p. 613.
116. *Duke Dangerfield Declaring How He Represented the Duke of Mon——* (London, 1685), p. 2. See also *A True Narrative of the Arraignment, Tryal, and Conviction of Thomas Dangerfield for High-Misdemeanors against His Present Majesty James the Second* (London, 1685). In Dangerfield's trial, Mr. Cellier testified against him.

Cellier also served as fertility counselor and midwife to James's wife, Mary of Modena; under her guidance, Mary conceived an heir. At once the culmination and termination of Catholic hopes, this Catholic male heir became the excuse for deposing James and ushering in William and Mary. With the "Glorious" Revolution and the securing of a Protestant succession in 1688, Cellier disappears from the historical record, as does any real hope of a Catholic succession. Unlike most other criminalized women, then, the sad ends of whose stories we know, Elizabeth Cellier disappears from the historical record with her writings in the late 1680s about midwifery. Perhaps she went into exile with James II's court in 1688.[117] But no one knows. The indeterminacy of Cellier's story depends on gaps in our historical knowledge—failures of evidence—as well as political turmoil and change.

In the late 1670s and the 1680s, the passage of a few months (between Langhorne's conviction and Cellier's acquittal, or between Cellier's two trials) or a few years (between the exclusion crisis and James II's accession, or between that accession and his departure) could drastically alter the prospects for individual Catholics and for their cause. Similarly, the shift in venue, from the crown-controlled King's Bench to the Whig-controlled Old Bailey, could affect the outcome. Yet many twentieth-century discussions of Cellier remove her from her lived present, in (unwitting) accord with the tragic and comic visions of her life and her cause that she herself defined as inadequate. Most political historians mention Cellier only briefly, depicting her cause as a doomed attempt to turn back the process of political change and restore a lost past. But they do not endow Cellier with any of the tragic grandeur this vision might suggest; instead, they dismiss her as "clumsy" and officious. Tim Harris twice refers to her "clumsy" attempt to deflect blame from the Catholics to the Presbyterians; John Miller also dismisses "the clumsy efforts of Elizabeth Cellier, the Popish midwife, and her little Catholic coterie to blame the Plot on to the Presbyterians."[118] J. P. Kenyon reproves her for being "busy" and for "very bad judgement," and J. C. H. Aveling describes her as "ardent and indiscreet"; Mark Knights links her to "an ill-conceived attempt."[119] These historians

117. Mary Hopkirk claims that upon James's accession, Cellier "was freed and given £90 from the secret-service money," and that she was briefly in residence with the exiled Stuarts: "Even Elizabeth Cellier, the Popish midwife, reached Saint Germain somehow, though she does not appear to have remained there for long" (*Queen over the Water: Mary Beatrice of Modena, Queen of James II* [London: John Murray, 1953], pp. 86, 171). The evidence for either assertion is unclear.

118. Harris, *London Crowds*, pp. 108, 119; Miller, *Popery and Politics*, p. 175.

119. Kenyon, *Popish Plot*, p. 189; J. C. H. Aveling, *The Handle and the Ax: The Catholic Recusants in England from Reformation to Emancipation* (London: Blond & Briggs, 1976), p. 213;

follow Cellier's detractors in disparaging her engagement in political action and her prominence in public discourse as voluntary and, in themselves, unseemly. Why did she insist on being such a "busie" body? Considering Cellier in the context of female rather than Catholic "involvement in affairs of state," Elaine Hobby, too, argues that Cellier represents a regression, espousing a regrettable "retreat . . . to virtue." Hobby's claim that Cellier tries to dissociate "social bravery" from "sexual boldness" does not necessarily lead to the conclusion that Cellier, in defending her own modesty, "exhorts women to quiescence and withdrawal from" political action.[120] To make this claim, Hobby must misread and dismiss Cellier's justification of women's involvement in public life. I read Cellier's assertion that "it is more our [women's] business than mens to fear, and consequently to prevent the Tumults and Troubles Factions tend to, since we by nature are hindered from sharing any part but the Frights and Disturbances of them," as a call to action, not to retreat (*MD,* sig. Iv).

In contrast to Hobby, Antonia Fraser closes *The Weaker Vessel* with a discussion of Cellier as a vivid representative of the trend toward women's self-determination, a feisty heroine who is, for "those that came after . . . a more engaging, even perhaps a more admirable character than the submissive Queen [Mary II]." In Fraser's view, Cellier suffered because she was ahead of her time; "her own society" was not yet able to appreciate her audacity and so "threw the stones."[121] This assessment assumes that the difference between Queen Mary and Elizabeth Cellier was simply that between submissiveness and self-assertion, draining it of political and religious content. It also assumes that Cellier's "society" was consensual; this assumption ignores the factionalism of London in the late 1670s and early 1680s, and seems inadequate to the picture of angry spectators throwing stones and Cellier parrying them with her wooden racket. Finally, Fraser's rousing finish promises that Cellier's day has come. All these narratives of change, whether they position Cellier as reactionary or as progressive, remove her from her moment and its political struggles. Because she cannot fit into either the narrative of progress (about women) or that of defeat (about Catholics, or, in Hobby's book, about women), Cellier's story falls through the cracks.

Historians otherwise attentive to the conjectural nature of purported Catholic plots seem to assume that there was a meal tub plot; this assumption enables them to confer more agency on Cellier than she may have

---

Mark Knights, *Politics and Opinion in Crisis, 1678–81* (New York: Cambridge University Press, 1994), pp. 61, 363.
120. Hobby, *Virtue of Necessity,* pp. 21–23.
121. Fraser, *Weaker Vessel,* pp. 454–61, 469–70, esp. 470.

had, but, like the Old Bailey, only in order to censure her for it. Most of these approaches accord Cellier a level of autonomy that it is hard to believe she had, given her double jeopardy as a Catholic woman. In these interpretations, then, we find Cellier freely choosing, with good or bad judgment, to perform actions, skillfully or clumsily, for which she may now be praised or blamed. I do not want to claim that Cellier was simply a pawn, as some of her detractors did; nor do I want to celebrate her heroic agency. Instead, I have sought here to explore how Elizabeth Cellier's gender and religious affiliation shaped her representation as a "wretched subject" and contributed to the particular conditions under which she entered into evidence and therefore into history.

Afterword

Like many scholars, I suffer from Mr. Dick's affliction in Dickens's *David Copperfield.* As you may recall, Mr. Dick's project of writing his "Memorial," or memoir, is constantly interrupted because the "trouble" in Charles I's head at the time of his execution reappears in Mr. Dick's head. As a consequence, Mr. Dick's account of himself and his life keeps returning to Charles I. David learns that "Mr. Dick had been for upwards of ten years endeavouring to keep King Charles the First out of the Memorial; but he had been constantly getting into it, and was there now." Mr. Dick's solution is to make kites out of the disrupted pages to "diffuse" the facts left over from that troubled past; then he begins again. But why not ask whether his troubles and Charles I's *do* belong together? What is Charles's head trying to tell Mr. Dick, anyway? Even Aunt Betsy Trotwood, who insists that the Memorial should not refer to Charles I because that would be unbusinesslike and unworldly, seems to understand why Mr. Dick might connect "his illness with great disturbance and agitation."[1] What kind of memorial could accommodate both Mr. Dick's and Charles I's "affairs," the addled head and the severed one, the small and the great disturbance, the personal and the historical and political?

For my own writing project, Charles I's head takes the form of various criminal women on whom, I tell myself, I *used* to work. Although I first approached this book as a departure from an earlier interest in domestic vi-

1. Charles Dickens, *David Copperfield* (New York: Pocket Library, 1958), pp. 194–97.

olence and the criminalization of women, I soon discovered that I could
not keep Catholic women separate from criminal ones. Take, for instance,
Mary Hobry, a French midwife who in 1688 strangled and dismembered
her husband after he had brutally sodomized her, then disposed of his body
parts in various places. When I was working on murderous wives, Hobry
was a crucial figure, and the many texts about her case helped me formu-
late some of my central arguments. But I did not, I must confess, think
much about the relevance of that year, 1688. Then, while perusing late
seventeenth-century topical playing cards depicting "The [Glorious] Revolution," I was surprised to discover three images of Mary Hobry, "cutting
her Husband to Peices," "putting his quarters in the privy," and, finally,
burning for her crime (see figures 8, 9, and 10). My first response to these
images was regret that I had not found them when I was working on domestic crime. Hard thereon followed the question: Why was Hobry's crime
considered part of a pictorial narrative of the 1688 revolution? In 1688,
how did Hobry's nationality and religious affiliation become crucial to the
significance attached to her crime, and make it so widely represented and
thus so available for study? In short, the appearance of a specter from my
last project in the evidence of the current one has forced me to recognize
my own participation in redrawing distinctions that I want to question and
break down—between the domestic and the national, between the private
and the public, between women's history and History.

What might these two Catholic midwives have in common as "wretched
subjects" of representation? One is French, the other married to a French-
man. Both claim to deliver themselves, one by murdering her husband,
the other by outwitting her accusers and judges. Furthermore, the words
and images on the playing cards that picture Hobry link her to Cellier. The
caption on one of the cards refers to Mary Hobry as the "Popish Midwife," the epithet often used to refer to Cellier; the illustrations dress her
in Cellier's characteristic hood. As a consequence, Robert Erickson understandably conflates the two popish midwives in his study of midwives in
eighteenth-century fiction, suggesting that the murderous midwife depicted on the playing cards may be Elizabeth Cellier.[2] Reconsidering Hobry's case in the context of anti-Catholic polemic suggests that what Hobry
shares with Cellier is a position—the feminized figure who, in the English
Protestant imaginary, stands for the disturbing intermixture of the personal
and the political.

2. Robert A. Erickson, *Mother Midnight: Birth, Sex, and Fate in Eighteenth-Century Fiction
(Defoe, Richardson, and Sterne)* (New York: AMS Press, 1986), p. 280n55.

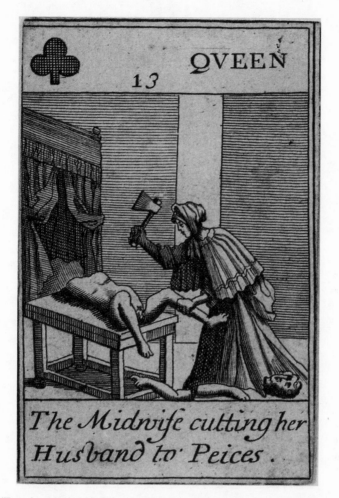

8. The "French midwife," Mary Hobry, killing her husband. Queen of clubs from playing cards depicting "The Revolution." (© Copyright the British Museum)

When the "mangled Body & Members" of Hobry's husband, Dennis, were "found in so many distinct places" around London in late January 1688, some people read the body parts as grim portents of yet another Catholic conspiracy, "as if it must needs be Acted on some Religious score, and but the Bloody Prologue to some greater Tragedy," as *Publick Occurrences Truely Stated,* a Royalist news sheet, reports. This news sheet, however, worked hard to reassure its readers that, in the end, the crime was only personal:

9. Mary Hobry disposing of her husband's body. One of spades from playing cards depicting "The Revolution." (© Copyright the British Museum)

"But after all, it appears to be a poor *French* man, destroyed on *private Malice* or *Revenge* by his Wife, the same Country-woman, and of the *same Profession* as to Religion with himself; so that there was not the least ground or colour in the world for any such Suggestions."[3] This writer attempts to convince his readers that since Mr. and Mrs. Hobry shared the same na-

3. *Publick Occurrences Truely Stated*, no. 1 (Feb. 21, 1687). On Feb. 23 and Mar. 6, *Publick Occurrences* reported that Hobry was not pardoned, as it had been rumored she would be because she was a papist.

10. Mary Hobry burning for her crime. Two of spades from playing cards depicting "The Revolution." (© Copyright the British Museum)

tional and religious identity, her murder of him could not have a meaning that extended beyond their marriage to the turmoil surrounding the succession, and English national identity and security.

Since Hobry confessed to her crime and there was no trial, Roger L'Estrange, who served both Charles II and James II as licenser and surveyor of the press, was concerned that there would be no published account to set the record straight. Therefore, he interrogated her, and published both her answers to his questions and her confession. In his role as interviewer, he particularly presses her as to why she disposed of her husband's quarters in "a House of Office at the *Savoy*, which was a way to bring so great a Scandal upon the Religion she professed, by laying the Murther at the Door of the Professors of that Religion." The Savoy was the center of the London Catholic community and the location of a notorious Jesuit college. It was also within the precincts of Somerset House, a site of Catholic female persistence; Catherine of Braganza was still living and worshiping there in 1688. In L'Estrange's text, Hobry insists that her disposal of the body there was not a political statement: "She had no Thoughts in what she did, as to that Matter, more than to part the *Limbs* and the *Body*, and hoped the Water might carry them away."[4]

This "private" grievance could incite rumors of political conspiracy in part because of the volatility of the political moment, when unidentified human "quarters" were more than usually likely to excite alarm. Even when both victim and culprit had been identified, rumors were not necessarily silenced. The fact that Hobry was a Catholic midwife combined with the recent announcement of Mary of Modena's pregnancy, which from the start was rumored to be fictitious, to create an early version of the rumor that would later fuel the "warming-pan scandal."[5] According to Count Terriesi, envoy of the grand duke of Tuscany, the story quickly gained currency that Hobry had been tapped to smuggle in a pretender whom the queen could pass off as the heir. When Hobry's husband discovered her secret, the story went, she had killed him.[6]

In this climate, and given the long association of Catholic women with the intertwining of private malice and political ambition, how consoling was it for L'Estrange to insist that this was all just a personal grievance? Even as such, the fact that Hobry burned for her crime—the punishment for petty treason rather than homicide—suggests that women's domestic murder could accrue political resonances, that "private malice" could be, as the news sheet attests, a "publick occurrence." The exact form of Titus Oates's charge against Catherine of Braganza suggests how conventional it was to assign political meaning to Catholic women's private grievances. Oates testified that he overheard a woman whom he assumed to be the queen, since no other women were in the room, tell conspirators that "she would assist them in the propagation of the Catholick Religion with her

4. *A Hellish Murder Committed by a French Midwife, on the Body of Her Husband, Jan.* 27 *1687/8* (London, 1688), sigs. F2v–3.

5. For the chronology of Mary of Modena's pregnancy and of the warming-pan scandal, see Rachel Weil, "The Politics of Legitimacy: Women and the Warming-Pan Scandal," in *The Revolution of 1688–89: Changing Perspectives*, ed. Lois G. Schwoerer (Cambridge: Cambridge University Press, 1992), pp. 65–82, esp. 67–69.

6. Martin Haile, *Queen Mary of Modena: Her Life and Letters* (London: Dent, 1905), p. 179.

Estate, and that she would not endure these Violations of her Bed any longer, and that she would assist *Sir Geo. Wakeman* [the queen's physician] in the poisoning of the King."[7] In Oates's testimony, the queen equates the country's lack of faith and her husband's infidelity; her desire to right both wrongs is deeply personal, yet the result, whatever the motive, would be treason. Like the conflation of Cellier and Hobry, Oates's predictable charge against the queen suggests that notorious Catholic women will eventually be suspected of plotting against their husbands, since that is just the most obvious manifestation of the crime that defines their status in the Protestant imagination: petty treason, betrayal from below, within, beside. Et tu, uxor?

Vituperations of Catherine of Braganza, like those of Henrietta Maria, thus resemble attacks on Elizabeth Cellier in raising the question: Is "stateswoman" an oxymoron or not? One contemptuous dismissal of Cellier's failed defense in her libel trial claims that "she talk'd abundantly more like a *Midwife*, than such a *Politician* and *Stateswoman* as she would be accounted."[8] Yet there was not as clear a distinction between midwives and politicians as this remark assumes; midwives had great authority in determining legitimacy.[9] Furthermore, stateswomen provoked anxiety not because they were unheard of but because they seemed to be on the rise. Their ascendance was associated with Catholicism; anticipating the restoration of the Whore of Babylon's regime, bossy women were coming into their own. In one pamphlet remarking on Oates's charges against Catherine of Braganza, the purported author, Margery Mason, Spinster, reminds readers: "Let no body wonder at this Attempt, as an Argument of overweening, when so many of our sex are become Statists."[10]

If women such as Elizabeth Cellier and Catherine of Braganza conjoin the political and the personal, this does not mean that the two were otherwise distinct; they were no more discrete than Protestants were indisputably

<hr />

7. *The Tryals of Sir George Wakeman [et al.] for High Treason for Conspiring the Death of the King* (London, 1679), p. 26.

8. *The Tryal of Elizabeth Cellier, the Popish Midwife, at the Old Baily, Septemb. 11 1680. For Printing and Publishing the Late Notorious Libel, Intituled, Malice Defeated* (London, 1680), p. 3.

9. Patricia Crawford, "Public Duty, Conscience, and Women in Early Modern England," in *Public Duty and Private Conscience in Seventeenth-Century England*, ed. John Morrill, Paul Slack, and Daniel Woolf (Oxford: Clarendon, 1993), pp. 57–76, esp. 63–64; Weil, "Politics of Legitimacy," esp. p. 75; and Merry E. Wiesner, "Early Modern Midwifery: A Case Study," in *Women and Work in Preindustrial Europe*, ed. Barbara A. Hanawalt (Bloomington: Indiana University Press, 1986), pp. 94–113, esp. 110.

10. Margery Mason, Spinster, *The Tickler Tickled; or, The Observator upon the Late Tryals of Sir George Wakeman, &c. Observed* (London, 1679), sig. A2. This pamphlet responds to Roger L'Estrange's pro-government spin on the charges in the *Observator*.

and reliably different from Catholics. Historians and literary critics debate what the terms "public" and "private" meant in the early modern period, and what other terms coalesced around each. For instance, did "personal" and "domestic" necessarily attach to "private"? They discuss whether or how those meanings changed. Did a new public/private distinction emerge? If so, when, in what discursive registers, and with what consequences? Print controversies surrounding Catholic women cannot resolve these scholarly debates. They do, however, lend support to the claim that in the seventeenth century, what Lawrence E. Klein specifies as "the magisterial public sphere—the State and its related agencies and the world of office-holding they circumscribed"—was increasingly being constructed as separate.[11] As part of this process of conceptual definition and separation, the magisterial public sphere more consistently and resolutely excluded women, defining itself against them, as it defined itself against Catholics and others.[12]

In seventeenth-century England, Catholic women, especially those inside the court, became figures for the challenge of keeping these realms distinct and of finding any safe sphere for women. As in eighteenth-century France, Catholic queens offered particularly vivid reminders that hereditary monarchies could not fully exclude women from even the most narrowly conceived of public spheres.[13] Queens consort inevitably exercised influence as wives and mothers. Charles II's mistresses, especially the Catholic Louise de Kéroualle, Duchess of Portsmouth, were also suspected of translating erotic intimacy into political influence. Catholic women revealed that the difference between the public and the private was a fiction

11. Lawrence E. Klein, "Gender and the Public/Private Distinction in the Eighteenth Century: Some Questions about Evidence and Analytic Procedure," *Eighteenth-Century Studies* 29.1 (1995): 103. See also Richard Cust and Ann Hughes, "Introduction," in *Conflict in Early Stuart England: Studies in Religion and Politics, 1603–1642*, ed. Cust and Hughes (London: Longmans, 1989), p. 38; Jürgen Habermas, *The Structural Transformation of the Public Sphere: An Inquiry into a Category of Bourgeois Society*, trans. Thomas Burger (Cambridge: MIT Press, 1995); Megan Matchinske, *Writing, Gender, and State in Early Modern England: Identity Formation and the Female Subject* (Cambridge: Cambridge University Press, 1998); Lena Cowen Orlin, *Private Matters and Public Culture in Post-Reformation England* (Ithaca: Cornell University Press, 1994), pp. 89, 244–45; Mary Beth Rose, *The Expense of Spirit: Love and Sexuality in English Renaissance Drama* (Ithaca: Cornell University Press, 1989), chap. 3; and Amanda Vickery, "Golden Age to Separate Spheres? A Review of the Categories and Chronology of English Women's History," *Historical Journal* 36.2 (1993): 383–414.

12. Carole Pateman, *The Disorder of Women: Democracy, Feminism, and Political Theory* (Stanford: Stanford University Press, 1989), p. 132.

13. Sarah Maza, "The Diamond Necklace Affair Revisited (1785–1786): The Case of the Missing Queen," and Lynn Hunt, "The Many Bodies of Marie Antoinette: Political Pornography and the Problem of the Feminine in the French Revolution," in *Eroticism and the Body Politic*, ed. Hunt (Baltimore: Johns Hopkins University Press, 1991): 63–89, 108–30; and Joan Landes, *Women and the Public Sphere in the Age of the French Revolution* (Ithaca: Cornell University Press, 1988).

that would have to be tirelessly reasserted, since it gained force and meaning only in such repetition. In the discourses that construct and constitute public life in this period, these female figures stand for what can neither be accommodated nor successfully excluded. These figures, all foreign or, in Cellier's case, married to a foreigner, yet all on intimate terms with English people and English power, also hold the foreign and the familiar in disturbing tension. Such women, then, vividly embody the particular threat that Catholics offer as "proximate others": they blur the boundaries defining English national identity and security by straddling, traveling between, and conflating categories of distinction, even those as basic as "me–not me" and "us–them."[14]

An effort to distinguish sharply and definitively between public and private was compromised from the start. As we have seen, the state was not comfortable leaving Catholics to their beliefs and observances in their own households, yet Parliament and individuals frequently balked at infringing on the prerogatives of male householders, husbands, and fathers, even when they were Catholics or tolerated Catholic dependents. Furthermore, anti-Catholic polemic obsessively imagined just what Catholics, whether women and priests or Henrietta Maria, might be up to in bed. If women were increasingly confined to the domestic, at least conceptually, their influence and activity there were also distrusted.

Furthermore, women's arena of public intervention often remains the private, albeit a private saturated with political meaning and consequence. Fantasies of the threat posed by Catholic queens and midwives acknowledge that in the realm of the bed, the bosom, the body, women are necessary, and therefore powerful; their power emerges from intimacy, yet it spills out to have consequences for public, political life. Catholic women lead their uxorious husbands astray through curtain lectures or wheedle them into deathbed confessions; they poison their adulterous husbands or hack those who know too much into pieces; they smuggle in presumptive heirs in warming pans. In seventeenth-century representations, Catholic women, invariably scandalous figures whether they are queens consort or popish midwives, reveal that the private is too important and dangerous an arena to leave to women.

Let us return to those playing cards depicting the Hobrys at home. In figure 8 the marital bed lurks to the left, looking like a kind of stage, but also reminding the viewer that the murder emerges out of the violence that occurred there, and that Mrs. Hobry, wielding her ax, is at home. On

14. The term "proximate other" is Jonathan Z. Smith's in "Differential Equations: On Constructing the 'Other,'" Thirteenth Annual University Lecture in Religion, Arizona State University, Mar. 5, 1992. I am grateful to Denise Buell for this reference.

what I like to think is the dining table, her husband sprawls before the
midwife in what resembles the birthing or gynecological exam position; he
seems to have lost his genitals, as well as his head and arms, although they
are not visible on the floor. Even in figure 9, in which Mrs. Hobry disposes
of his dismembered body in a privy, that final destination for stillborn and
murdered infants, Mrs. Hobry still seems, illogically, to be inside. We see
her outside and in "the public sphere" only when we see her burning to
death in figure 10. How safe, then, is the domestic? What are the advantages
of keeping women there? In anti-Catholic discourses, as in representations
of domestic murder, the domestic—whether one's own household or England itself—was not viewed as safe or as defensible against invasion from
within. Catholics and women, especially Catholic women, threaten through
their very proximity. If the private was coming to be viewed not only as separate but as equal in importance to the public, then this changing status
only heightened anxiety about what happened there, how women might
be empowered there, and what the consequences for men and for the nation might be.

Rather than champion the inclusion of Catholic women in existing narratives of change, then, I wish to argue that attention to the many texts by
and about them might challenge the boundaries separating, say, political
history from women's history. For instance, considering Elizabeth Cellier
as both a woman and a political activist (a "Stateswoman"), considering her
not "singly and alone" but in relation to other representations of Catholic
women, reveals how conventions shape these representations and how
and why scandalous Catholic women, "whores of Babylon," played so crucial a role in English Protestant discourses. Similarly, I do not want to end
by simply suggesting that texts about Mary Hobry look one way if you read
them against other representations of Catholic women and the gendered
menace of Catholicism, and another if you read them against other representations of murderous wives. My point is that the boundary between
those two approaches, or between Catholic women and criminalized
women, is arbitrary, anachronistic, a mirage. It makes most sense to read
Hobry's case as one nexus of many at which such distinctions were articulated and thereby created. Her case can be read in the contexts of a history of domestic violence and a history of "The Revolution," a history of
gendered subject formation and a history of highly politicized religious
conflict, for these histories, like Protestants and Catholics, are not clearly
distinguishable. If, as I have argued, Catholic women became prominent
in seventeenth-century polemical and legal representation precisely as
figures for the intertwining of intimate and frightening, familiar and foreign which made Catholicism more generally so threatening, then to assign

them to one history or the other, one category or the other, is to miss the point. My goal here has not simply been to recover the gendered representations of Catholicism, or even to shift the focus onto them, but rather to shake our confidence in categorical distinctions that are figments of the seventeenth-century English imagination, born in anxious confusion, fostered by hatred, and perpetuated through our own desire for historical certainty.

Index